Chicamacomico

Chicamacomico

How it was back then

ELVIN HOOPER

Best wishes
Elvin Hooper
Enjoy the Book

CHAPEL HILL
PRESS, INC.

FRONT COVER PHOTOGRAPH Chicamacomico Lifesaving Station, Rodanthe, North Carolina, 1974. Originally built in 1874, the station was decommissioned in 1954, and was the scene of numerous rescues. Now fully restored and open to the public. Image courtesy of Michael Halminski.

BACK COVER PHOTOGRAPH Wreck of the G.A. Kohler, four-masted schooner, beached in a 1933 hurricane. The remains, usually covered by shifting sand, still resurface from time to time. This photo was taken in 2000. Image courtesy of Michael Halminski.

ISBN 978-1-59715-103-0
Library of Congress Catalog Number 2014936689

Third Printing

To my only daughter Kristina A. Hooper,

who has brought much joy into my life

Contents

Acknowledgments

I really enjoyed writing these fictional stories about the Chicamacomico area. I have used many local names and would like to thank these folks for the use of their names. I sincerely hope they approve of how I have used them to name the characters in these stories.

I would like to thank several more folks who have helped me during the course of this work. I would like to recognize Elizabeth Oliver, an editor affiliated with the North Carolina Writers Guild, who edited the rough draft. A special thank-you goes out to Gee Gee Rosell of Buxton Village Books. Her encouragement, guidance, patience, and vast literary knowledge guided me through this process.

Hugs, kisses, and a great big thank-you go out to Georgia Hardee, Geanna Hardee, and Lori Townsend. Their endless hours of editing, formatting, and rewriting the text have made this book possible. Thank you, Martin Garrish, for the use of the quote "how it was back then." This quote is found in the lyrics of one of his songs.

I would like to thank Michael Halminski for his research and the photography used on the cover and inside flaps of this work. Thank you to Drew C. Wilson for the author's photograph.

Also many thanks to Edwina Woodbury and the folks at Chapel Hill Press for their assistance in making this book come to life.

The willingness of these folks to share their knowledge, talent, and encouragement has made it possible for me to achieve my dream and publish this book.

PROLOGUE

This story is centered around the three villages located on the northern end of Hatteras Island that used to be known as Chicamacomico. Today, the area is called the tri-village. If you are native-borne to the area, the rest of the native islanders refer to you as a Rodanther. However the local people who have chosen to move and live here refer to you as living in the tri-village.

With the increase in the number of vacation homes, these villages have grown together. In fact, there are three different villages in this area. Beginning from the north, they are Rodanthe, Waves, and Salvo. In the days before U.S. post offices were established on the island, these were known, respectively, as Northard Woods, Southard Woods, and Clarks.

This is a collection of adventures about life in this area, and up and down the Eastern Seaboard, in the time of the sailing vessel. Today, Interstate 95 stretches from Maine to Florida and supports long-distance trucking. However, in the days of yesteryear, all travel and the transport of goods and services were conducted on the waters of the Atlantic Ocean, the inland sounds, and rivers along the Eastern Seaboard.

This work covers several rescue procedures employed by the United States Lifesaving Service, today known as the U.S. Coast Guard. It covers the days of horse-and-cart travel, local holidays and celebrations, hurricanes, ice storms, and a large marsh fire. It provides some insight into the harmony between the local people and the wildlife of the island.

The natives were mostly hunters, gatherers, and fisherfolk. They used the natural resources of the area but also respected them, making good of everything they harvested.

All the adventures in this work are purely fictional. Although some historical facts are mentioned, they may not be completely accurate. Most of the material has been passed down through stories told by old-timers around local gathering places. I would seek out these gatherings and remain absolutely quiet, taking in their stories about the good old days. They frowned on being questioned, and if a stranger walked in, they would clam up and begin to size up the intruder. If you passed muster, you would get a simple nod as you walked in. Then all you had to do was sit and listen.

Each one of these older folks is a wealth of knowledge. They are experts on the weather and have skills in carpentry, plumbing, and electrical work. Most of them have built the houses they live in, and can fix most anything. They're very proud of their heritage and are willing to share everything, with the exception of their favorite fishing, hunting, and gathering locations. If you are fortunate enough to be involved in some of these sessions, listen and learn about the area you now call home. It's perfectly fine to stretch the number and the size of fish caught, or to change the stories to make them more interesting. Just remember to pass them along!

The adventure begins in the city of Boston, near Little Brewster Island, located in the outer portion of Boston Harbor. This island contains the Boston Light, the first lighthouse built in the United States. Kristina Peterson could see the flash of the light through the window. She was sitting in the great room of her Cape Cod–style house, across the bay from the lighthouse. It was the beginning of May, and in just three more days, she would be ninety years old. She had married a military man many years ago, and they had made their home in the Boston area. They had seven children. Her husband had passed away just three years ago, and her eldest son and his family had moved into the large house to take care of her. She was very excited because all seven of her children, accompanied by seventeen grandchildren and four great-grandchildren, were coming to her birthday celebration.

Finally the day arrived. The house was full of energy, and she was very happy. After a huge evening meal, and the blowing out of a few candles on her birthday cake, they settled in the great room. It was the first day of a three-day northeaster. The spray was flying high in the air as the waves crashed onto the rocks bordering her backyard. Sea foam was beginning to accumulate at the edge of the yard.

"This type of weather reminds me of down home," she told her family. They all knew exactly where "down home" was and what she was referring to. That's all it took. One of her grandchildren begged her to tell them stories about growing up in the Chicamacomico area. She looked at all of them and realized how very fortunate she was. She shifted her pain-ravaged body in her wheelchair and let her mind drift back over the years. Thoughts of Barnacle, Hazel, and Cocoa began to flood her mind. A huge smile developed on her aged, weathered face, and she began.

$$❧ \; 1 \; ❧$$

BARNACLE, THE CHICAMACOMICO STALLION

The sun was high, the sky was clear, and the wind was light from the north-east. The sailing vessel, *Sylvia*, slid smoothly out of Baltimore's outer harbor. Aboard the schooner were the sea captain, his wife, and small daughter, along with a crew of six deckhands, the cook, quartermaster, ship's carpenter, two riggers, and two cabin boys. *Sylvia* was owned by a textile company and transported raw cotton from Charleston to Baltimore for processing.

The trip was very smooth and enjoyable for the first few days. The only choppy water on their journey to the Port of Charleston was through the passage around Diamond Shoals. Upon arrival in Charleston the work of loading cotton would begin. During this time the sea captain would take his family inland to stay at a friend's plantation. The young daughter enjoyed the plush plantation lifestyle, which was quite a contrast to the life she lived in the crowded inner city of Baltimore. In the green fields of the plantation she had plenty of room to explore and seek all types of adventures. There was a small lake for fishing and canoeing and a large barn with many farm animals where she would feed the chickens and ducks. She had even learned to milk a cow! Most of all Kristina loved to ride the horses, especially a gentle mare named Emily. One day, when she went to ride Emily, a baby colt joined them, staying very close to the mare. The plantation owner told Kristina that Emily was the colt's mother.

Soon Kristina was spending most of her time with the small colt and had become quite attached. Her father worried about her feelings as the time drew near for them to return to Baltimore. The day before their departure, when Kristina begged her father to purchase the colt for her, he continued to insist that they had no place to keep the colt in the city and that it would be much happier with its mother. Still, his daughter begged and pleaded, to the point of making herself sick, and like many other loving fathers, who have only one child who happens to be a daughter, he gave in and allowed Kristina to have the colt.

The colt did not like boarding the vessel, and there were problems from the start. Kristina had to keep him in sight at all times, and feed him and clean up after him. He got away from her several times, which caused complete panic on ship. It took the young horse several days to calm down to life on the sea, and he cried for his mother constantly.

As the *Sylvia* was approaching Diamond Shoals on her return voyage north, the barometer was dropping fast. The sea captain warned his crew that they were in for a blow. He told Kristina to take her colt below deck so that it wouldn't wash overboard. He cautioned her to do this right away because, hereafter, the crew would be too busy tending the ship to worry about the safety of the colt.

The wind began to blow gale force from the northeast. The *Sylvia* had rounded Diamond Shoals and was quarter to the pounding sea. The captain ordered all hands to rig for storm conditions and to strike all sails with the exception of the forward jib. Then all hands were ordered below deck, with the exception of the quartermaster, riggers, and carpenter. The *Sylvia* was fighting for her life. She was taking on water and in danger of sinking.

Daylight brought on a new peril. During the night, the *Sylvia* had been driven dangerously close to the beach by hard winds. Large waves could be seen by the wheelhouse crew, crashing onto the outer bar, just off the port side. At this point, there was no way the crew could keep the *Sylvia* from grounding, so the sea captain ordered all hands topside, where lifejackets were distributed and quickly donned by all aboard.

Suddenly there was a lurch, and as the *Sylvia* hit the sandbar she twisted, bow to the beach, tearing away the rudder. The next wave broke over the stern, flooding the deck with water and debris. Then the *Sylvia* bumped bottom near the stern, twisted side to the pounding breakers, and rolled on her port side, completely filling with water. All hands had to scramble to the top of the wheelhouse and latch themselves to what was left of the mast and riggings.

The lookout at Gull Shoal Lifesaving Station had picked up the *Sylvia* in his glass as soon as she had entered sight. He could see that she was having trouble and possibly headed for disaster, so he sounded the alarm, ordered out the beach cart, and sent a message to the Chicamacomico keeper about the endangered ship. Since the *Sylvia* was grounded closer to the Chicamacomico Station, their crew would reach the wreck first, and the Gull Shoal crew would come quickly to assist with rescue efforts.

To begin the rescue, the beach cart was positioned, the sand anchor was buried, and the Lyle gun and shot-line were prepared. The first shot flew squarely over the vessel. The Hauser was pulled seaward and secured to the upper portion of the broken mast. The crotch was positioned, the hauling lines were attached, and the breeches buoy was sent to the wreck. Then, one by one, all aboard the *Sylvia* were transported to safety, with the exception of a small colt, still trapped below the deck. The sea captain's daughter was crushed by the thought of losing her colt to the sea. She begged her father not to leave the beach until all hope of finding him was exhausted, so they stayed until the *Sylvia* was completely broken into pieces, and all evidence of the vessel was gone.

Tangled in broken rigging, cold, and very scared, the colt was fighting for his life. Only a small space of air below the deck of the ship allowed him to breathe, and only self-preservation kept his legs kicking. He was becoming exhausted, to the point of blacking out, until a bale of cotton bumped him, allowing him to grab a hold with his front legs and rest a spell. Then he slowly began to untangle himself from the rigging. As other bales floated past him, he was finally able to drift to a hole in the deck. From there, he scrambled to the upper deck and spent the rest of the night hanging on to cotton bales for dear life.

In time, the sea calmed and the cotton bales began to wash ashore, all except the bale carrying the colt. It had drifted into another large piece of ship wreckage, and once again, the small colt had become trapped in rigging, full of sharp barnacles. Once again, the colt struggled to keep afloat. His lips were swollen from lack of fresh water, and this time his legs were bleeding terribly from barnacle cuts.

Surfman Number Four was leaving the Chicamacomico Lifesaving Station for daily patrol duty when the lookout shouted down from the tower about something "funny-looking" he had just seen in the surf, like a box with a head on it. Upon topping the dune line, the surfman found a small colt, clinging to a bale of cotton, unable to stand as he was tangled in the knotted debris.

Surfman Number Four returned to the station, carrying the wounded colt in his arms. Just as he entered the stable area, the Chicamacomico keeper was coming out of the barn. He wanted to know what the surfman had in his arms and why he was not patrolling the beach as expected. The surfman told the keeper that he had a half-drowned colt, which was badly cut by barnacles, and asked to be excused from patrol duty for a short time so that he could look after the colt. The keeper agreed, provided the surfman could find a volunteer replacement for his shift. Then the keeper suggested that the colt be given a name. Without any hesitation, Surfman Number Four named the colt Barnacle! Both the keeper and surfman laughed and went on their way with their daily duties.

This is how Barnacle came to live at the Chicamacomico Lifesaving Station and was given his name.

❦ 2 ❧

HAZEL THE HEALER

Surfman Number Four's name was Barney, and he always had plenty of daily duties to perform in order to stay in the good graces of the station keeper. Still, he was very concerned about the well-being of the small colt he had named Barnacle. He liked the colt's name because it was similar to his own name. Each day Barney tried his best to care for the young horse. Most of the cuts had healed and the swelling of his lips had gone down, but Barnacle drank very little water and refused all food. It seemed the colt was heartsick and had lost his will to live.

Initially the other surfmen teased Barney about Barnacle. They told him that Barnacle looked like him and acted like him. Still, they were very concerned about the colt and helped Barney take care of him, but the colt would not take any food. Because his condition was getting worse daily, the keeper told Barney that he should put the colt down. Then he gave Barney until the end of the week to make a decision about the colt. The solution would come from a strange old lady named Hazel.

Hazel lived near Clarks, across the floating marsh, at the edge of Cedar Hammock Swamp. She lived in a small shack and preferred the company of animals to that of people. Most children were scared to death of her. Hazel's clothes were old, faded, and very threadbare, and she always wore a large bonnet that hid most of her face. She only came out among people when she needed supplies. Mr. Midgett, from the local store, knew the old woman well and had become very good friends with her over the years. She had helped him with horse problems in the past, and he knew Hazel had a gift when it came to helping animals. One day, the Chicamacomico keeper was in Mr. Midgett's store and told him about Barnacle. Mr. Midgett suggested that they ask Hazel to take a look at the colt.

After the keeper returned to the station, he requested the presence of Barney out at the boathouse. When Barney arrived, the keeper was checking lines on the beach cart and told Barney what he had heard from Mr. Midgett about Hazel. The keeper reminded Barney that he had to do something about Barnacle soon and suggested a trip to Cedar Hammock to visit Hazel. Barney agreed right away and asked if another surfman could accompany him, but the keeper would not allow anyone else to leave the station because it would leave them two men short. They were still in the middle of hurricane season, and the keeper was expecting more beach rescue operations. Barney borrowed a horse and cart and began his journey, four miles south, to the village of Clarks. He wanted to visit Mr. Midgett at his store and talk to him about Hazel.

Mr. Midgett laughed when Barney requested his company and said he was uneasy about the impending visit. He told Barney that he could not accompany him and leave the store but that he would ask his nephew, Norman Scarborough, to go, insisting that Norman knew Cedar Hammock like the back of his hand. He had crossed the dreaded floating marsh many times on guided hunting trips.

Norman agreed to go with Barney, so they began their trip one mile south, from Clarks to Cedar Hammock. On arrival at the edge of the Hammock, there was no visible path or trail to take. As both men got off the cart and put on hip boots, Norman told Barney to stay close behind him and to stay within reach of the small, scrubby trees. If either man got stuck in the bog, they could only escape if one of them had a firm grip on a tree branch.

As Norman led the way, all of a sudden he disappeared from view beneath the muddy bog. He soon surfaced a few feet in front of Barney and was able to keep himself afloat long enough for Barney to get a small branch to him and pull him out of the mud. They rested for a bit, then started out again, making their way across the outer pond area. Norman informed Barney that the inner pond was the worst part of the floating marsh. Upon entering the inner pond area, both men sunk up to their knees in the floating bog, out of reach of all trees. Norman instructed Barney not to move, explaining that the more he moved and struggled, the more he would sink.

Hazel was resting on her back porch, brewing up a jar of sun tea, when she heard the men's cries. She put on a pair of boots and walked to the inner pond area. She was surprised to see Norman and inquired about the other man with him. She wanted to know what Norman was doing in her hammock. It wasn't cold enough for him and his hunters to shoot the wild ducks she fed and protected in her swamp. She was not very happy to see them and told them she should let them slip below the bog and drown.

Norman politely told Hazel the story of Barnacle and how the colt would surely die unless she helped them. She agreed to help them out of the bog, only because she was concerned about the small colt. Before doing so, she made Norman promise to keep his future hunts clear of her swamp. At first Norman balked at her request, so she waited until both men sank to their waist. With pressure from Barney, Norman finally promised Hazel he would stay off her property. Then she tossed Norman and Barney a rope and pulled them out of the bog. She told them to wait while she gathered a few things she needed for the trip, and then she led them out of the swamp without any problems.

Barney, Norman, and Hazel arrived in Clarks around dusk and stopped to see Mr. Midgett at his store. Mr. Midgett agreed to put Barney and Hazel up for the night so that they could strike out for Chicamacomico Station early the next morning. Barney thanked Norman for guiding him to Hazel. Then Norman wished them well, bid everyone a good night, and went home.

The next day dawned sunny and pleasant. Hazel and Barney arrived at the Chicamacomico Station around ten o'clock. After examining Barnacle, Hazel said that the colt was fine physically, but he appeared to have some emotional problems. According to Hazel, in order to help Barnacle, she had to get inside his head. She insisted that every scrap of information known about the colt's background would be necessary and helpful.

Barney began his story with how he found the colt on the shore side, tangled in a cotton bale by ship debris, near death. He explained that, according to station rescue records, the colt had been aboard the *Sylvia* when she went down off the shores of Chicamacomico, after being taken from his mother and his South Carolina home by the sea captain and his daughter.

After listening to Barney, Hazel instructed him to take the colt to the stall of the keeper's mare and allow him to remain there for a few days. Upon entering the stall of the big, gentle mare, the colt tried to stand stronger as the mare nudged him with her nose. Shortly, for the first time since his rescue, Barnacle ate a small portion of hay and tried some oats. Hazel's next instruction was for Barney to arrange for a small girl about the age of the sea captain's daughter to visit the colt.

Surfman Number Three had a young daughter who was very glad for the chance to spend time with the colt. Over the next two weeks, Barnacle's condition improved to the point that he was able to accompany the mare when she helped pull the surfboat wagon. On drill day Barnacle proudly trotted along with the beach cart.

Hazel knew her work had been completed. Ready to return home, she headed for Clarks, stopping at Mr. Midgett's store to gather supplies before returning to Cedar Hammock. In the meantime she asked Mr. Midgett to contact Norman so that she could speak to him. When Norman answered the phone, Hazel reminded him of his promise to stay off her land—and the dangers of the floating marsh if he didn't keep his promise. Then she was off to her beloved swamp and its animals.

The keeper told Barney that, as long as Barnacle was helpful around the station, he could stay and earn his keep just like the other horses. Barnacle would have to be introduced to the saddle so that he could help with beach patrols. He would have to learn how to pull the surfboat wagon and the beach cart. The keeper also instructed Barney to begin the process of contacting the sea captain and his daughter because Barnacle belonged to them.

Barney knew that the sea captain and his daughter had gone back to Baltimore. He also knew the captain's normal route up and down the East Coast.

Still, the captain would have to be contacted by mail, so Barney found the address he needed from station rescue records and began the process of contacting the sea captain. All outgoing mail was collected at small post offices within the villages and then shipped to a larger sorting area in Elizabeth City for further distribution by sea. Sometimes it took weeks to get a letter to a city like Baltimore.

Edward was very surprised to receive a letter from Surfman Number Four at the Chicamacomico Lifesaving Station. The letter contained familiar information about the rescue and wreckage of the *Sylvia*, reminding the sea captain of everyone's escape to safety except for Kristina's colt, which had been trapped below the deck during the storm. All efforts to rescue the young horse had been in vain. The sea captain would never forget the look in his daughter's eyes as she watched the ship go down below the pounding waves.

Edward's mind returned to the letter he was holding in his hand. The surfman went on to talk about a small colt he had found a few years back, washed up on the beach near the station, tangled in a bale of cotton and barely alive. He shared how the station crew had nursed the colt back to good health. Over the past few years, the little colt, which they had named Barnacle, had become a strong and responsible horse. Barnacle was also becoming a very important part of their lifesaving and patrol duty operations. However, as much as the surfmen wished to keep Barnacle at the station, the Chicamacomico keeper insisted that the sea captain of the *Sylvia* be contacted first, since he was Barnacle's rightful owner.

Kristina was livid as she read the letter her father had received from the surfman at Chicamacomico. She had thought about the little colt every day since the shipwreck, and now, after four years of believing the colt had drowned, she was pleading with her father to get him and bring him to her. When she found out that her father was scheduled to take a load of white oak timber to a shipbuilding operation in South America, she begged him to take her to Chicamacomico, but he refused her request, mainly because she would be starting high school soon. He told Kristina that the trip would have to be arranged the following summer, after she got out of school. Presently, all Kristina could do was to answer the surfman's letter and inquire about the well-being of her horse named Barnacle.

Over the period of the winter months, Kristina and Barney set up correspondence and Barnacle was always the main topic. Barney told her how well Barnacle had adapted to life at the station and of his many adventures with the station crew. Kristina told Barney how much she had missed the colt and couldn't believe she was going to see him again!

Finally, Kristina's school year ended, and her father started making plans to return to Chicamacomico to get her horse as promised. Only father and daughter went this time, traveling by schooner to Norfolk, then by a fishing vessel to Elizabeth City, where they spent the night in a hotel. The next day Edward booked passage on a sailing vessel headed south to Northard Woods.

As they sailed out of the Elizabeth City harbor, Kristina became very excited about seeing her horse again. A fair wind was blowing from the northeast, helping them make good time across the Albemarle Sound. Kristina and her father ate their evening meal as the vessel entered the upper Roanoke Sound, and afterward, Kristina fell asleep in the padded dining chair. As her father carried her to their stateroom, he could tell from the smile on her face that she was dreaming of Barnacle and new adventures along the Chicamacomico beaches.

❦ 3 ❧

The Reunion

The *Coastal Rambler* was the name of the schooner that traveled the inland waters between Ocracoke and Elizabeth City. Her master, Logan Mansfield, knew the sound's waters well and had made many trips to Northard Woods, in Chicamacomico, to transport passengers and supplies to and from the area. This time he was taking Kristina to be reunited with her beloved horse. With a fair wind from the northeast, they slid out of the harbor in Elizabeth City and into the Pamlico Sound.

It wasn't long before the wind shifted to the southwest and kicked up considerably, causing the *Coastal Rambler* to pitch and roll a bit. Awakened by the sudden movement, Edward and Kristina headed topside to check the weather, then to the dining room for a light breakfast. Edward was concerned about their current position and possible arrival time at Chicamacomico, and Kristina just wanted to know how much longer it would take to get there. Edward asked one of the cabin boys to seek permission for him and his daughter to visit the wheelhouse.

Upon hearing that another shipmaster was on board, Captain Mansfield invited Edward and Kristina up into the wheelhouse. The two captains greeted one other, and the quartermaster took the wheel. The *Coastal Rambler* was on a southwestward tack, away from the island. Captain Mansfield explained that, once they completed two more tacks, they would be able to anchor at the mouth of Southard Channel, just off the village of Northard Woods and the Chicamacomico Lifesaving Station.

Kristina was elated with anticipation and could hardly contain herself. Seeing how excited she was, Captain Mansfield offered his glass to her and pointed out the location of the station. Kristina could actually make out the tower and some of the outbuildings, and although she strained to see the stable, she was sure she saw movement in the barnyard area. Captain Mansfield informed Edward that they would arrive at the mouth of Southard Channel around noon. At last, the *Coastal Rambler* completed her final westward tack and headed directly toward the station tower. Upon entering the edge of the channel, the quartermaster turned the vessel into the wind and told the crew to anchor up.

The much smaller *Sea Mullet*, skippered by Logan Farrow, headed out to meet the *Coastal Rambler*. Mr. Farrow lived in the village of Northard Woods and had a contract to transport mail and cargo to and from the area. Each time the *Coastal Rambler* arrived close to shore, his job was to bring the *Sea Mullet* to her leeward side, near the offloading platform, to pick up or deliver mail, cargo, and often passengers. Upon boarding the *Sea Mullet*, Kristina waved good-bye to Captain Mansfield and the *Coastal Rambler*, then turned her eyes to the landing area ahead.

After they reached the dock, Kristina wanted to run ahead to the station, but her father instructed her to wait, explaining that Barney had agreed to meet them at the dock with a horse-drawn cart to carry them to the station. Kristina could see the cart from the landing, but the horse was blocked from view by a large parcel on the dock. She hoped the horse would be Barnacle and was a bit disappointed to see a golden-colored mare hitched to Barney's wagon. She could hardly wait to see Barnacle. Her excitement returned immediately as Barney greeted them and introduced them to Jason Gray, Surfman Number Three, from the Chicamacomico Lifesaving Station.

Jason had two children with him; their names were Stan and Shanna. Stan looked to be about a year older than Kristina, and Shanna looked a bit younger. Edward and the men began talking about the weather and such, while Kristina grilled Stan and Shanna, begging them to tell her everything they knew about Barnacle. They told her that Barnacle had been earning his keep around the station by working with the surfmen, completing daily assignments, and assisting with patrol duty.

As they entered the station yard, Kristina jumped off the cart and ran toward the stable. Edward yelled and tried to stop her, but to no avail. As Stan and Shanna ran after her, their father warned them to slow down and be careful in the stable area. When Kristina reached the stable, it was empty, and her heart sank. A surfman was cleaning out the stalls, and when she asked him if he knew the whereabouts of Barnacle, he told her that the horse was on wood-gathering detail at the beach with the keeper.

Edward and Jason reached the stable shortly after Stan and Shanna and heard the news about Barnacle. Edward told his daughter that they needed to go to the boardinghouse to make arrangements for their stay and that, by the time they checked in and unpacked, Barnacle would most likely be back at the station. Although her father's wishes made sense, Kristina couldn't stand to wait another moment. She had come too far and had waited too long for this reunion, so Jason took the kids to the beach to find Barnacle and the keeper.

The Chicamacomico keeper, Mr. Ervin Daniels, had worked many long hours training Barnacle to master the wood-gathering cart. All he had to do was call Barnacle from the stall, and he would trot over to be hitched up. Keeper Daniels was able to make Barnacle move forward and stop on command. As the two were making their way back up the beach with a load of wood, Keeper Daniels could barely make out four people coming toward them. They were still too far in the distance to see their faces or call out to them.

Kristina saw the keeper and Barnacle in the distance, and she began to run with Stan and Shanna at her heels. She called out to the horse, and Barnacle immediately started running toward her. Keeper Daniels tried to stop Barnacle, but to no avail; all the wood spilled off the cart, and the constant up-and-down pounding of Barnacle running on the hills began to break the cart apart, completely destroying it. Barnacle galloped on until his nose was resting in Kristina's hands. Keeper Daniels was very upset, and he scolded Barnacle about his behavior.

Kristina's mind was on the last time she had seen Barnacle, when he was a small colt aboard the *Sylvia*. Now standing before her was a beautiful full-grown stallion, about eighteen to twenty hands high. He was a reddish chestnut color with a white blaze on his forehead, four white socks, a black tail, and a beautiful mane. Kristina was so happy to see her horse, and she wrapped her arms around Barnacle's neck. In the meantime, Keeper Daniels and Jason fashioned a temporary sled from what was left of the cart and piled the wood on top. Then they all made their way back to the station. When Edward returned from the boardinghouse, they told him of the beach caper and the destruction of the wood cart. Edward could not believe how Barnacle had grown.

The evening was beginning to turn into night, so Jason told Stan and Shanna to run on home, assuring them that they could show Kristina around the next day. Then he and Keeper Daniels unloaded the wood and returned Barnacle to his stall, where Kristina rubbed him down, fed him, and bedded him down for the night. Edward and Kristina said goodnight and headed for the boardinghouse, which was not far from the station. After a supper of stewed chicken and pie bread, they also went to bed. When Kristina knew her father was asleep she took two blankets and headed back to the stable to spend the night with Barnacle. Just as she reached the stable she ran into Stan and Shanna, who said they had a feeling she would be sleeping in the barn.

Edward awoke in the night and noticed that Kristina was not in her bed, so he lit a lantern and headed for the stall. On the way he met up with Jason, who was also looking for his children. When the two men arrived at the stall, they found a huge chestnut stallion and three children all curled up together asleep. Both fathers decided to let their children remain asleep in the stall, knowing full well that, if they made them get up, they would probably sneak back out anyway.

The next day dawned bright and sunny, and when Keeper Daniels found the children asleep in the stall with Barnacle, he could not believe his eyes. He woke them up and told them to go home and get cleaned up, and that Barnacle had work to do. As the children were leaving the stable, Keeper Daniels could not get Barnacle to respond to any commands, so he gave in and told Barnacle to go on with the kids. When Jason got to work, he was very surprised that Keeper Daniels had given Barnacle the day off.

A little later, Edward met up with the children and told Kristina she had to go with him to the telegraph office in Northard Woods to receive a message. She pleaded with her father to let her stay with Stan and Shanna, and he agreed if—and only if—it was okay with their mother. Of course, Mrs. Gray was glad to keep Kristina for the day.

The following morning, after breakfast and making up beds, Kristina, Stan, and Shanna planned their day. Stan knew how to make a kite, and he asked his mother for some old newspaper, plus a bit of flour and water to make glue. They asked Mrs. O'Neal at the post office for a ball of string. With all the materials for the kite, Stan began the assembly process by binding the sticks together and then stringing from stick to stick to make the frame. Once the newspaper was cut out and glued to the frame, and after the glue dried, the kite would be finished. In the meantime Mrs. Gray told the kids that she would make homemade blackberry tarts for them if they would go to the beach hills and gather some fresh blackberries. They eagerly agreed, then hitched Barnacle up to the family cart and headed for the hills.

The blackberries grew large and juicy in the sand hill area, and it didn't take long for the children to gather three tins of berries and return to the house. As promised, they had delicious blackberry tarts and cold milk for a snack. Afterward, Barnacle ran along with them as they flew the kite. Stan tied the kite off to a tree after letting out most of the string, and they took turns riding Barnacle bareback around the yard until it was time for lunch.

Edward returned with the telegram, knowing that Kristina would be upset at the message within it. He had promised her that they could stay with Barnacle for at least a month. However, the telegram stated that Edward needed to return to Baltimore right away for a special trip to South America.

Kristina was indeed very upset when her father told her the news, and she begged to stay with the Grays until she had to return home. Edward told her that they would need her mother's permission, and he sent his wife a telegram the next day. At first, Beth would not agree until she received a letter from

Kristina begging for permission to remain on the island until her summer vacation was over. At this point, Beth told her daughter that she would pack up and come spend the rest of the summer at Chicamacomico, too.

When it was time for Edward to leave Chicamacomico, Barnacle and the children took him to the dock at Northard Woods Landing. From there he took the *Sea Mullet* to catch the *Coastal Rambler* and headed for Elizabeth City, where his wife would be waiting for him in a hotel room.

The next day the sea captain departed for Baltimore while Beth waited for the crew of the *Coastal Rambler* to offload cargo of salted seafood from the coastal ports. Once the *Coastal Rambler* was reloaded with supplies for the return trip, Beth boarded the vessel and continued her trip south, back to the village of Northard Woods, where her daughter was.

When Beth arrived at the dock, she was met by Kristina, Stan, Shanna, and Barnacle. After greetings and hugs, they loaded her luggage onto the cart and climbed aboard. Then Stan told Barnacle to head to the station. Beth and Kristina would be staying at the boardinghouse, and Mrs. Miller had agreed for Barnacle to stay at the boardinghouse barn, if it was okay with Keeper Daniels. The keeper agreed, convinced that Barnacle would only follow the commands of the children anyway.

June was coming to an end, and there was a big celebration in the works for the Fourth of July. All three villages would be joining together for a beach party and picnic near Southard Woods, midway between Clarks and Northard Woods. Some of the adult men would set up large shades for the gathering. Stan and a few boys would go clamming and crabbing down at Clarks Bay, and Shanna and Kristina would go down to Mr. Gutheries' to collect plums, mulberries, and blackberries for the special occasion.

On the day of the party, nearly everyone came from all three villages. The children swam and played in the surf, the teenagers gathered in groups, and the older folks enjoyed fellowship with one another. As night approached, everyone gathered around a roaring fire and sang songs. Then, after cleaning up the beach, they lit the oil lamps on their carts and returned to their homes.

Jason was driving the cart that Barnacle pulled. While the exhausted children slept in the back, Beth and Mrs. Gray talked about the day's activities. Jason noticed the clouds racing across the sky from the northeast and suddenly felt uneasy. Riding alongside them, Keeper Daniels also expressed his concern about the sky, and both men agreed that they should arrive at the station early the next day.

❦ 4 ❦

THE RESCUE

Keeper Daniels had the coffeepot on when Barney and Jason walked into the galley the next morning. The cook was setting the table for breakfast. As the rest of the crew came in, Keeper Daniels told them that they were in for heavy weather; he had seen the early signs of a blow on his way back from the Fourth of July celebration the night before. After the crew was gathered he divided the men into groups to prepare for the storm. Some of the men were to check out the beach cart and all the equipment in it, while the others readied the surfboat and all the gear. As soon as the crew finished breakfast, they headed off to perform their duties.

Outside they found Barnacle pawing the ground and acting excitedly. "Something is wrong with that horse," Keeper Daniels told the men. As they continued to walk toward the outbuildings, Barnacle nipped at Jason's heels. "Scat!" Jason told Barnacle, who then began to aggravate Keeper Daniels. As Barnacle ran ahead, the men saw why he was upset. The ocean water had covered the marshy buffer area between the sand hills and the boathouse.

Keeper Daniels scratched his head in confusion. The wind was light from the northeast, perhaps ten to twelve knots, and the sky was fairly clear, but the upper clouds were racing from the northeast to the southwest. "We could be in for a big storm," he told his men. Then he sent Jason back to the station for tower duty, insisting that Barnacle go with him.

"This water's got you uneasy, huh, boy?" Jason said as they returned to the station.

Kristina and her mother were finishing breakfast when they heard a fuss outside. "It's Barnacle, and he is ready to start the day," her mother said.

As soon as Kristina went outside, she hopped on Barnacle's back, and they headed to the Gray house to see if Stan and Shanna were awake. The brother and sister were just coming off the front porch when Kristina and Barnacle arrived. "The surf's up," Stan said. "I can hear it crashing on the sand from here. Let's go to the beach and see how rough it is."

When the children got near the low buffer area, they found it covered with water. Barnacle led the way as they scampered from dune to dune, between the waves. Shanna was knocked down by a large wave and began to wash out with the returning current, but Barnacle ran to her and knelt down, allowing her to grab his tail so that he could pull her to safety. After Kristina and Stan helped Shanna to her feet, they made a game out of trying to outrun the waves. Barnacle would protectively nip at their heels if he thought the wave was too big or if they did not have enough time to make the next dune.

Jason was up in the tower, carefully scanning the horizon for any sign of a vessel in distress. The ocean was white as far as the eye could see, with fifteen- to twenty-foot breakers on the inside and outside bars. Through his glass he could see the keeper and his crew double-checking the beach cart, surfboat, and gear. He could also see the kids making their way south, scampering from dune to dune with Barnacle by their sides. It aggravated him to see the children taking such chances with a rough sea, but somehow he felt better because Barnacle was with them.

Suddenly Jason caught sight of something just offshore, in the outer surf line, and scampered to the tack room for a stronger glass. He returned to the tower to get a better look at what appeared to be a small piece of wreckage just off the beach, near the area where the kids were headed. When Jason yelled to Keeper Daniels and the crew to report what he had seen, the keeper told him to come and assist with the rescue.

Jason took the tower steps, two at a time, and ran to the beach, carrying the glasses with him. When he approached the crew, Keeper Daniels asked him for the more powerful glass as Jason pointed in the direction of the wreckage. Then Keeper Daniels began to bark orders to his men. "Too close for the surfboat, and no time for the beach cart. Grab a life vest and those coils of rope and head down the beach," he commanded.

Stan had just toppled off a dune, falling forward as he overran his mark. He scrambled up the next dune just as a wave broke where he had fallen. The three children sat down to rest before testing the next wave, but Barnacle was ready to keep going. He was pawing the sand and making whimpering noises, excited and ready to go farther down the beach.

Then the kids heard a faint cry for help. At first they didn't know where the noise was coming from, until they saw the wreckage between the outside bar and the surf line. Two adults and two children were clinging to a small mast and the forepeak of a small vessel. When the next wave passed, Barnacle and the children ran to the dune in front of the wreckage but were unsure of what to do next. They felt helpless. There was no time to run back to the station for help, and they knew they could not swim out in the pounding surf and strong current to help the victims.

Suddenly Barnacle jumped off the dune and headed seaward. Kristina called for him to return to the dune, but he continued forward into the water. A large wave broke over his head as he entered the surf line, but he came up on the other side and continued to swim toward the wreckage. As Barnacle reached the victims, the man placed the little girl on his back and he swam back to shore, where Kristina, Stan, and Shanna helped the little girl up onto the dune. Barnacle returned to the wreckage three more times until all the victims were safely atop the dune.

Keeper Daniels had witnessed the rescue through his glass as his crew made their way to the scene, and he had reported his sighting to his men along the way. Sure enough, when the station crew arrived, the four victims were standing on the dune next to Shanna, Stan, and Kristina, with Barnacle by their side. As the crew rested, Keeper Daniels gave everyone a drink of fresh water and began to explain how they would leave the beach and proceed back to the station with the rescued family.

Upon arrival at the station, Keeper Daniels inquired about the family whom Barnacle had rescued and found out that they were the Johnson family from Cape Charles, Virginia. They were sailing to the west coast of Florida for the remainder of the summer when their small family-owned schooner got caught in rough seas and started taking on water.

Luckily, the Johnson family had only suffered minor scratches. They were treated by the medical officer at the station, and after some hot soup and cornbread they wanted to meet Barnacle and the children. The medical officer told them to rest for the afternoon, and Keeper Daniels promised that he would invite the children for supper that evening, and they could visit with Barnacle.

The station cook fixed a meal of red drum, boiled potatoes, and meat cracklings, along with a large pan of cornbread, and served it on two large picnic tables on the station porch. Beth, Kristina, Stan, Shanna, and Mrs. Gray were asked to join the station crew and the Johnson family for the meal. Afterward, Keeper Daniels hitched his mare to a cart and took Mr. Johnson to the telegraph office to let his folks in Virginia know that he and his family were safe in Chicamacomico. The children took turns riding Barnacle around the station yard until dark.

Upon returning to the station, Keeper Daniels told Kristina that, in reward for the heroic rescue, Barnacle had earned a larger portion of oats and hay than he normally received. Barney commented about how Barnacle had acted so nervously and anxiously prior to the rescue, but he now seemed so calm and settled. "I knew there was something special about him the first time I saw him, half-drowned and clinging to the tangled rigging of the *Sylvia*," Barney said.

"I knew there was something special about him the first time I saw him at the plantation in South Carolina," Kristina said. Then Barney lifted her up so that she could give her horse a big hug.

Mr. Johnson told everyone how amazed he was to see Barnacle swimming toward his family and how thankful he was that Barnacle kept coming back until everyone was safe. He, too, was convinced that there was something very special about Barnacle and his dedication to protecting people.

The next day, Stan and Shanna went to the boardinghouse to wake Kristina. They wanted to go back to the station to visit the Johnson children again. While Barnacle waited for them to come outside, he scratched his back in the front yard by rolling over and over in the dirt near the apple tree. Then he stood very still, bobbing his head in appreciation, while Stan scratched his back with a stick he had picked up from the ground.

When the children arrived at the station, Barney told them that the keeper had taken the Johnson family to the landing to book passage for their journey back to Virginia. He told them that they would be welcome to wait on the front porch until the Johnsons returned. In the meantime, the cook gave each of them a glass of cold lemonade.

Soon the Johnson family returned to the station. Barney had the day off and offered to take the young ones fishing, after they got permission from their parents. The station cook packed lunches for them, and then Barney hitched Barnacle up to the cart and off they went. After stopping in Southard Woods to buy hooks and fishing line, Barney took them to a cane field and helped them cut the cane for their fishing poles. Then he tied their lines on for them and placed the bobbers and hooks. When they reached the sound, Barney showed the children how to catch crabs and small minnows for bait as they proceeded to Opening Creek to the fishing hole.

Two summers earlier, Opening Creek had been dredged very deeply by the running water of a hurricane. It was a known place for puppy drum and speckled trout to ambush smaller baitfish looking for the safety of the marsh grass. The gang unloaded their gear and began to fish, but every time they waded out past their knees, Barnacle would scold them by whining, pawing the ground, and bobbing his head until they returned to knee-deep water. Still, the children ended up with a good catch of fish. They ate their picnic lunch, then headed back to the station at Northard Woods and had fish for dinner that night.

Mr. Johnson had arranged passage for his family to return to Virginia the next morning. Barney, Stan, Kristina, and Shanna took them to the landing in a cart pulled by Barnacle, and Skipper Logan Farrow helped them board the *Sea Mullet* at the dock. Everyone said good-bye to the Johnsons as the *Sea Mullet* slipped away to meet the *Coastal Rambler.*

Barney asked the children if they wanted to stop by Zack's Place on the way back, and they all screamed, "Yes!" Zack's Place was a sweets shop where most of the teenagers hung out. Mr. Zack always turned a freezer of vanilla ice cream in the afternoon, and he had all types of toppings to flavor the cold treat. He also made his own type of cocoa-flavored waffle cones, which Barnacle especially liked—without the ice cream. Stan and Shanna had plain vanilla. Barney had a chocolate-flavored topping, and Kristina chose strawberry. As they licked their ice cream cones on the way back to the station, each wondered what adventures the next day would bring.

❧ 5 ❧

The Roundup

The very same storm that had just passed the Chicamacomico area was also making life complicated for Edward, the sea captain, as he mastered the *Edith Marie* out of the mouth of Chesapeake Bay. He had sailed from Baltimore, heading for South America with a load of white oak, and would be returning with a load of coffee. The sea captain had ordered the *Edith Marie* to be readied for storm conditions. She was a sturdily built freighter, suited for heavy weather. The captain tried to stay close to the shore, but as the storm grew worse he headed the vessel offshore and sailed southeast, toward Bermuda. The storm was less threatening offshore, so he decided to sail around it. As the conditions improved he could not help but wonder about the weather at Chicamacomico and how his family was getting along.

The weather at Northard Woods was very hot. The older folks referred to this time of year as "the dog days of August." With little wind, the mosquitoes were very thick, and the greenhead flies were unbearable. When Kristina went outside, Barnacle was swishing his tail to drive the flies off his back and rump. Kristina broke a small branch from a nearby tree to keep the pests off of her as she and Barnacle headed to see Stan and Shanna.

When she arrived at the Gray house, Kristina met Stan and Shanna out on their front porch. She told them that Keeper Daniels wanted to see them as soon as possible, so all three headed for the station with Barnacle at their heels. When they arrived Keeper Daniels was sitting on the screened side porch. "Come on up," he said. "I thought of something you kids might like to be a part of."

The children listened intently as Keeper Daniels continued. "Each year, headquarters sends a man down here from Washington to treat all the livestock in the area for ticks and fleas. He inspects each of the domestic animals and dips them in a solution that kills anything attached to their hides. I am in charge of this operation at the local level, which includes meeting the government man at the landing; helping him get his solution down to the dipping vat, south of Clarks; and most of all, rounding up all the animals for treatment," he said. "Rowan Austin, the junior officer, will be in charge of the station, while Barney, Jason, and Michael will assist me with roundup," he told them. The children could hardly believe their ears when the keeper said that they were welcome to come along, provided it was okay with their mothers.

"You mean an old-fashioned roundup of all the domestic animals?" asked Stan.

"Yes," Keeper Daniels replied. "You will be on horseback, camping, and eating out of a chuck wagon for a few days." Then the children took off immediately to seek permission for the upcoming adventure.

As Jason was busy getting his gear ready for the trip, his wife scolded, "You watch out for them young'uns, you hear?"

"They'll be fine," he said. "They'll have the time of their lives!"

Jason packed the wagon and called for Stan and Shanna. They were over at the boardinghouse, trying to convince Beth to let Kristina go along on the roundup. Whatever concern Beth brought up, the kids had an answer. When Jason pulled up at the boardinghouse, he assured Beth that he and Barney would watch out for the children.

"Who will watch out for you and Barney?" Beth responded.

"Keeper Daniels is in charge and will watch out for all of us," Jason replied. "Just think how unhappy Kristina will be if she has to stay here while her friends are on an old-fashioned roundup."

Beth gave Jason a hard look. She wanted Kristina's last month of summer to be a happy one, so she gave in, helping Kristina pack her gear for the journey.

Then Jason and the children set off for the station, with Barnacle following very close behind them.

Barney and Keeper Daniels were in the stable area, preparing two big wagons to carry the dipping solution. Soon they headed for the landing area to meet up with the government livestock agent, and as they arrived the *Sea Mullet* was just nearing the dock with a load of passengers. The livestock agent was the first man off the boat; his name was David Wilson. After introductions were made, Keeper Daniels suggested that Mr. Wilson continue south aboard the *Coastal Rambler* and meet them at Clarks Landing, where they would offload the dipping supplies and gear.

Barney, Jason, and Keeper Daniels headed their wagons south toward the village of Clarks. As they passed Southard Woods they could see the *Coastal Rambler* anchored up in Southard Channel and the *Sea Mullet* headed back to her. "We'll be in Clarks about the same time as the livestock agent," Jason said, "but we must stop by Mr. Midgett's store and purchase food for the week."

After the chuck wagon was stocked with needed supplies, Barney noticed a yellow Labrador puppy on the porch, lying on a blanket underneath a rocking chair. "Where'd you get the new pup?" he asked Mr. Midgett.

"You remember Old Hazel, who lives in Cedar Hammock marsh?" asked Mr. Midgett. "She has three more to give away."

"Who in the world would be crazy enough to go there and confront her?" Barney asked. "They would have to be out of their mind!"

"Whoever wants a new pup," laughed Mr. Midgett. "As I remember, she helped you quite a bit when Barnacle was ailing."

Kristina had heard the story of how Old Hazel had helped nurse Barnacle and knew there was something mysterious about her. She knew a horse such as Barnacle would be hard to take back to Baltimore, but perhaps a dog would be alright—if only she could get her mother to agree. First she would have to convince someone to take her to Old Hazel's, and she was already dreading the visit.

The keeper, Barney, and Jason watered the horses and headed for Clarks Landing to meet the livestock agent. At the fork in the road, Keeper Daniels and Barney turned down the landing road while Jason continued to the dipping vat area with the children to set up camp. Keeper Daniels instructed Jason to start building a temporary fenced area leading up to the entrance of the dipping vat. The children also had duties. They would assemble the mess tent, unload and situate the supplies, and help Jason with the fence for the horses.

Just as Jason and the kids finished their work of setting up camp, Keeper Daniels, Barney, and Mr. Wilson arrived with supplies to dip and treat the animals. They unhitched the horses and allowed them to graze nearby under Barnacle's watchful eye. Barney asked the kids if they would like to accompany him on a berry-picking trip to the beach hills. He told them he knew of a nice patch, close to their camp, and that they could have a berry-flavored dessert after the evening meal. Shortly they set off to pick the berries with Barnacle leading the way.

"How does Barnacle know where we're going?" asked Shanna.

"All he knows is that we are headed for the beach, and he loves the beach," Kristina answered.

That evening they ate their meals and berry desserts, then gathered at the fire to discuss the roundup of the animals. Keeper Daniels began by assigning the horses. "Kristina can ride Barnacle, Stan can ride the bay, and Shanna can ride my mare. I'll ride the pinto. Shanna and Barney can ride the two paints pulling the largest wagon. We'll be responsible for all the livestock from the Gull Station area north to the village of Clarks. Aaron Hooper will drive his animals to the vat from the Southard Woods area, and Nathaniel Ambrose will drive his group from Northard Woods. I have extra folks coming to help Mr. Wilson with the examining area and the mixing of the dipping solution for the vat. Before it gets too dark, we need to check the vat for cracks and make sure the steps are in good shape so that the animals can walk out of the vat once they have been dipped. We will be rounding up all the domestic horses, cows, and goats for treatment. The horses will have to be penned up at night so they don't run off with the wild Banker ponies."

"What wild Banker ponies?" asked Kristina.

"The ones that roam these islands from shipwrecks," said Keeper Daniels. "They are led by a black stallion called 'the Raven.' He protects the ponies and will not let anyone get near them."

"Will the Banker ponies be dipped with the rest of the stock?" asked Stan.

"Are you kidding?" Jason replied. "That Raven will not let anyone get close enough to rope a single one of 'em!"

The next day was sunny and hot as they began the four-mile ride south toward the Gull Shoal Lifesaving Station, with Keeper Daniels in the lead. On arrival they were greeted by the Gull Shoal Station keeper and his men. They rested for a while and listened as Keeper Daniels explained the roundup. He told the group that they had to spread out and cover the entire area, from the ocean to the sound. They had to gather all the livestock they could find and drive them to the dipping vat area. He placed Jason to the east with Stan next to him. Kristina was next, with Shanna and Barney next to her, and Keeper Daniels took up the westward position.

The drive was going well until they reached the open meadow about a mile away from the dipping area. Suddenly the Raven appeared with about fifty other wild ponies. He stopped short when he saw the herd of mixed animals being driven by Keeper Daniels and his group, then ran over to Barnacle and Kristina, pawed the ground, and snorted.

Barnacle answered the challenge with a snort as he pawed the ground in return. For the next few minutes, the two stallions sized one another up, but Barnacle held his ground and would not allow the Raven and his herd to pass. "Hold 'em tight," warned Keeper Daniels as they neared the dipping area. "If the Raven breaks through, he'll take our animals with him."

The Raven's herd was caught between Aaron Hooper and his group to the north, and Keeper Daniels and his group to the south. As they neared the entrance to the vat area, the Raven charged Keeper Daniels's position. Keeper Daniels closed off the stallion's path, forcing him into the sound. The Raven swam to a shoal, close to the bank, and called for his herd. In response they also charged the keeper's position. It was all Keeper Daniels and his group could do to contain the domestic animals while the Raven's herd escaped to the south, out into the sound.

Keeper Daniels drove his animals to the holding area at the entrance of the dipping vat. Agent Wilson examined each animal before they entered the dipping vat. He checked their ears, nose, throat, mouth, and feet. Then they were dipped and made to swim in the solution to the other end of the vat.

After Aaron Hooper secured his animals in the entrance to the vat, he stopped to speak with Keeper Daniels. "I thought we had that Raven and his bunch."

"We wouldn't be able to examine them or dip them, as long as the Raven's around," Keeper Daniels replied.

At the end of the day—after all three groups of animals were examined, dipped, and released—Keeper Daniels told the kids to go tend to their horses and bed them down for the night. Then he, Aaron Hooper, and Nathaniel Ambrose sat around the fire and told tales about past roundups.

Before the day was over, the Raven reappeared at the camp with his Banker ponies several yards behind him. A smaller stallion ran up to join him, but the Raven nipped him and made him return to the herd. Barnacle broke free and charged the Raven, and soon both horses were pawing the ground, challenging each other. The Raven circled Barnacle before they went at it, biting, kicking, and pawing at each other—raising such a fuss that everyone came to see the cause of all the racket.

Kristina wanted to approach the horses, but Keeper Daniels stopped her. After what seemed to be a lifetime to Kristina, Barnacle was able to land a sound kick to the Raven's hindquarter, knocking him off his feet. When the Raven got up and limped back to his herd, Kristina called for Barnacle and he came to her. Shanna helped Kristina clean Barnacle's small scrapes and bruises, and Mr. Wilson brought the girls some salve to help soothe and cure the scrapes.

"I guess the Raven had all of Barnacle he wanted," Aaron said to Keeper Daniels, and they both laughed.

"You have a very special stallion," Nathaniel Ambrose said to Kristina. Kristina hugged Barnacle but could not help thinking of the Raven and his wild ponies with no one to care for them.

The next morning, everyone helped break camp and head back home. Agent Wilson would be returning to Elizabeth City on the *Coastal Rambler* to pick up more dipping solution and supplies. A government-owned dipping vat was located every fifteen miles apart on the islands, and Agent Wilson was responsible for treating all animals from Northard Woods to Ocracoke.

Stan, Shanna, and Kristina had many stories to share with their friends when they returned to Northard Woods. On the way back, Kristina asked Barney about Cedar Hammock and Hazel.

"You're thinking about them pups, aren't you?" he asked. "We passed Cedar Hammock about three miles back," Barney told her. "We don't have time to fool with any pups today, and we must get back to the station before nightfall. Anyway, you need to talk to your mother before considering a trip to see Old Hazel about those pups. She's a very scary person, and I feel uneasy when I'm around her."

Kristina settled down in the back of the wagon to take a nap between Stan and Shanna, who were already asleep. She thought to herself, *Mom will be no problem, but finding someone to go with me to visit Old Hazel could be complicated.* Then she thought of her dad. She knew he would do anything for her. If only her father would return before she had to go back to Baltimore at the end of the summer. She smiled to herself and drifted off to sleep.

6

MULLET FISHING

Loaded with coffee, the *Edith Marie* was just beginning to enter the Florida Straits. The sea captain's mind drifted to Northard Woods and his family. If only the weather held fair, like the past few days, they would be off Hatteras Island in about three days. He and his first officer had discussed a possible long-boat landing, near the Chicamacomico Station, so that Edward could surprise his wife and daughter. They were not expecting him for another three weeks, until after he delivered the coffee in Baltimore and booked passage back to the island.

Kristina woke up early in the morning to Barnacle's constant snorting and complaining outside in the corral, where he was pacing and prancing nervous-ly. She walked out on the front porch and tried to calm him. "Be quiet or you'll wake the entire neighborhood," she said to him. "What's the matter with you? Why are you kicking up such a fuss?" she asked him. No matter what she did, Barnacle would not calm down.

Beth walked outside, yawning, and said, "He wants to go for a run this morning. Eat your breakfast and take him out."

After breakfast Kristina saddled Barnacle and looked forward to a nice, quiet ride along the sound side, which was always so beautiful early in the morning. They went out the gate at the boardinghouse, and Barnacle turned in the direction of the beach. "We are not going to the beach," she told him, then turned him toward the landing road, where he walked a few steps, stopped, and refused to go any farther. "Come on, Barnacle," she said, kicking his sides, but he would not move. "What in the world is the matter with you?" Kristina asked. "I thought you wanted to go for a run this morning."

Kristina decided to take Barnacle back to the corral, but as they reached the gate he refused to enter. Instead he turned his head in the direction of the beach. "You always want to go to the beach," she said. Then she gave in and let Barnacle lead the way. He soon quickened his pace to a trot, followed by a slow gallop, then a full gallop. "What is your hurry?" Kristina asked. "Slow down, you fool horse," she said, pulling back hard on the reins but to no avail. Barnacle galloped on.

The *Edith Marie* had about five miles to go on her shoreward tack when Edward picked up the Chicamacomico Station tower in his glass. He knew it was Chicamacomico because of its color. The lifesaving stations were spaced about seven miles apart along the coast, and each was painted a different color to help ships establish position.

Barney was on lookout duty in the tower. "Here comes a vessel with a bone in her teeth!" he shouted to Keeper Daniels. The surfman was referring to the white water being kicked up by the bow of the freight schooner as she made a beeline for the shore. This phrase had originated from the white water resembling a dog running with a bone in its mouth.

"If she stays on her course, she will soon be on the outer bar. Stay on her," Keeper Daniels shouted to Barney, "and I'll ready the men at the boathouse."

"She is striking sail, making ready to anchor," Barney shouted.

"Hold fast until I can figure this out," Keeper Daniels told his crew.

"She appears to be okay," Barney said. "Just decided to anchor up off the outer bar."

Why in the world would a vessel decide to anchor up in open water, near the outside bar? Keeper Daniels thought to himself.

Kristina could not slow Barnacle down until they reached the surf line, where she almost fell off in the water. Then she saw the schooner, which puzzled her. She had seen many sails in the past weeks, but only on the horizon. Kristina could not believe her eyes as she watched a smaller boat being lowered to the water—and now someone was rowing to shore. She tried to urge Barnacle out of the surf line, but he would not budge. Instead he turned his head from side to side and pawed the water-soaked sand.

Keeper Daniels and the station crew arrived in two wagons. "Someone is going to land in that longboat," Keeper Daniels said.

As the small boat neared the shore, Edward waved to the group. "That's my daddy!" Kristina shouted as she ran to greet him.

The station crew helped Edward with his luggage, and the group made their way back to the village as the longboat returned to the *Edith Marie.*

Kristina hugged her dad as they rode Barnacle to the boardinghouse. "I am so glad to see you, Daddy," she said, "and Mom will really be surprised! We were expecting you in a couple of weeks. I'm happy that you surprised us. I have somewhere I want you to take me."

"Where might that be?" her father asked.

"I want you to take me to see Old Hazel," Kristina said.

"Isn't that the old lady who knows and cares for animals?" he asked. "The one who helped Barney when Barnacle was ailing?"

"The very same one. She lives at the edge of Cedar Hammock marsh, near the floating bog," Kristina replied.

"Why in the world would you want to go there?" her father asked.

"That's a secret, and we'll need Mom involved to discuss the reason."

"Something that involves animals, I'll bet," her father said as they rode on.

"You'll see," she replied.

As they entered the gate at the boardinghouse, Kristina ran, yelling to her mother that her father was home. Beth came out on the porch and could hardly believe her eyes. As she greeted her husband, she said, "We were expecting you in a couple of weeks."

"I thought I'd surprise you," he replied.

"You sure have," she told him.

"Kristina has something she wants to discuss with us as soon as she returns from the barn," Edward told Beth.

Kristina took Barnacle to his stall and gave him a rubdown while she formulated her plan to visit Hazel and see the pups. "You knew my dad was on that ship," she told Barnacle as she hugged him. "How do you know about things before they happen? You seem to know a lot of things before they take place, and I believe you truly have a gift," she told her horse as she finished his rubdown. Then she walked back to the house, wondering how she would convince her parents to allow her to have a puppy.

Kristina's parents were setting the table for lunch when she arrived. "What do you want to talk to us about?" her mother asked.

"I want Dad to take me to Old Hazel's to see some new pups Mr. Midgett told us about. I want to take one back to Baltimore when we leave. Barnacle is too big to go with us, and I have to live with that," she said. "It is not fair, and I wish I could live here with Barnacle, but since I can't, I think I should at least be able to have a puppy."

"We've been over that," Beth told her daughter. "Your education is very important to us. The opportunity for a variety of subjects and a more comprehensive course of study is much better in the Baltimore area. It is close to your father's work and our family."

"I think I should be able to take a puppy home with me to remind me of the area and Barnacle," was Kristina's reply. Without much hesitation, Edward gave in and agreed to arrange the trip to see Hazel.

"You always give in to her," Beth told him. "She is completely spoiled and gets everything she wants." Edward knew his wife was right. Kristina just smiled. After all, she was his only daughter.

Kristina ran toward the Gray house, completely forgetting that Barnacle was waiting for her. Barnacle began to whine and complain as he realized that Kristina was leaving him behind. Beth was looking out the window and said, "Edward, come look at that fool horse. Kristina has left him, and he is going to jump the fence!"

"That's not possible," Edward exclaimed. "That fence is six feet high!"

"There he goes," Beth said, as Barnacle easily cleared the fence and caught up to Kristina. She could hardly wait to tell Stan and Shanna about her plans to visit Old Hazel and ask for one of the pups. As she neared their house, she saw Shanna on the front porch teasing a yellow kitten with an empty cotton spool tied to a string. She told Shanna about her plans and asked if she and Stan wanted to go with her to Cedar Hammock.

"My dad and Barney have a week off from duties, so they are going mullet fishing up to New Inlet, and Stan is going with them," Shanna explained. "They're at the landing preparing the net skiff now."

"We should go and talk to them," said Kristina. "I really want them to go with us to see Hazel. Barney knows her better than anybody else. She helped him with Barnacle."

Shanna and Kristina rode Barnacle bareback to the landing. "He is so smart," Shanna said. She was seated in front of Kristina with a handful of Barnacle's mane.

"He sure is," Kristina replied as they entered the landing road.

"Look at that," Stan said, when he saw Kristina and Shanna approaching on Barnacle. "That horse goes along just like he is bridled. He even knows where to go without being told."

"Yes, he does," Jason replied. Then Stan asked the girls what they were doing.

"We're going to see Hazel about a pup for Kristina," Shanna told him, "and we want you to come with us."

"We're going mullet fishing," Stan replied.

Barney said, "You need to be careful when dealing with Hazel. She knows a lot about animals, but there is something strange about her. I will talk to Norman Scarborough and see if he will go with you. At least Hazel seems to tolerate him."

The next morning Barney talked to Norman about escorting Kristina and her father to Cedar Hammock. Norman told Barney that he was too busy to go with them, but he suggested that they go to Clarks and borrow Aaron Hooper's small sprit sailboat and avoid the floating marsh. Edward, Shanna, and Kristina gladly took his advice and told Barnacle to head for Clarks. When they arrived at the Hooper cottage, they talked to Aaron about their journey. He was glad to loan them the small sailboat and mapped out a route for Edward to follow. He also agreed to stable Barnacle until their return.

Edward used a shove stick to push the boat away from the dock and into the mouth of the creek. Then they would raise the sail to begin their journey southward. As they pulled away, Barnacle began to whine, snort, and protest about being left behind. Just as they reached Cedar Creek Point, Barnacle jumped the fence and shot through the marsh to catch up with his friends. Then he kept pace with the boat.

"Well, I guess he is going with us after all," Edward told the girls, and they all laughed.

Meanwhile, Barney, Jason, and Stan paddled out the entrance of the Northard Woods harbor in a sixteen-foot net skiff containing the mullet net. From there, they paddled out to the *Flying Fish* and tied the net skiff to the stern. The *Flying Fish* was a double-master, with a cabin that could sleep four people.

As soon as they boarded the vessel, they raised sail and headed for New Inlet and Pea Island to do some mullet fishing. As they sailed along, Jason thought of previous fishing trips and wondered how this one would turn out. If all went well, he planned to be back home by the weekend. He knew that mullet started schooling up near the end of August to prepare for their migration south and could usually be found in the sheltered areas close to shore, hiding in the grass beds.

With the net skiff in tow, the fishermen sailed north, around the shallow water of New Inlet, and entered the sheltered area of Pea Island Bay. After anchoring the *Flying Fish*, they boarded the net skiff once again and started shoving through the shallow water, back toward the shore, to catch their mess of fish.

The three fishermen would have to shove the net skiff, containing a fifteen-hundred-yard-long net, until they spotted a school of mullet. The net contained a wooden staff tied to each end. Once the fish were sighted, the skiff would be paddled as fast as possible toward them. One man would jump overboard with one end of the net, holding the staff in a vertical position with lead weights downward and corks atop. Then the boat would be paddled quickly around the school of mullet, paying the net out over the stern to surround the fish.

If this procedure was successful, both ends of the net would be brought together, trapping the fish inside. The man outside the boat would take one end of the net and walk inside the other end, making the circle smaller and forcing the fish to become hung up in the webbing. The two men in the boat would then remove the fish as the net was pulled back in. This procedure would be repeated until the desired catch was made.

The fellas shoved onward, searching for mullet. Jason hoped he and Barney would have a good catch, especially with the fall coming on. His son, Stan, wanted to make money to help buy school clothes for himself and his sister. He also wanted to purchase some new trout fishing equipment.

Edward and the girls sailed into Clarks Bay, and Barnacle ran along the sound side. Just before they reached Clarks Island they spotted a large school of mullet darting in and out of the grass lumps between the shore and the island.

"I'll bet Barney, Stan, and my dad would like to be here right now to set on these mullets," Shanna said.

"That's what they are looking for?" Kristina asked as she pointed to the fish.

"Yes," was Shanna's reply, "and that is a big school."

After passing No-Ache Point, Edward said, "Okay, girls, we're here! There's No-Ache Island on the left and Cedar Hammock Island on the right." He pointed and said, "There's the creek that leads up to Old Hazel's sandy beach, if Aaron's map is right." Then they saw a large sign that read, *Keep your distance. No one is welcome here. Stay away. You have no business here. There is nothing here for you.*

As they passed the sign, they entered a sheltered bay area with a nice white sandy beach. A rowboat was pulled up on the beach and tied to an old tree stump next to a path leading into a well-hidden hammock area. As their skiff landed, the girls jumped out and began cautiously walking up the path, with Barnacle at their heels.

"You girls wait for me," Edward called after them, but they continued to creep slowly up the path.

Overgrown with bushes, there was very little sunlight along the path, and the girls could only see straight ahead. Finally they came to a clearing and Old Hazel's shack. In the dimming light, in her front yard, Hazel was standing next to a big pot of boiling water, pushing something down into the mixture that looked like the hand of a small child.

❦ 7 ❧

Pot of Boiling Children

Barney, Jason, and Stan shoved the skiff all night looking for mullet. Just before daylight they spotted a very large school headed south. They decided to return to the *Flying Fish*, sail past the mullet, and wait for them. By the time they could make sail, the mullet were way ahead of them, so they sailed on, trying to catch up to the fish. When they got close enough to see the mullet, the fish entered the Southard Channel area. "We'll have to wait until they come out of this deep water to set on them," Jason said. The men sailed to the edge of Opening Shoals, anchored the *Flying Fish*, and readied the net skiff.

Just as the fish came out of the deep water, Jason jumped overboard with the staff tied to the end of the net, and Stan shoved the skiff to the south as fast as he could. Just as he turned the skiff to the east to circle the fish, the entire school turned and swam in an eastward direction. Then Stan shoved the skiff as fast as he could to the east. He was able to turn the school back to the west and surround them with the net. Then he shoved the boat back to Jason in order to trap the fish inside the net. "I think we've got the entire school!" Barney said with excitement.

Barney and Stan started pulling the net back in the boat while Jason made the circle smaller. When they finished taking in the net and were shoving back to the *Flying Fish*, they noticed the shoreline. "We are almost to the Cedar Hammock," Barney said. "I wonder how Kristina, Shanna, and Edward are making out with Old Hazel."

When Edward caught up with Kristina and Shanna, he found them peeking at Hazel through the bushes. She was in her front yard, standing in front of a big boiling pot.

"Why are you kids hiding?" he asked.

"Quiet," warned Kristina. "We think she's cooking children in that pot."

"That looks like a small hand she's pushing down with that stirring stick," Shanna whispered.

As Edward strained his eyes to see what Hazel was boiling, Barnacle walked out in the open and made a soft whining sound.

"Who is there?" shouted Hazel as she wheeled around. "What are you doing here, and what do you want?" Her bonnet half-covered her worn-looking face.

"She looks like a witch," whispered Kristina.

Barnacle walked right up to Hazel and nuzzled his head in her hands. "Well, hello, big fellow," she said. "My, haven't you grown up? If memory serves me right, Barney should be close behind you.

"Come on out, Barney," Hazel said. "I know you're around here somewhere."

"It's not Barney," Edward said as he stepped out of the bushes.

"Who in the blazes are you, and how did you find this place?" Hazel asked.

"My name is Edward. Barney was too busy to lead us out here," Edward continued. "He asked Norman Scarborough and Aaron Hooper to help us find you, but they were also unavailable. Aaron Hooper drew us a map to your place."

"I knew I should have let them disappear in that floating marsh when I had the chance," Hazel exclaimed. "What do you mean by 'us'?" Hazel asked. "I only see you and this horse."

"My daughter and her friend are hiding in the bushes."

"Well, tell them to come on out so I can see what I am dealing with," Hazel replied.

"They're scared of you," said Edward. "They think you're boiling children in that pot. Those branches resemble small hands from a distance, according to the children."

Hazel laughed. "I keep to myself and prefer the company of animals to that of people," she said. "I try to keep folks away from here as best as I can," she told him. "As for the pot of boiling water, I am making bayberry candles for my cabin. Tell them to come on out so you can state your business here. I know you want something or you wouldn't have gone to all the trouble to get here."

"Come on out, girls," Edward said as they slowly crept out of the bushes, keeping their eyes on Hazel and the boiling pot.

"Come closer," Hazel told them. "I am boiling the wax off the bayberries in this pot. It is easier to boil the berries while they are still on the branches rather than pick them off. If you pick them, you have to fish each berry out of the pot one at a time. If you leave them on the branches, they come out together."

Hazel pointed to Shanna and said, "I remember you. You're the one who helped Barney with this horse when he was ailing." Then she spoke to Edward: "If you will help me remove this pot, you can use the fire to cook your supper, and I'll finish the candles tomorrow morning." Hazel told them they could sleep in her net house, down at the shore side. At last, she wanted to know why they had ignored her warning to stay away.

"Mr. Midgett showed us a puppy at his store and told us that he got it from you," Kristina told her.

"So, it's a pup you want. Well, I have two of them left, one black and one brown, but they cannot be separated. The brown pup depends on the black one for everything. They need to stay together until they are a bit older. You will have to take both of them or leave them here," Hazel said.

"We can sleep on it tonight and decide by morning," Edward said as he helped Hazel remove the pot from the fire. Afterward, they cooked and ate their supper, and then retired to the net house for the night.

Upon their return to Hazel's shack the next morning, they found her boiling more bay branches in the pot. "You girls can help me with the candles," she told them. "First we will boil the bayberries until the waxy covering melts off and floats to the top of the water. Then we will scoop it up and pour it in the candle molds containing the wick strings. Once the wax hardens, we'll remove them from the molds, and the candles will be ready for use. They will light up my cabin and fill it with the pleasant smell of bayberry. We'll make enough so you can have some, too," she told the girls.

Kristina and Shanna helped Hazel make up enough candles for her own use as well as an order to sell at Mr. Midgett's store—and a few dozen to take home with them. Then Hazel said, "Well, you have earned the pups, but you have to take both of them with you when you leave."

"Stan and I can keep one if we can convince Mom to let us," Shanna said.

While Hazel walked them down to the net house, she politely said, "The next time you need me for anything, send for me, and I'll come to the villages to see you. Please destroy that map and tell Barney, Norman, and Aaron that I will deal with them later. Be sure to tell everyone that this was not an enjoyable experience for you, because I want to keep as many people away from here as I can," she told them. Then Edward, Kristina, and Shanna loaded the pups, waved good-bye to Hazel, and promised to keep her secret.

"Old Hazel is really a nice person, isn't she, Dad?" Kristina asked.

"Yes, but she likes to keep to herself, which is why she acts mean and mysterious," replied Edward.

They raised sail and began their trip north to Clarks. As they sailed around No-Ache Point, they spotted Barney, Stan, and Jason aboard the *Flying Fish*, sailing north with their load of mullet.

"What are they doing way down here?" asked Kristina.

"They probably couldn't find any mullet up at New Inlet," Shanna replied.

"Let's catch up to them and check out their catch," Kristina replied.

Soon they were sailing alongside the *Flying Fish*. "How many fish did you catch?" Edward hollered.

"We caught about five hundred pounds!" Barney hollered back. "We have to head up to the Loran Meekins Fish House at Northard Woods to sell them."

Shanna asked her father if she and Stan could have a puppy. "That's up to your mother," was Jason's reply.

"We'll see you back in Northard Woods," Edward said as he turned the boat shoreward toward Clarks Landing. As they approached the landing, Barnacle was waiting for them on the edge of the marsh. They tied up the boat, loaded the wagon, and stopped by Aaron's cottage. Aaron was in the backyard mending net, and he smiled as they approached. "How is Old Hazel?" he asked.

"She said she would deal with you, Barney, and Norman later," Edward replied.

Aaron shuddered. "That old woman gives me the creeps. Some folks say she has the power of black magic and can place hexes."

"She is very strange and likes to stay to herself," Edward said. "She gave us these pups and hurried us on our way."

They gave Aaron some of the bayberry candles, dropped Hazel's order of candles off at Mr. Midgett's store, and told Barnacle to head north. Just as they were entering the open grounds, south of Northard Woods, they noticed a group of horses coming toward them, heading south. The herd was being led by the wild black stallion, the Raven.

Barnacle perked up his ears as they neared the group of horses. The Raven stopped his small herd and ran up to the wagon, snorting at Barnacle. Returning the challenge, Barnacle snorted, pawed the ground, and began to shake his head from side to side.

"Steady, boy," Edward said to Barnacle.

The Raven positioned himself between his herd and Barnacle as they continued past the wagon on the right. Barnacle kept himself between the Raven and the wagon and never moved—until the Raven trotted back to his herd and directed them south.

"They're not finished with each other," Edward told the girls.

When they got back to Northard Woods, Kristina and Shanna headed for the boardinghouse. They unhitched Barnacle, gave him a rubdown, and fed him. Then they took the pups inside to show them off to Kristina's mother.

On their return from mullet fishing, Jason and Stan stopped by the boardinghouse to pick up Shanna. As soon as she saw her father, she told him that she wanted a puppy.

"Come on in for some lemonade," Beth said. "The kids can decide who wants to keep which pup!"

"Old Hazel said that they couldn't be separated until they were older," Edward reminded them.

"I like the black one," said Stan.

"Good," added Kristina, "because I like the brown one!"

"I like them both," said Shanna as the pups played on the porch. "We'll take the black one to show Mom."

As soon as they were separated the pups began to cry. Jason placed the black pup in the wagon, and they both began to scream. When Barnacle heard the pups, he jumped the fence and ran in front of their wagon to block their path. "Even Barnacle knows the pups should stay together," Edward said. Then Kristina climbed on the wagon and placed the brown pup near the black one, where they huddled together, stopped crying, and stared up at everyone.

"We have a mess on our hands," Jason observed as they traveled north.

"Kristina and the brown pup can spend the night with us," Shanna said.

"I guess that will be alright, until we can figure this out," Jason replied. Then he, Stan, Shanna, Kristina, and the pups headed for the Gray cottage, with Barnacle leading the way.

As Edward and Beth relaxed at the boardinghouse, Edward said, "I guess Barnacle is spending the night with the Grays, too!"

"Try and stop him," Beth replied, and they laughed.

When they reached the cottage, Mrs. Gray was standing on the front porch. "How was your catch?" she asked Jason.

"The catch was good!" was his reply. "Your daughter has a surprise for you." Then Shanna held up the black pup. "Can we keep him, Mom? Can we, please?" she asked.

"For heaven's sake, I thought you went to get Kristina a pup," was her reply.

"I have one," said Kristina, holding up the brown one.

"Lord, have mercy," said Mrs. Gray. "Not two of them!"

"They cry when they are separated," added Jason.

"I want to keep the black one, Mom," Stan told his mother. "He is so black, he shines when the light hits him just right!"

"Well, they are too young to stay in the house tonight. I know they are not housebroken yet," replied Mrs. Gray. "They can sleep in the stable with Barnacle until we can make a decision. Shanna, you and Kristina take Barnacle and the mare to the stable, along with the pups, and bed them down."

"After you finish, return to the house and wash up for supper," Jason told them.

While they were gathered at the table, Stan told the mullet fishing tale, then Shanna and Kristina told about their time with Old Hazel. It wasn't long before the children said goodnight and went off to bed.

Jason woke up in the middle of the night and sat up in bed.

"What's wrong?" his wife asked.

"I thought I heard something out in the stable area," Jason replied. Then he lit a lantern and they walked out to the stable, where they found Kristina, Shanna, Barnacle, and the pups curled up, fast asleep.

"Should we wake them?" asked his wife.

"No. That horse won't let anyone or anything get near them. You can count on that," he replied.

8

COCOA AND TAR

The end of the summer was drawing near, and soon Edward and his family would return to Baltimore. Kristina was moping around like she had lost her last friend.

"What is the matter with you lately?" her mother asked.

"I don't want to go back home and leave Barnacle and my friends," she replied.

"There are some things we must do, like it or not," her mother said. "You should go over to the Grays to see Stan and Shanna so that you kids can name these pups today. It would be good to try separating them for short periods of time so that they can get used to being apart. Barnacle is waiting for you outside the fence, ready to start his day."

Kristina picked up both of the pups from their constant play of rolling and biting on one another. When she opened the gate and called Barnacle, he came over and kneeled down so that she could climb up on his back. "Let's go to the Grays," she told him, and Barnacle slowly began walking that way.

"Here comes Kristina," said Jason as he started off for a day of work. "Look how slowly Barnacle is walking along. It's as if he knows Kristina has a pup in each hand."

"He does know! Barnacle knows everything," stated Shanna. "The pups would not stop growling and yapping during their play last night, so Kristina volunteered to take them home and give Mom a rest."

49

"I will see y'all around suppertime," Shanna's father said. "We're drilling every day now, and Keeper Daniels is on edge with hurricane season approaching." Then Jason waved good-bye and headed off toward the station.

"Mom said we should name the pups and try separating them for short periods," Kristina told Stan and Shanna.

"That is a very good idea," Stan said.

"Well, you can have some breakfast first," added Mrs. Gray, standing just inside the screened door. "I've made some nice blueberry pancakes from the berries you kids picked yesterday."

After breakfast the kids relaxed on the front porch. "What should we name the pups?" Shanna asked.

"I think we should name the black one 'Tar,'" Stan stated. "He's so black, he shines when the sunlight hits him just right."

"That's a very good name for him," added Kristina. "The brown one looks like the cocoa your mom makes us at night, to go with the cookies she bakes."

"That's it, then," Stan said. "The black one will be named Tar, and the brown one is Cocoa. From now on, that's what they'll be called."

"We should try small periods of separation today," Kristina suggested.

"Let's take Tar and Cocoa to the beach later," said Stan. "Miles Midgett and I are going drum fishing later. He found some very good sloughs north of the station while he and his dad were gathering wood from the beach yesterday. We can separate the pups at the beach—for short distances, where they can still see each other." Shanna and Kristina agreed and went in the house to ask permission for the beach trip. They returned shortly with smiles on their faces.

"Mom said she would pack us a lunch," said Shanna.

Stan went to the shed to check on his hand line and swarping wire. He would use the hand line to catch large fish near the surf line. The swarping wire was a long piece of copper wire with one end bent back to form a handle. It would be used to smack the water in small creeks to stun the baitfish so that they could be caught.

Stan called Barnacle and hitched him to the family wagon, then loaded up the pups and their gear. They had to stop by the boardinghouse to tell Kristina's mom where they were going.

"Be sure to tell your father," Beth said. "He's at the station with Keeper Daniels, discussing the finer points of navigation."

Stan, Shanna, and Kristina picked up Miles and stopped by the station to see Kristina's father. Edward, Keeper Daniels, Barney, and Jason were in the chart room, going over navigation maps. Edward was showing them how to take latitude and longitude information from the wireless transmissions and plot the progress of approaching hurricanes.

"We're going drum fishing today," Stan told them. "Miles and his dad found some very good spots north of the station yesterday during a wood-gathering hunt at the beach."

"It's a beautiful day for drum fishing," Barney said. "I saw plenty of bait up at Cut-Through Creek the other morning while I was walking beach patrol to New Inlet Station."

"Thanks for the information," said Stan. "Cut-Through Creek is on our way to the fishing hole."

On their way to the beach, Kristina asked Stan about beach patrol. He explained how surfmen from each station walked the beach twice a day. "The stations are located seven miles apart, and one man from each station walks toward the other until they meet in the middle. Then they exchange patrol badges to prove they completed their duty," Stan said. "Patrol duty also allows the exchange of written messages from station to station."

They stopped at the creek to catch some bait, but every time Stan started to the creek, Barnacle moved to block his path. "Kristina, can you do something about this fool horse of yours?" Stan asked. "He will not let me and Miles in the creek to catch bait!"

"There must be some sort of danger near that creek," Kristina responded. "He only acts like that when a threat is near."

Stan and Miles tried to go around the back of the wagon, but Barnacle backed up, blocking their path. "We'll never get any bait this way," Miles said.

"We can climb over the wagon. He can't stop us then!" added Stan.

When they tried to cross the wagon, Barnacle walked a few steps ahead, taking them away from the path entrance. Then Stan told Miles, "You go around the back, and I will go around the front. He can't block both of us."

Barnacle moved to block Stan, and Miles made it to the path entrance. Barnacle pawed the ground and snorted his disapproval at Miles. Then Shanna said, "You better be careful, Miles. Barnacle knows when something is wrong and always protects us."

At that instant, a large cottonmouth water moccasin slithered out of the path near Miles's bare feet and coiled up, ready to strike. Barnacle moved swiftly to the side, placing one of his hooves on the snake's tail, near the end of the coil. The snake bit at Barnacle's leg, but its fangs bounced off the thick covering of Barnacle's hoof. Then Barnacle kicked his leg, sending the snake across the path and out of the way.

"Whoa! That horse just saved me. I will never doubt him again!" exclaimed Miles.

"I told you," Shanna said as Barnacle relaxed and stood still, shaking his head up and down in an approving gesture.

As Stan and Miles walked in the creek, Stan smacked the surface of the water with the swarping wire, and Miles picked up the stunned fish until they had enough bait. They got back in the wagon and headed for the fishing holes north of the station.

When they arrived at the beach, Stan stopped the wagon at one of the largest sloughs, which looked to contain the deepest water. During the fall, the drum fish migrate to the south for the winter, swimming in deep water along the outer edges of the bar until they find an opening. Then they hug the edges of the outlets and swim into the sloughs, looking for baitfish. Stan and Miles decided to fish on the north side of the slough and lay their bait up on the north edge of the sandbar, near the outlet.

Stan baited his hook, which was attached to the end of seventy-five yards of nylon cord. The fishing line contained about five leads attached to it for weight. The other end of the line had a short wooden staff tied to it, which was buried in the sand. The fishing line was laid out on the beach in big, separate half-circle shapes, to allow a tangle-free fling into the ocean.

The boys swirled the hand line above their heads, casting the net into the fishing hole. When they were satisfied with the position of their hand lines, they settled on the beach to talk of previous fishing trips and the drum they had caught in the past.

Kristina and Shanna unhitched Barnacle, took Tar and Cocoa out of the wagon, and went for a walk down the beach. "Look at that," Miles said to Stan. "That horse is walking between the surf and the girls, with the pups close behind them."

"Yes," Stan said. "Dad thinks he has a special gift when it comes to protecting us, and after today I am beginning to believe him. Shanna and Kristina seem to know it already! He's really smart. The girls ride him without saddle or bridle. They just tell him where they want to go, and he takes them there. When he pulls the wagon, you can allow the reins to go slack, and he still leads the way."

Suddenly, as the boys were talking, Stan's staff pulled out of the sand and headed for the surf.

"Stan, you have a bite!" shouted Miles.

Stan jumped up and chased the end of his line, and just as the wooden staff entered the edge of the surf, he grabbed it and yanked back, hard. "Lost him," he said.

"Spit the hook, I bet," Miles said.

Stan retrieved his bait, examined it, and said, "This bait was drum crushed, alright. See where he had the bait in his crushers? It's flat as a pancake! The crusher in a drum's throat is capable of crushing the shell of a clam," Stan told Miles. Then he baited his hook, cast it back on the edge of the bar, and settled down to talk to Miles again.

"I think it's time we try to separate these pups," Kristina said to Shanna.

"Okay," Shanna replied.

Kristina took Cocoa up the beach, ahead of Shanna and Tar. The puppies looked around for each other and began to yap. The yapping became louder until the girls placed them on the ground. Then they ran back together and rolled and played in the sand. "Maybe we should wait until we get home. Perhaps our parents will have some advice for us," Kristina said, and Shanna agreed. Then they turned around and headed back to check on the boys.

Just as they were nearing the wagon, Tar and Cocoa found an old, half-rotten shark someone had caught and left on the beach. The dogs wallowed in the dead fish remains, covering their coats with a putrid stench.

"What is that awful smell?" Stan asked as the girls approached the wagon.

"The dogs found a rotten shark," Shanna told them.

"Wash them off in the ocean," Stan said.

"I'm not picking them up," Shanna replied.

"At least take them downwind so we can eat lunch," Stan stated.

After they ate their picnic lunch, Kristina coached Tar and Cocoa to wade into the surf, which helped remove some of the smell.

"Look at your fishing lines!" Shanna shouted, as both staffs were rapidly headed for the surf. Both boys grabbed up their gear and began to struggle with the large fish on the ends of their lines.

"Double hookup!" Stan hollered.

"What luck!" said Miles. They both landed their drum fish at about the same time, and then loaded up their gear to head home.

"Put the dogs in the wagon," Stan said to Shanna.

"I'm not picking them up! You do it," was Shanna's reply.

"Perhaps they will follow behind us," Miles said as they started off.

The puppies followed behind the wagon for a short distance, and then they sat down and started to yap. Stan stopped the wagon and used an empty burlap bag to pick them up. Then he tied some fishing line around the end of the bag, allowing their heads to stick out. The pups seemed to be happy with this situation, as they licked each other's faces and then settled down to sleep.

"What is that awful smell?" asked Keeper Daniels as they entered the station yard.

"Tar and Cocoa rolled in a rotten shark some fisherman left on the beach," Stan said.

"Bring them over here to this number-ten tub, and I'll help you wash them. I've just received a new brand of livestock soap that will rid them of that smell," said the keeper.

While Keeper Daniels helped Stan wash the pups, Jason and Barney helped Miles clean the fish. When everyone had been dropped off and the Grays' wagon was returned, Kristina and Barnacle headed back to the boardinghouse.

"We'll work more on separating the dogs tomorrow. They can stay here for the night," Shanna called to Kristina.

"That's fine," Kristina replied, but her mind was not on the dogs. She was thinking of the dreaded day when she would have to leave Barnacle to return to Baltimore and begin school for the winter term. She tried to think of a way to convince her mother to let her stay with Barnacle, but Kristina knew it was hopeless because of her mother's plans for her future education. As Barnacle entered the corral, she thought to herself, *Someday I will come back and never leave!*

❦ 9 ❦

THE PAINFUL PARTING

The weather was clear and the wind light as Barnacle galloped along the surf line with Kristina on his back. She told Barnacle to head back home, and without hesitation he turned in the direction of the boardinghouse. In just three days, her family would be leaving Chicamacomico to go back to Baltimore for the winter.

She waved to Barney and Keeper Daniels as they passed the station. "It still baffles me how she rides that horse without saddle or bridle, and he goes wherever she wants to go," Keeper Daniels said to Barney.

"She just tells him where she wants to go, and he takes her there," replied Barney.

When Kristina went into the boardinghouse, her mother was busy packing for their return journey to Baltimore. "We only have today and two more days," Beth said to her.

"Please don't remind me," Kristina replied.

Then her mother said, "You have to get yourself ready to leave in more ways than just packing. You have to say your good-byes to all of your friends, including Barnacle."

"I'm saving that for the last day, before we leave. I plan to enjoy the time I have left," she said to her mother. "Stan, Shanna, and I are meeting up with Miles and some of his friends to go clamming and have a clambake," Kristina said as she went out the screen door.

A little later, they met up with Miles and his friends south of Clarks, at the entrance to Clarks Bay. Miles offered to tie Barnacle up with the rest of the horses where he could graze on the saw grass, but Kristina politely refused and told Miles that Barnacle would probably walk out in the water with them.

"Don't tell me he knows how to catch clams!" Miles said.

"Of course not," was Kristina's reply, "but he likes to roll in the shallow water, especially near the grassy-topped shoals."

Tar and Cocoa raced ahead of the group, chasing the shorebirds. The clams were located on the outside of Clarks Island, near the edge of Clarks Channel, between Cedar Creek Point and No-Ache Point. It didn't take long for the kids to catch plenty of clams for their clambake. Then they went ashore to the white sand beach and built a fire to roast their catch.

While they enjoyed their feast, Barnacle rolled on the grass-covered shoals nearby, and Tar and Cocoa retrieved sticks that the boys were throwing into the shallow water. On their return to the shore, Barnacle stopped suddenly near an inside slough and started bobbing his head and blocking their path to shore.

"There is something dangerous in the water," Kristina told the group.

"He always does this when something is wrong," added Shanna.

"They're right," Miles added. "I remember the day he protected me from the snake."

"We need to check out the slough before we wade across," Stan said. Sure enough, upon closer inspection they found the slough filled with stinging nettles.

"We can walk up north of the island to the head of the slough where it shallows. Then we'll be able to see the nettles and avoid them," Stan told the group.

As they reached the shore, one of the girls who came with Miles asked Kristina where she got Barnacle. Kristina told the group the entire story of Barnacle, beginning with the South Carolina voyage. "I have never used a bridle or saddle. I just tell him where I want to go, and he goes there. He always senses danger and protects us from it. Barnacle is a very special horse, and it aggravates me to no end that Cocoa and I have to leave him here when we go back to Baltimore. We live in the inner city, and there is no room to stable a large animal like him. I will miss him so much, I can't stand to think about it," she sighed.

On the way home, one of the boys suggested that they stop by Mr. Midgett's and grab a snack. As they munched at the store, Norman Scarborough told them about how he had just seen the Raven and his group of Banker ponies between Clarks and Southard Woods. Then he reminded them of the bad blood between Barnacle and the Raven. "They're not finished with each other," he warned them. "Be careful as you head north."

As the kids entered the meadow south of Southard Woods, they came upon the Raven and his herd of wild ponies. The Raven ran up to Barnacle and snorted his disapproval at their intrusion in his territory. Barnacle answered his challenge by pawing the ground.

"No, Barnacle!" Kristina shouted.

"Get Stan!" Miles yelled.

The Raven retreated to his herd and stood firm while Barnacle and the kids passed by. One small mare left the Raven's herd and trotted over to Barnacle. Then she bobbed her head and neighed to him, and Barnacle answered her in a soft voice.

"Barnacle has a friend in that group," Stan said. When the Raven called to the small mare, she looked at Barnacle, then slowly trotted back to the wild ponies.

When Kristina returned to the boardinghouse, her parents had most of their large things packed. "I can't believe we only have two more days here," she lamented to them.

"I think the dogs have been separated enough that they will be alright," her father said, "but you'll have to come up with something to trick Barnacle when we leave."

"Trick him? As smart as he is? That will be impossible!" Kristina replied. She and Shanna had worked with Tar and Cocoa until the pups were comfortable spending longer periods apart. It was apparent that the dogs could live away from each other without a lot of discomfort to themselves and everyone around them.

"We will bed Barnacle down for the night and sneak out early in the morning before he knows we are gone," her father suggested.

"That will never work," Kristina said. "I'll have to ask Stan to help me. He is the only other person who rides Barnacle, besides me and Shanna."

As Kristina walked to Shanna's house, Barnacle fell in close behind her. When they arrived, the Gray family was having an after-supper snack of lemonade and cookies on the front porch. Jason offered Barnacle a cookie, which he gobbled up with one swallow before sniffing Jason's hand for more. "That's all, big boy," Jason told Barnacle. "Any more might give you a bellyache."

"We are leaving day after tomorrow, early in the morning," Kristina told the Grays. "Dad thinks Barnacle will cause a fuss and try to follow the boat out into the sound when we leave." Then she asked Stan if he would take Barnacle for a run until they got out of sight.

"I'll do that for you," Stan told her.

"It might be a good idea for you to take him out in the morning and get him used to the idea," Jason said.

"Alright, I'll take him out both days," Stan replied.

"Okay, thanks! I'll see you tomorrow," Kristina said. Then she and Barnacle headed for the boardinghouse.

The next morning Stan got up early and went to the barn for Barnacle, but the horse stopped at the gate and would not move until Kristina came out of the boardinghouse and told him it was okay. After Barnacle got the go-ahead from her, he took off for the beach in a gallop with Stan on his back.

"I hate lying to him," Kristina told her mother when she went back into the house.

"That is the only way he will go," her mother replied. "You have a lot to do and a number of people to say good-bye to today. You should get started."

Kristina went to the station to see Keeper Daniels and the station crew, then to Zack's Place, where most of the kids hung out. She spent the day saying good-byes to all of her friends. Then she spent the evening with Shanna and Stan.

"I am going to spend my last night with Barnacle in the stable," she told her parents as they prepared for bed. "In the morning, when Stan comes, I will be there to see them off."

"Sleeping in the stable . . . ," her mother began.

"Let her go," Edward said. "After all, it is her last night with him."

"I love you, Barnacle," Kristina told him as they settled down for the night.

The next morning Stan found Barnacle and Kristina asleep in the stall. "Kristina, wake up," he said as he shook her. "It's time for me to take Barnacle for his run."

"Go with Stan, boy," she told the big horse. Her eyes began to swell with tears as she hugged Barnacle's large neck for the last time of the summer. "I will miss you, but someday I will return and never leave you again!" Barnacle walked a few steps, then turned to look at Kristina. "Go on, boy," she told him, and waved her hands in the direction of the beach. Slowly he turned and galloped off as Kristina ran, crying, back to the boardinghouse. She grabbed Cocoa off the porch and went inside.

"Hurry and get cleaned up and dressed. Barney will be here soon to give us a ride to catch the *Sea Mullet*," her mother said.

When Barney arrived, they loaded the wagon and started off for the landing.

Barnacle and Stan had only gone a short distance down the beach when Barnacle spun around and headed back in full gallop. "I hope they've had enough time to get off," Stan thought as Barnacle increased his speed to a full run. As they reached the corral, Barnacle stopped short and put his head down, causing Stan to slide down his neck and hit the ground with a thump. Then Barnacle took off for the landing in a full gallop.

Kristina and her parents were aboard the *Sea Mullet* and almost out of sight when Barnacle plunged into the sound and began to swim toward them.

"Dad, Barnacle is going to drown!" Kristina cried out.

"He will stop and turn back soon," Edward told her.

"Go back, Barnacle!" yelled Kristina. Cocoa began running back and forth on the boat and barking loudly. "Go back!" she commanded to Barnacle again. Then he turned around and headed back toward the shore.

Cocoa's barking turned to a whimper as she curled up in Kristina's arms. Beth tried to console her daughter, but Kristina cried uncontrollably. "Don't worry, dear," her father told her. "He has a lot of friends to look after him until you can return."

Barnacle climbed back up on shore and shook himself. Stan called to him, but he would not come. He just stood on the end of the marsh and stared offshore. Stan and Shanna tried to get him to take food and water, but he refused. Keeper Daniels, Jason, and Barney tried to take him back to the corral, but he stood his ground and would not leave the landing.

Barney became increasingly worried about Barnacle, so he asked Norman Scarborough to get in touch with Old Hazel for help. Hazel met Barney and Norman at Mr. Midgett's store in Clarks so that they could tell her what was going on.

"He feels like he has been betrayed by the very people he loves and trusts," Hazel told them. "Animals are like people in that sense. He will get over it in time. Then it will be up to him to decide what future relationship he will have with people," Hazel explained. "All we can do at this point is support him."

Shanna and Stan went to visit Barnacle every day at the point. Then one morning he was gone.

❧10❧

LIVING FREE

The *Sea Mullet* struggled with the brisk southwest wind as she neared the *Coastal Rambler*. The smaller schooner dropped sail and moored to the loading platform, on the leeward side of the larger vessel. Then all passengers, mail, and cargo were transferred to the vessel.

Kristina and her parents entered their cabin and began to settle in for the trip to Elizabeth City. Cocoa paced the cabin floor nervously. She was not accustomed to being below deck on a vessel. Between sobs, Kristina picked up the dog and tried to calm her. "I know you don't like leaving them anymore than I do," she told the dog. "I really hate deceiving Barnacle and sneaking away from him. I will be lucky if he ever has anything to do with me again," she sobbed.

"You know better than that," her father said. "Barnacle loves you and will always be there for you."

The *Coastal Rambler* had a fair tailwind all the way up the Pamlico Sound to Elizabeth City. Once there, Kristina and her family changed schooners and headed up the Albemarle Sound toward Baltimore.

Barnacle was totally exhausted as he climbed up on the marsh. Kristina had left him. The very person whom he loved and trusted, and for whom he would do anything, had gone away and left him behind. He had always been able to follow her and protect her in the past, but now she was gone from his sight. He did not know where she was going or when she would return. He had lingered on the point for a few days, waiting for her, watching the *Sea Mullet* come and go, hoping to see her. Slowly he realized that she was gone and wasn't coming back.

Finally, Barnacle turned his attention to the place he loved best. He was eventually observed galloping along the surf line, up and down the beach. He would not come to anyone or allow anyone to approach him. One day Stan and Shanna were able to get close enough to talk to him, but he would not return to the corral or allow them to touch him.

On one of his runs, Barnacle encountered the Raven and the Banker ponies. The Raven came up to Barnacle and nipped at his mane, but Barnacle ignored him and galloped off. When the small chestnut-colored mare tried to follow Barnacle, the Raven kicked her, causing the mare to topple over. She cried out in pain, hobbled off a few feet, and looked at Barnacle.

The Raven stood between them and tried to move the mare back to his herd, but she kept walking toward Barnacle. When the Raven charged the mare, Barnacle caught him off-balance and kicked him hard in the chest, causing the Raven to stagger. He stared at Barnacle and walked toward the mare, but Barnacle blocked his path and would not allow him to approach her.

The Raven circled Barnacle and tried to find an opening to strike, but Barnacle turned with him, countering, always facing him. The Raven charged in and reared up on his hind legs, trying to strike Barnacle in the head and neck, but Barnacle spun quickly and kicked the Raven's hind legs out from under him. Finally, the Raven turned completely over in the air and landed on his back. He stayed still for a few moments while Barnacle stood his ground, then the Raven got to his feet and slowly hobbled back to the herd of Banker ponies.

The Raven walked off a few feet and called to his herd. At first, none of the ponies moved, but when he called to them again, about half the herd went to him. The others joined Barnacle and the small mare. The Raven snorted his disapproval and tried to retrieve them, but Barnacle blocked his path and challenged him by pawing the ground. The Raven turned and headed his much smaller herd in a northward direction, while Barnacle, the small mare, and their new group of Bankers headed southward.

Keeper Daniels and the Chicamacomico Station crew were practicing the breeches buoy drill when they spotted Barnacle with a small group of Bankers headed their way. "That's the first time I have seen Barnacle since he left the point, after Kristina left," Keeper Daniels told Jason and Barney.

"He sure is looking fit," Barney replied.

When Jason called to Barnacle, the young stallion turned and brought the other horses within a few feet of the men but would not allow them to approach him or the ponies. When Jason walked toward Barnacle, he galloped off, and the Bankers followed him.

"Shanna got a letter from Kristina yesterday, wondering about Barnacle," Jason said. She will be glad to know he is well, but she'll be concerned about him running free, with little human contact."

Upon returning home that night, Jason told Shanna that the station crew had seen Barnacle with a herd of ponies, and that Barnacle was in good health, although he was still avoiding contact with people. As soon as Shanna heard this news, she wrote back to Kristina to let her know that Barnacle was living free—taking care of himself and a small herd of Banker ponies.

When Kristina read Shanna's letter, she told her parents that they should go back to Northard Woods right away. "We must go back and rescue Barnacle!" she exclaimed.

After reading Shanna's letter, Edward said, "It seems to me that Barnacle is doing just fine. He's enjoying a carefree lifestyle with other horses."

"But he needs me," she told him.

"He is fine at the present time. Perhaps when I return from this next trip to South America, we can go back during Thanksgiving. You have to start school this week anyway," her father told her.

Kristina answered Shanna's letter and told her of their plans to return for Thanksgiving. Then she pondered the thought of how she could go back sooner. She started school, but it was boring for her. She was having a terrible time focusing on her studies as her mind kept drifting off to the Chicamacomico Banks and Barnacle.

Each afternoon when Kristina came home from school, Cocoa was waiting for her, ready to take a walk in the park near their house. After dinner each night Kristina would curl up in a large padded chair with Cocoa in her lap. They would both fall asleep, staring out the window into the night, and dream of when they could return to Northard Woods.

Barnacle was living the good life. His herd could roam the entire island. In the fall, they grazed on the sweet grass of Pea Island. One afternoon, as they were approaching the meadow, a funny feeling came over Barnacle. He sensed that he should take his ponies south, near the cape, to a higher and more sheltered area for a few days. As Barnacle and the ponies neared the station, Barney spotted them from the station tower. "Here comes Barnacle and his new family," he told Keeper Daniels.

"Where are they headed?" the keeper asked.

"Looks like here!" Barney told him. Barnacle brought his ponies within a few feet of his old corral, then he began pawing the ground and prancing around in circles.

"Fill the water trough for them," Keeper Daniels told Barney.

After the horses drank, Barnacle ran up and nipped Barney on the sleeve. "What in the world is he up to now?" Keeper Daniels asked Barney.

"I don't have the slightest idea," Barney replied.

For the next few days, Barnacle kept his ponies near the station and aggravated anyone who came out to see them. When Stan and Shanna came to visit the ponies, Jason suggested that they go to the beach. "Barnacle likes the beach," he said.

Just as the kids started toward the beach, Barnacle blocked their path. "He senses some sort of danger at the beach or in the ocean," Shanna said. "That is the way he acts when he is protecting us from harm."

Barnacle ran up and grabbed Stan by the shirt sleeve and pulled him a few feet toward the south. Then he let go of Stan's sleeve and ran a few more feet before he stopped, neighed at Stan, turned around in quick circles, and trotted back. "It's as if he wants us to follow him," said Keeper Daniels, as Barnacle gathered up his ponies and headed them southward. He ran back several times, trying to get everyone to follow them.

"He is telling us we are all in danger," Shanna told them.

"We should be careful in the upcoming days," Keeper Daniels warned the group, as they watched Barnacle and his ponies disappear from sight.

Within a few days, while Keeper Daniels, Barney, and Jason were in Clarks, Norman Scarborough saw them and told them about seeing Barnacle and a small herd of Banker ponies as they passed in the distance. "They were moving south, along the beach road," Norman said.

Barnacle continued to move his small herd steadily in a southerly direction. He did not know why, but he knew he had to get the ponies to higher ground. Just as they were nearing the meadow to the north of Gull Shoal Station, they encountered the Raven and his group of Banker ponies.

The Raven galloped up to Barnacle and challenged him to fight. Barnacle circled him, then stood in front of his ponies and snorted his disapproval. After Barnacle moved his herd past the Raven, he ran back, stopped short, and reared up, pointing his front legs to the south. He galloped back and forth between the herds of ponies, then to the back of the Raven's herd, and tried to push them southward. Finally, Barnacle nipped at the Raven's tail and galloped off, stopping once more to neigh at him. At that point, the Raven called for his herd to join Barnacle and together they took off, with Barnacle in the lead.

While on tower duty, the Gull Shoal lookout remarked to his station crew that he had seen Barnacle and the Raven with a large herd of Banker ponies moving quickly to the south. He instructed his northbound surfman to pass a message to the southbound surfman when they met and exchanged patrol markers that night about the movement of the ponies. "This could be important," said the Gull Shoal keeper. "Those animals can sense a sudden change in the weather."

When Keeper Daniels read the message from the south he immediately checked the barometric pressure. "The glass is holding steady," he told the station crew.

The next morning Jason noticed flocks of gulls, cormorants, pelicans, and various other seabirds leaving the beach, flying toward the sound. During breakfast he told Keeper Daniels and the station crew about the birds' behavior. When the crew went outside they saw flock after flock of shorebirds headed for the mainland. Keeper Daniels told the men to pass the information on to the Gull Shoal and Pea Island Stations during their beach patrols. Then he sent Barney to the telegraph office to contact the weather station at the Cape and inquire about any storms that were approaching the area.

When Barney reached the telegraph office, a crowd was gathered in front of the building; word had already been received about an approaching storm. He went inside and asked the operator if any numbers accompanied the transmission from the weather station. She gladly wrote the information on a piece of paper and handed it to Barney. He thanked her and headed back to the station, where some of the men asked Barney what the numbers meant. He told them that the numbers were points of navigation for plotting the location and progress of storms, as well as the movement of ships.

"Keeper Daniels has navigation charts given to him by Edward, the sea captain," Barney told the men. "Edward taught Keeper Daniels and Jason how to plot the movement of approaching storms on the charts by using latitude and longitude. As time goes by and we receive more information, we will be able to determine the direction and speed of the wind. This is very important information, and we will need all updates as soon as they come in."

"We will arrange for one of the young boys to bring all updates to you as soon as they are received," one of the men shouted to Barney, on his way to patrol duty. When Barney arrived with the numbers from the weather station, Keeper Daniels and Jason already had the charts spread out on the table in the tack room.

Keeper Daniels exclaimed, "There it is, boys, northeast of Haiti, headed northwest, toward the Florida Straits!" Then he pointed to the chart. "The weather station at the cape is also plotting the storm, and they will inform the lifesaving stations at Cape Woods, Trent, and Hatteras. As soon as we receive updated numbers we must immediately pass the information to the Gull Shoal and Pea Island Stations, and to the people of Northard Woods, Southard Woods, and Clarks."

The hurricane moved near the east coast of Florida and then turned in a northeastward direction, hugging the Atlantic coast line. Due to a large high-pressure system moving off the Delaware coast, the hurricane began to slow down and intensify in strength as it approached the warm waters of the Gulfstream. It moved slowly up the Gulfstream and stalled, just off the coast of Hatteras Island. The wind blew from the southeast at hurricane force for a day. The next day, it came around to the east, and finally from the northeast by the third day.

Every bit of sound water was blown up into the creeks and rivers on the mainland, creating inland flooding for miles. The Pamlico Sound shoals were completely visible and dry as far as the eye could see. Fish were flopping in the muck, and the blue crabs and hermit crabs were scampering to and fro. The entire island was under ocean water, with the exception of a few high hills in the Cape Woods area.

As the hurricane crawled slowly by, the eye of the storm hovered for several hours, creating an eerie calm over the island. Then the wind switched to the northwest and blew at hurricane force once again. A couple of days later it shifted to the southwest, and all of the water blown inland came rushing back, covering the island with muddy, stinky sound water. After all was said and done, the hurricane battered the island for about seven days before following the high-pressure area off the Virginia and Delaware capes out to sea.

As the hurricane moved away from the island, it acted like a large vacuum cleaner, sucking all the clouds along with it and leaving the area with extremely hot and humid air from the tropics. The temperature was almost unbearable as the sun baked the island from a cloudless sky.

❦ 11 ❦

The Hurricane

Barnacle hurried his ponies along by constantly nipping at their heels if they slowed down. The wind was already blowing hard from the southeast and rain was coming down in buckets, stinging their faces and making it difficult for them to see very far in any direction. When the horses reached the safety of Cape Woods, the Raven and Barnacle moved them into a small sheltered hammock and bedded them down.

Barnacle was content that his new family was safe from harm, up on the high, sheltered ground of Cape Woods. His mind drifted north to his friends in the Northard Woods area. Suddenly he got up and shook himself. His mind was made up; he had to return to Chicamacomico and help them. The small mare tried to follow Barnacle, but he stopped and scolded her, forcing her back to the safety of the hammock.

Coming out of the woods of the cape, Barnacle was in knee-deep water as he galloped northward. Soon the water began to shallow as the island curved coming out of Cape Woods. With the wind to his back he galloped along until he reached a new inlet, just north of Cape Woods, which had been cut by the hurricane. He tried several times to swim across the inlet, but each time he was caught in the strong current and then dumped on a shallow shoal at the end of the cut.

Barnacle knew he had no choice but to ride the current north until he could find the bottom and regain his footing. He entered the water, which was over his head, and was thankful when the current released him, about a mile

71

out into the sound. Exhausted, he returned to his family and the safety of the sheltered hammock. At this point he could only wonder about the fate of his friends at Northard Woods.

Kristina, Edward, and Beth received news about the hurricane that was threatening the North Carolina coast. Edward knew that the island was the eastwardmost point of the coast and would be subjected to the maximum influence of the storm. His frantic daughter could not be comforted, so worried was she about Barnacle and the Banker ponies.

Kristina questioned her father on Barnacle's ability to care for himself, out in the open, during the wrath of such a storm. "He will be fine," Edward told her. "Barnacle is a survivor! He has survived two shipwrecks, and he watched out for you and your friends all summer. He knows how to take care of himself and all those around him."

"I am still worried sick," she told her father.

"Write Shanna and ask if she has seen Barnacle lately. This weather will clear in a few days, and your letter can be mailed," her father told her. Then Kristina sat at Edward's large desk, with Cocoa curled up near her feet, and wrote to Shanna.

At the station, Keeper Daniels plotted the last set of numbers and told his crew to go home, batten down their hatches, gather up their families, and return to the station.

Jason and his family busied themselves right away to prepare for the storm. He told Shanna to make sure at least one window was open, just a crack, to equalize the sudden pressure change to which the house would soon be subjected. Then he instructed Stan to remove the covers from the float-out panels on the floors, underneath the roll-out rugs. The float-out panels would allow the floodwater to seep in and help keep the house on its foundation.

Jason went to place the wooden storm shutters on the windows and hollered to Stan to hurry and come help him. Mrs. Gray was busy moving their belongings to the upper level of their home. At last, they checked on their animals to make sure of their safety and protection. Then the Gray family headed to the station to await the coming storm. The wind was beginning to blow hard from the southeast.

Keeper Daniels had explained how the island was shaped like a "backwards letter L" and how the north beach usually fared pretty good during a hard southeaster, where the wind surge tended to run parallel to the beach. However, the south beach, from the Cape to Hatteras, would usually get blistered during a southeaster from full-force wind and tidal surge attacks. The lower end of the island would often be completely covered with ocean overwash, with the exception of the higher ground, in the woods at the cape.

The southeast wind blew hurricane force and battered the island. As the wind went around to the east, the ocean water began to recede from the southern part of the island and rise on the northern end. When the wind switched around to the northeast, still at hurricane force, the entire upper end of the island was covered with ocean water, and every item that was not secure or did not allow water to seep in floated away with the surge.

Four days later dawned bright and sunny, with no wind at all. Not a cloud could be seen in the sky in any direction. "The storm is over!" shouted the children as they ran out of the station into the sunlight, and they found the area in shambles. Things were strewn about in all directions. Many large structures and outhouses had floated into the sound and were lodged on the shoals, which were completely dry. Before the adults hurried out to check on their dwellings and livestock, Keeper Daniels warned them to be back before nightfall, reminding them that they were currently within the storm's eye, and that the storm wasn't over.

During the eye of the storm, Barnacle's mare woke him early in the morning. She was pregnant with his foal and was in distress. He knew he had to find help for her before the wind switched, so the two of them left Cape Woods and began their journey northward. When they came to the newly formed inlet, Barnacle took the mare out into the sound, and they swam around the cut. There was no wind at all—only an eerie calm as they waded ashore and continued north along the surf line.

As they reached Kinnakeet, Barnacle stopped to let the mare rest and noticed splotches of blood on her hind legs. He urged her on, hoping to make it to the Gull Shoal Station before the winds started blowing from the northwest. However, it became apparent that the soon-to-be-mother was in no condition to go much farther. Then Barnacle thought of Old Hazel. He trusted her. She had helped him in the past, and he needed her help again. However, crossing the floating marsh was not an option.

Barnacle decided to approach Hazel's cottage from the west. He led the mare out the mouth of Station Creek to the sound, which was still completely dry from three days of the battering northeast winds. They were making good time on the shoals, about one hundred yards from the shore, when the wind became stronger, from the northwest. Just as they were about to reach the white sand beach, near Old Hazel's shack, they heard a swishing sound, which quickly became a roar.

When Barnacle saw the wall of water coming toward them from the west, he got behind the mare and grabbed her tail in his mouth. As he tried to push her to shore, the water overcame them and knocked them off their feet, rolling them over and over to the shore. The force of the water, full of debris, sent them crashing through briars, cactus, and sharp water-bushes, past the entrance to Hazel's shack. Struggling to catch their breaths, they became separated in the marshy thicket. When Barnacle gained his balance and looked around, the whole marsh was covered with water. He did not see the mare anywhere.

Barnacle thought he heard the mare's small voice. Then he spotted her lying on her side, pinned against a large oak tree by the rushing current. He swam over to the mare but could not free her, so he took off, through the debris, in the direction of Hazel's shack. The water was still flowing at a fast pace, which slowed his progress, and by the time Barnacle reached Hazel's porch, the wind had reintensified to hurricane-force strength.

Old Hazel could not believe her ears when she heard a horse in the middle of the howling wind. *That's not possible,* she thought. She opened the door on the leeside of the shack and there was Barnacle, with his front legs resting on her porch. She tried to pull him up onto the porch, but instead he grabbed her sleeve and yanked her off into the floodwater. All she could do was hang on, as he swam away from the safety of her shack. *Where are you taking me?* she thought, as they moved along in the debris-filled water. Then, when Hazel saw the mare, she knew exactly where they were going.

The mare was still clinging to the tree as the water rushed by, and Hazel would not be able to free her until the force of the water let up. They spent the rest of the night huddled together in the darkness, with debris from the current constantly bumping into them. Hazel could not determine the extent of their injuries in the dim light of night.

Around daybreak the wind shifted to the southwest, causing the direction of the water to change just enough to free the mare. After some difficulty, the three of them made it back to Hazel's shack. She led the horses onto her porch, where she examined them and cared for their cuts and bruises. Hazel tried to take them into her shack, out of the weather, but Barnacle insisted on staying outside. By the light of a lantern, Hazel spread blankets on the floor in preparation for a new baby colt while Barnacle stood guard on the porch. Just before dawn, the mare gave birth to a small male colt, with four white socks and a white blaze between his eyes, just like his father.

Barnacle hung around the shack while the mare and colt grew stronger. In the meantime, Hazel ridded her yard of storm debris and gathered her animals. When she and Barnacle took the colt outside for the first time, his legs were shaky, and he wobbled as he tried to stand. As Barnacle watched his baby colt try to walk, he thought about his herd to the south and his friends to the north, hoping they were all safe. He was overjoyed and couldn't wait to show off his son! As soon as his family could travel he would decide what to do next.

After seven long days the storm moved offshore, leaving the islanders to assess their damages and begin to put their lives back together. Many structures had been completely destroyed by the wind, and most of them were full of mud and sand brought in by the tide. In the village of Kinnakeet, nearly all of the dwellings had been washed out onto the beach by sound-side flooding. So much work would have to be done in order to return to normal life. Incredibly, there was no loss of life during the storm, although there were reports of people spending the night clinging to floating debris and hanging on to trees. To the amazement of all the station keepers, no shipwrecks were reported during the storm either.

❧12❧

THE NEW ARRIVAL

Barnacle, the mare, and the new colt stayed with Hazel for about two weeks while the mare regained her strength, grazing on the fall grass of Cedar Hammock marsh. Barnacle took the colt on a few trips to the beach, to introduce him to carefree runs along the surf line. Soon the mare joined them.

On one of these trips, two boys from Clarks spotted the horses returning to Hazel's shack and gave chase. They tried to capture the colt, but each time they got close, Barnacle charged them and finally chased the boys away, straight to the floating marsh, where they sunk to their waists in the bottomless bog. The more they tried to free themselves, the farther they sunk, and they were soon up-to-their-shoulders deep.

Barnacle circled the boys a few times, then kicked a small pine tree, breaking it near the ground. He picked the branch up in his mouth and placed it so that the boys could grab the top. Then he pulled the boys to the safety of stable ground. As they were getting to their feet, Barnacle reared up on his hind legs and scolded the boys as he chased them out of the hammock. Then he led his family back to the safety of Hazel's corral. When they arrived, Hazel washed the mud off them, watered and fed them, and gave all three of them a rubdown.

Later, the same boys who had tried to capture Barnacle's colt were in Mr. Midgett's store, in Clarks, and told their story to everyone, including Keeper Daniels. *The large stallion described by the boys couldn't be Barnacle*, the keeper thought to himself. He knew that Barnacle was moving around the island with a much larger herd of Banker ponies, not living with a mare and baby colt. The part of the boys' tale that seemed most odd was when the ponies ran into the floating marsh, near Cedar Hammock. Keeper Daniels knew that all the Banker ponies stayed away from the bottomless pools of the floating marsh. The skeletal remains of many large animals had surfaced there, including horses. There was a tale of two men who went missing from a hunting party a few years back; the area was searched for days, but no sign of the men was ever found.

The keeper knew that Old Hazel would soon come to Clarks to trade her handmade bayberry candles and trinkets for supplies. Keeper Daniels asked Mr. Midgett to send for him the next time she came in. If anyone or anything had entered the Cedar Hammock marsh, Old Hazel would know about it.

One afternoon as Barney was returning from his beach patrol, he saw Norman Scarborough gathering a load of wood on the beach. The two friends stopped to talk for a spell, exchanging local news over a drink of water. Norman asked Barney to pass a message from Mr. Midgett to Keeper Daniels to let him know that Old Hazel was coming to town the next morning for her monthly supplies. Barney thanked Norman for the information, and the two friends parted ways and went about their business.

When Barney returned to the station, he gave Keeper Daniels the message from Mr. Midgett about Hazel. "I'll be busy tomorrow," the keeper told Barney, "but I would like for you and Jason to meet Hazel at the store and talk to her about the horses. We need supplies for the station, and you can pick them up while you are there."

The next morning, Barney and Jason arrived at Mr. Midgett's store around noon, right when Hazel was fixing to leave. She already had her wagon loaded with supplies and was tying down the canvas cover. "Got caught in the mud lately?" she asked Barney.

"Not lately," Barney replied.

"We would like to talk to you before you go," Jason said. "Have you had any unexpected visitors lately?"

"I have all types of visitors stopping by all the time. Mostly animals," Hazel said.

"We are looking for three horses," Jason said. "One of them might be Barnacle. We heard a tale of some horses being chased by two boys from Clarks into the entrance of Cedar Hammock Marsh."

"Anything entering that marsh is probably still stuck there, and it's doubtful if it is still breathing," she told them.

"Have you seen a large chestnut stallion, mare, and small colt near your hammock?" Barney asked her directly.

"What do you want with them, to pen them up and use them for work purposes?" Hazel asked. "These Banker ponies are free to roam as they please. They are friends of mine, and the sooner you realize that, the better you will get along with me and the animals."

"We are not looking to catch them or use them in any way," Jason said. "We are just asking about their well-being, because no one in this area has seen Barnacle since the storm. My daughter, Shanna, received a letter from her friend in Baltimore inquiring about his whereabouts."

"You mean the girl who left him? The one person he trusted and loved most?" Hazel asked.

"Yes, she is the one," was Jason's reply.

"She didn't have a choice. She had to leave," Barney said.

"Yes, she had to leave, but she tricked her horse and did not take time to explain to him why she had to go," Hazel replied.

"Explain to a horse why you are leaving?" Barney scratched his head and went on, "I don't get it."

"That's the problem with most people and their understanding of animals," Hazel said, "the very reason I prefer the company of animals to people. They never lie or mislead you," Hazed explained. "Yes, I have seen them and they are well, but I don't control them. They go where they please. I'm just a friend they trust. You can tell your daughter that Barnacle now has a mate and a male offspring."

"Shanna will be happy," Jason said, "now that she can answer Kristina's letter with good news." Then he and Barney thanked Hazel and began to head back to Chicamacomico. Barney continued to the station while Jason went home to share the good news about Barnacle with Shanna.

"Barnacle has his own family to think about now," Shanna's father told her.

"I want to see Barnacle for myself, to be sure he is safe, before I answer Kristina's letter," Shanna said.

"I've never been to Hazel's shack, and I don't know the way," her father replied.

"I have been there, and I do know the way," said Shanna.

"Old Hazel frowns on folks who snoop around in her hammock. Word has it that she possesses the power of the dark side," Jason told his daughter.

"Don't be silly, Daddy! We stayed with her, and she showed us how to make bayberry candles. She'll be glad to see us again," Shanna exclaimed.

"She tolerates Barney and allows him to enter the hammock more than anyone else around here," Jason said. "Perhaps he will go with us to see Hazel."

"I'll go to the station to see Barney tomorrow," Shanna replied.

The next day when Shanna talked to Barney, he said, "You're in luck! I'll see Old Hazel today when I return from beach patrol at Gull Shoal Station. I have to drop off some lantern wicks to her, and you're welcome to come with me, if you like."

Later that afternoon, Barney and Shanna walked south to meet the surfman from Gull Shoal Station and exchange patrol markers at the halfway point. As they were returning, Hazel was waiting abreast the Cedar Hammock marsh for her lantern wicks, and Shanna asked about Barnacle.

"Oh yes, that one," replied Hazel. "He moves around, mostly before the break of day and after dark, and trusts very few. I'm the only one he will allow to come near his mare and colt."

"All I want to do is see him," Shanna told Hazel.

"Then you will have to get up really early or stay up very late and place yourself along the surf line to see the ponies on their runs," Hazel replied. "Barnacle knows this marsh better than anyone, and he only comes out when no one is around. He can sense danger and smell you if you are upwind. He comes out of the marsh a different way each time and returns in the same fashion, especially after those Clarks boys almost caught his colt. He moves his herd in a large circle, to and from the beach, always sniffing the air, and is very hard to approach. I let Barnacle come to me. I will not trick him or help you catch him. If you want to see him, you are on your own." Shanna thanked Hazel for the information and headed back to the station with Barney to tell Keeper Daniels about Barnacle.

"So he has a family now," stated the keeper. "He will be much harder to approach and bring back now. We may have lost a valued friend and protector."

Shanna filled her dad in on the meeting with Hazel. "You have to take me to the beach near Cedar Hammock so that I can see Barnacle and his new family. I must see Barnacle for myself before I can write to Kristina," she told her father.

"I have duty for the next few days," Jason explained. "I can't spend the night in the sand hills with you and work during the day, but perhaps your brother will go with you, if you ask him nicely. Maybe you could take a couple friends with you and make an outing of it."

"That's a great idea. Thanks, Dad!" she said, and went off to find her brother.

After some persuasion, Shanna convinced her brother, his friend Rowan Hooper, and Rowan's sister, Nettie, to accompany her to the beach across from Cedar Hammock marsh. They would spend the night in the sand hills and watch for Barnacle and his family. As they were leaving, Tar started barking and throwing a fit.

"If you go, you will have to take this dog with you. He'll be unmanageable if you leave him home alone," Mrs. Gray told her children.

"But he will bark and run ahead, and we won't be able to get close to Barnacle and his family," Shanna told her mother.

"You wanted him, now you deal with him," was her mother's answer.

"Alright, come on, Tar," Shanna told the dog, "but you must behave."

When the children got to the beach near Cedar Hammock, they set up camp, ate supper, and settled down on top of the highest hill to watch for the horses. Stan had borrowed two long glasses from Keeper Daniels. Beginning at dark, he and Rowan watched north and south for any sign of the horses.

They couldn't see a thing until about midnight, when the moon came out from behind a cloud bank, directly over their heads. Then Rowan saw the three horses southeast of their position.

Stan woke Shanna. "I think you should see this," he told her, pointing to the horses. Then Shanna saw the horses headed to the west. Barnacle was in the lead, a colt was in the middle, and the mare was bringing up the rear, their coats shimmering in the moonlight.

"The colt looks just like Barnacle!" Shanna said.

Suddenly Barnacle stopped and sniffed the air, and all three horses in an instant galloped out of sight to the south. "That's all I wanted to see," Shanna told her brother. "Now I can answer Kristina's letter."

Shanna shivered as she began her letter to Kristina. The summer's southwest winds had ceased, and the fall northwesters had begun. As her father was lighting the fireplace he said, "It looks like winter is going to come early this year."

❦13❦

THE FROZEN SOUND

Kristina could hardly wait to get back to Chicamacomico. Her mother was having lunch with her at school and told Kristina that a letter had arrived from Shanna. She apologized for not bringing it with her, but assured Kristina that the letter was waiting for her at the house. "Now finish your lunch so you won't be late for your afternoon classes," she said. After school, Kristina ran all the way to her house. When her brown Lab, Cocoa, saw her coming, he started barking and pacing the floor.

"That dog acts up every afternoon just before Kristina gets home," Beth said.

"She's just excited to see her," Edward replied. Cocoa was jumping up and down and barking near the door, waiting for Kristina to come in. The door flung open, and Kristina busted into the room. "Where is it? Where is my letter?" she asked her mother.

"I put it on the nightstand, beside your bed," her mom replied.

Kristina ran past them to her bedroom as Cocoa followed with a leash in her mouth, ready for their afternoon walk. "Not now, Cocoa," Kristina told the dog. "I want to read my letter first." As she tore open the envelope, the dog settled near her feet. After reading the letter, Kristina ran to her father and said, "Daddy, we must go to Northard Woods right away! Barnacle is fine and he has a new family. They are living at Cedar Hammock, near Old Hazel, and we must go see them!"

"Thanksgiving holidays are in a couple of weeks. We'll try to go then," her father replied. "You have time off from school, and I don't have to sail until after the holidays."

"Do you promise?" she asked.

"Yes, I promise," he replied. "Now take your dog for a walk. She's been waiting for you all afternoon. You can answer Shanna's letter later, and I will drop it off in the mail for you tomorrow on my way to the harbor."

"Come on, Cocoa," she said as she skipped out the door with the dog at her heels.

The weather had turned violently cold for the beginning of November. There was a skim of ice on the sound, and the *Sea Mullet* was having trouble meeting the *Coastal Rambler* for the weekly exchange of mail, passengers, and supplies. The ice extended from the shore to the deep water on the back side of the reef. The larger schooners had deep, ice-free water to travel in, but the smaller sailing vessels from the shore ports were having trouble navigating out to meet them.

The winter northwesters had come early, and one low-pressure front after another kept the temperature well below freezing. Smaller rowboats were used to get the mail and supplies to and from shore, with two men in the bow to break the ice while one man did the rowing. There was no room in these small boats for passengers, so anyone who wanted to get to the upper end of the island had to travel to Hatteras and then go by wagon to the northern villages, adding two extra days to their trip. This information was given to anyone booking passage from Elizabeth City, south to Ocracoke, including Kristina and Edward.

Kristina was devastated by the setback. She pleaded with her father, yet he would not book passage for fear of becoming stuck on the island for the duration of the winter. "As time goes on, the ice will only become thicker," he told her. Kristina asked about the next possible time they could go to Northard Woods, and her father said, "It depends on the weather and how long the ice remains in the sound. It will probably be sometime in the spring."

Kristina felt her heart sink. This was not what she wanted to hear. Now there was a big, empty feeling inside her. She could only wonder about

Barnacle and his new family and would have to wait several months before she could see him and meet them. Thankfully she had Shanna's letters to keep her informed about Barnacle until she could return to the beach.

The weather was very harsh on the islanders. Due to the extreme cold, completing any task outside was difficult. Because the free-roaming Banker ponies were having trouble finding enough to eat, the islanders would leave food outside the corral fences and in places the ponies frequently visited, trying to help them make it to spring.

Barnacle and his family were spending the winter with Hazel. Each day Hazel had to break ice out of the water trough so that her horses could drink. She would leave the corral gate open so that they could come and go as they pleased, and each morning Barnacle would take his colt and mare for a run along the beach. On one of these mornings, they came into contact with the Raven and his herd of Banker ponies.

The Raven was leading his herd south after having spent several months up north, seeking winter grass. When they met up with Barnacle's herd, near Gull Shoal Station, the reunion was a joyful one! They had not seen each other since the big storm. The Raven allowed Barnacle to take the lead without putting up any fuss. Barnacle knew that there was not enough food near Cedar Hammock to support the Raven's herd until spring, so he gathered his mare and colt and led the herd south to the Cape Woods area to find ample food and shelter for the remainder of the winter.

Hazel noticed that the food she left for Barnacle and his family had not been touched for a couple of days. *Now where could they have gone?* she thought to herself. She kept looking for them to return to the hammock but saw no sign of them anywhere, and after a few days she stopped leaving food out for them. *I just hope they are alright and can make it through the winter,* she thought as she fed her stock.

A few weeks went by, and Hazel still had not seen Barnacle. When she went up to the store in Clarks for supplies, she asked everyone if they had seen the horses, but no one knew a thing about them. Then she received word that the beach patrol from the Little Kinnakeet Station had seen a large herd of

Banker ponies heading south, led by a big chestnut stallion, and she knew it must be Barnacle. He had waited until the colt and mare were strong enough to travel south with the rest of the horses.

So that's what you're up to, she thought. She had wondered why Barnacle had taken his mare and colt on runs so often in the bitter cold. Now she realized that he had been preparing them for a long trip to the south, where the winter conditions were milder.

Barnacle moved the herd steadily southward. They rested in the Cape Woods area for a few days and then continued south. As they entered Trent Woods, they found enough food and fresh water to last for a couple of days, but Barnacle knew they needed to keep going. The herd reached the Hatteras area around midday and the southernmost tip of the island by early afternoon. From there, they could see the green grass of Ocracoke on the sand hills, across the inlet.

Barnacle knew they had to cross to the other side. He stayed near the herd and the smaller colts, while the Raven and one other stallion tested the current, finding it way too strong. They would have to wait until the tide changed, so they found a sheltered grove of oaks and bedded down for the night. The next morning, the tide was running through the inlet, strong from the ocean, so Barnacle took the herd to the sound side of the inlet and waited for slack water. The colts and mares crossed first, followed by the stallions. By the time the tide changed, all of the horses were safely across the inlet, resting on Ocracoke Island.

The herd traveled south until they found a large freshwater pond, plenty of winter grass, and a large meadow in the shelter of Molasses Creek Hammock. The weather was a bit milder, and the ground was not as frozen as the ground up north. Here, they could paw and dig in the ground for the sweet soft roots of the winter grasses. The large meadow would provide ample space for the colts to enjoy running and playing, making an ideal place for them to ride out the cold-weather spell.

Captain Logan Mansfield, master of the *Coastal Rambler*, was crossing the inlet between Hatteras and Ocracoke when he noticed something strange in the water and reached for his long glass. He could not believe his eyes. Swimming the inlet was the largest herd of Banker ponies he had ever seen, led by a large chestnut stallion. He had seen this horse in the Northard Woods area and wondered what the herd was doing this far south, knowing very well that it must have taken them days to travel this far. As the horses made their way across the inlet, the captain made a note in the ship's log so that he would be sure to tell the folks up north what he had seen.

As the *Coastal Rambler* neared Northard Woods on her return trip to Elizabeth City, the ice was still too thick for the *Sea Mullet* to meet her. Instead, a smaller rowboat came out with two oarsmen, assisted by a man in the bow breaking ice with a hook. Captain Mansfield sent a message to the keeper at Chicamacomico Station about seeing the Banker ponies led by the big chestnut stallion.

Keeper Daniels soon spread around the news about Barnacle and the Banker ponies. At last, Shanna had something to tell Kristina about Barnacle.

Jason cautioned his daughter, "We do not know for sure if it is Barnacle or not. That's a bit far south for him."

"Yes," she replied, "but it has been weeks since Hazel has seen them. The harsh winter is almost over, and the good news will give Kristina a new ray of hope."

When Kristina received Shanna's letter about Barnacle and the Banker ponies going to Ocracoke for the winter, she was elated, and she pondered her return trip to Northard Woods. She would be graduating from high school in the spring. "We're going to Chicamacomico right after my graduation!" she told her mother.

"We will have to plan the trip when your father gets home," her mother said.

"Daddy will go, I know it!" Kristina said.

"We will have to wait and see what his schedule is like when he arrives. He will be here for your graduation, but I don't know if he has to go right back out or not," Beth told her. As Kristina sank down in her father's big chair, she looked at the calendar. Her graduation was still three weeks away, and she could hardly wait until her father came home.

Edward and his crew were entering the outer portions of the Norfolk Canyon on a landward tack for the mouth of the Chesapeake Bay. They had a load of raw coffee beans and were headed for Baltimore to the processing plant. Edward would be home in a couple of days and was eager to see his family.

❧ 14 ❧

Return to Northard Woods

As spring arrived on the islands, Barnacle and the Raven were ready to head northward with the ponies. Heading out of Ocracoke they had a peaceful meeting with a group of Ocracoke ponies. Both herds contained many yearlings, including Barnacle's son. As the Bankers continued north, they stopped at Hatteras Inlet and waited for the turn of the tide. Then they crossed over and made their way to the beach, to the Cape Woods area, where they stayed the night. Barnacle led the way, with the group of colts behind him, then the mares, followed by the younger stallions. The Raven was bringing up the rear. Together they moved the horses steadily to the north. The lookout at Big Kinnakeet Station spotted the horses in his glass as they passed to the east of the station and sent word of his sighting to Chicamacomico by the northbound beach patrolman.

Keeper Daniels received the news by late afternoon. Then he sent for Barney and Jason. When they met, Keeper Daniels told them to make ready for the largest group of spring Banker ponies they had seen in many years. "They have somehow survived the winter and are headed up our way, led by Barnacle and the Raven," the keeper told them.

"Perhaps we can feed them and make friends with Barnacle again," Keeper Daniels continued. "Barnacle was becoming one of the best lifesaving horses I've ever seen, until the sea captain's daughter returned to Baltimore. That horse could really help us save many lives. And besides that, the service is considering the use of horses for surfmen to ride on future beach patrols, instead of walking."

Barnacle led the herd up to the east of the Cedar Hammock area and turned leadership over to the Raven. Then he cut out his mare and young stallion, taking his family to the west to find Old Hazel. A few of the younger ponies tried to follow Barnacle, but the Raven forced them back to the herd as he moved them to a meadow near Clarks.

Norman Scarborough had spotted the horses in the meadow. The next day, when he saw Keeper Daniels at the store, he told him about his sighting. He explained that the Raven was leading the herd and that he had not seen a large chestnut stallion in the group. Keeper Daniels told Norman that he had no idea where Barnacle was; the keeper, however, figured Barnacle was up to something.

Old Hazel was elated when she saw Barnacle and his family moving toward her through the floating marsh. He had led them safely to the hammock, straight into her front yard. All three of them came up to greet her. Hazel chatted with the horses for a minute, then gave them food and water. After she rubbed them down and brushed them, she watched as they moved out to the marsh to nibble on the new green grass.

Hazel nailed the gate in the open position to allow them to come and go as they pleased, along with her domestic stock. To avoid human contact, Barnacle would move in and out of the hammock very early in the morning and late at night. It was hard for anyone to see them, except for Hazel. She seemed to be the only one whom Barnacle trusted.

When Keeper Daniels saw Hazel at the store in Clarks, he asked her about Barnacle and if she had seen him or his family. "Maybe I have, and maybe I haven't," she replied. "That one is special, you know. What do you want with him? To hitch him up to your surfboat wagon and work him to death, I suspect."

"That's not exactly true, although Barnacle has a natural talent for lifesaving activities and would be a huge asset to our station," the keeper replied.

"I don't control any of the animals I look after," Hazel said. "I'm their friend, and I do not trick, fool, or take advantage of them in any way. Most importantly,

I never lie to them. People say I can talk to the animals when, actually, anyone can talk to them! The hard part is to understand them. They're just like people, with a few exceptions: They haven't learned to lie, cheat, or steal. They deal only with the truth and its effect on their daily lives."

Keeper Daniels nodded his head as Hazel swore she would not ever help anyone chase, catch, or bother Barnacle and his family in any way. She went on to inform the keeper that he was on his own. "Barnacle is very smart," she told the keeper, "and goes to great lengths to protect his family. The only one who can help you at this point is that sea captain's young daughter, if she ever comes back." Then she went about her business, unloading the bayberry candles, mosquito smokes, and birdhouses she had brought to trade for supplies, and bid the keeper good-bye.

Barnacle and his family were coming out of Cedar Hammock just as Hazel was going in. She stopped the wagon, and all three horses came up to her. "You better be careful for the next few days," she told Barnacle. "That keeper is set on having you as part of his lifesaving crew." After hearing this, Barnacle bobbed his head, turned around, and followed her back to the safety of the hammock.

Barnacle's son was becoming bored with staying in the hammock, not being able to run carefree along the surf. Soon Barnacle gave in to him and began taking his family to the beach late at night and very early each morning, which seemed to satisfy the young stallion for a while.

As soon as her graduation was over, Kristina began to aggravate her folks about going back to Northard Woods for the summer. Edward and Beth tried to put her off, but to no avail; she would not let up on them. They tried to convince her to wait until the Fourth of July, but she had a hissy fit. "The summer will be over by then," she told them, constantly moaning and complaining, until Edward finally gave in and booked their passage.

"Congratulations," Beth told Edward. "You just allowed your daughter to manipulate you, and you always give her everything she wants."

Once they arrived at the harbor in Elizabeth City, Edward, Beth, and Kristina waited as the *Coastal Rambler* was unloaded and reloaded for their trip south to the islands. Kristina could hardly contain herself as they boarded the vessel and began their trip. Soon she begged her father to ask Captain Mansfield if they could visit the wheelhouse.

"It's been so long, he probably doesn't remember us," Edward told his daughter.

"Please, Daddy? He might have some news about Barnacle," she said.

"You might as well give in," Beth said. "She won't stop until she gets what she wants."

"Oh, alright," Edward said, and escorted Kristina up the stairs to the wheelhouse. Captain Mansfield did remember Edward and his daughter, welcoming them aboard. When Kristina asked him about Barnacle, the captain said he had definitely seen Barnacle, swimming in the inlet toward Ocracoke with a large herd of Banker ponies. Kristina was delighted to hear this news and thankful that Barnacle and his family were okay. Still, she wondered what in the world he was doing so far south. Suddenly she felt depressed because she wouldn't be able to see Barnacle right away. She had no idea where to go and find him.

"Daddy, maybe we should continue on to Ocracoke. Barnacle may have moved his family down there," said Kristina.

"We will go to Northard Woods as planned, and you can begin looking for him there," Edward replied. "Even if Barnacle is in Ocracoke, he will return to Northard Woods. It's been his home since he was a small colt, and I believe that is where you will find him." Kristina accepted her father's instruction and continued to stare at the shoreline through Captain Mansfield's glass as they passed Oregon Inlet.

The *Coastal Rambler* had made a long tack to the west and was now about to start an eastward tack, which would take them to the lower portion of Old House Channel, and then to the reef off Northard Woods. Because it was very late at night, Captain Mansfield told them they would anchor up on the reef, spend the night, and meet the *Sea Mullet* early the next morning. Kristina had trouble getting to sleep that night. She could see the dim lights of Northard Woods from the bow of the vessel and thought of Stan and Shanna. She could hardly wait to see her friends.

The next morning, after the passengers and supplies were loaded, the *Sea Mullet* headed for the harbor at Northard Woods. They were greeted by Barney and Jason, and as soon as Kristina got a chance she asked them about Barnacle.

"You will have to talk to Keeper Daniels about that," Jason told her. "He has talked to Old Hazel and she has seen them, but she isn't volunteering much information."

"How are Shanna and Stan?" Kristina asked.

"Shanna is home with her mother, canning figs. She wasn't sure if you would be returning this early or waiting until later in the summer, so she'll be extremely surprised and excited to see you," he told Kristina. "Stan has joined the lifesaving service and is spending the summer training to become a surfman up in the Manteo area with Captain Etheridge. He'll be home for a long weekend tomorrow, and y'all can spend some time together," Jason said.

Edward had made arrangements to rent a cottage for the summer, and as soon as they arrived Kristina ran over to the Grays' cottage to find Shanna. Mrs. Gray and Shanna were finishing up two dozen quarts of figs when Kristina busted in and greeted them with big hugs. Then she told Shanna to hurry and said, "We must go see Keeper Daniels. He has news about Barnacle!"

"Well, hello, Kristina!" said Mrs. Gray. "It's so nice to see you. How was your trip?"

"I will explain later," Kristina hollered as the girls ran out.

"Don't slam that screen door," Mrs. Gray hollered after them as the door crashed with a loud bang. *Always in a hurry*, she thought to herself. *Just like their fathers, still kids at heart!*

The girls ran all the way to the station to find Keeper Daniels but found the station empty. They were headed out to the boathouse when Barney hollered to them from the tower. "It's Thursday, Drill Day," he said. "All hands are at the drill fields, practicing the breeches buoy drill."

With this information, Kristina and Shanna ran toward the beach where the drill pole was set up. Keeper Daniels was in the middle of a drill and could not stop right away to talk to them. When drill practice was finished, he walked over and asked the girls if they wanted to be victims and ride the buoy down from the drill pole.

"We are here about Barnacle," Kristina said to him.

"Ah, that one," Keeper Daniels sighed. "He has the best lifesaving skills of any horse I have ever seen."

"Yes," said Kristina, "but have you seen him?"

"Nope, but Old Hazel has," the keeper said. "According to her, Barnacle is hanging around Cedar Hammock and only comes out late at night. She said he works very hard to hide his family from everyone, except her. When I mentioned that Barnacle would be a tremendous asset to the lifesaving service, she refused to help me. However, she did say that Barnacle would probably come to you, when you returned for the summer, if you could regain his trust. If so, perhaps you could help with his training." Then he returned to his men and the drill practice, reminding Kristina that she would have to go to Cedar Hammock to see Barnacle. Kristina and Shanna left the beach immediately to go find Edward and convince him to make a return trip to Hazel's house.

❧15❧

TRASHED COTTAGE

Kristina and Shanna entered the rental cottage and found it empty. Their luggage was still on the floor in the front room, but her parents were nowhere to be seen. "I wonder where they could have gone so fast?" Kristina said to Shanna. Then she checked the kitchen table for a note from her mom. Sure enough, a note there said, "We have gone to the store for supplies and will be back soon. Love, Mom."

"What shall we do?" Kristina asked Shanna.

"We'll probably meet them on the way, so we might as well wait here until they return," Shanna replied. Kristina agreed but could hardly cope with the excitement. She was ready to see Barnacle! Then she heard the soft whine of her dog and realized she had completely forgotten about Cocoa. Her parents had put the dog in one of the bedrooms before they left for the store.

Barnacle felt a very strange sensation. He could not shake a strong urge to go to Northard Woods to the station corral. Finally he made a decision to head north. The mare and colt tried to follow him, but he scolded them and made them return to the hammock, insisting that he would make this run alone.

Barnacle left the security of the marsh just as darkness was falling. Quickly he maneuvered the floating marsh and galloped toward the beach. When he reached the surf line, he turned northward and ran along the surf at a full gallop, reminding himself of his younger carefree days. As he passed to the east of Clarks he could see the lights from the village, and from Southard

Woods he could see the lights from the Chicamacomico Station tower. Soon Barnacle climbed the highest dune he could find and cautiously scanned the area around the corral.

Kristina and Shanna walked out to meet Edward and Beth as they returned from the store. The moon was just beginning to rise over the ocean. Suddenly they heard a horse snort and clear his throat, followed by a soft whinny. On top of the highest hill around stood a very big horse with the moon to his back.

"Look, Daddy, it's Barnacle!" shouted Kristina.

"That's a big horse, alright," Edward said, "but he is too far away to identify."

"Oh, it's him. I know it," Kristina said, running toward the horse and shouting. "Barnacle, I have come back for you!" Then Barnacle reared up on his hind legs, whinnied very loudly, and disappeared on the ocean side of the hill.

Cocoa reached the hill just as Barnacle went down the back side to the surf. They greeted by touching noses, and then the horse raced off in a southward direction with Cocoa at his heels. By the time Kristina and Shanna reached the hill, the horse was gone, and only his tracks remained in the sand.

"That was him. I know it was," Kristina told Shanna. "Now he's gone!"

"But he knows you're back," Shanna replied.

"Yes, I suppose," Kristina sighed, then she called Cocoa. "Here, Cocoa. Come back, girl." Cocoa could hear Kristina calling her, and even though she wanted to go on with Barnacle, she hurried back when Kristina called her again. "Good girl," Kristina said, patting the dog's head.

When the girls returned to the house, Beth and Edward were in the process of storing the supplies and unpacking the luggage. "Did you girls get close enough to determine the identity of the horse?" Edward asked.

"It was him, alright," Kristina replied. "Even Cocoa knows it."

"Well, maybe Cocoa will be able to help you reacquaint yourself with Barnacle," Edward said.

"That's a good idea," Kristina replied. "Maybe we can take Tar along, too. What do you think, Shanna?"

"That might be a problem," Shanna replied. "Since Stan went to Manteo to work with Captain Etheridge on lifesaving training, Tar has been spending a lot of time away from home. I think he's running rats in the marsh. When Tar comes home at night, he is always muddy and full of stickers, and we have to clean him up before he can be fed. He takes off in the morning, just as soon as we let him out."

"Well, if you spend some time with him, he'll go with you," Beth said. "I bet he'll be glad to see Cocoa."

The girls went out on the front porch and called for Tar. "Here, Tar! Here, boy!" they hollered. Then they heard a faint bark coming from the sound side. The more they called, the louder the barking became, until Tar was standing before them, muddy and full of water-bush stickers. Happy to see the girls, he jumped up and covered them with mud, stickers, and dog kisses while Cocoa barked from inside the cottage.

"Don't open that door," Edward warned, "at least until you clean him up." Then Beth opened the screen door just a crack, allowing Cocoa to go outside. The dogs greeted each other and began to roll and play in the front yard. Before they could be stopped, they ran off in the direction of the beach. "Let them go," Edward told the girls. "Maybe they will wash off in the ocean."

On his way back down the beach, Barnacle stopped at a freshwater pool to rest for a while and take a drink of water. He could tell the dogs were headed in his direction from the sound of their barks. Having sniffed their way south, the two dogs ran up to Barnacle and rubbed his nose to greet him. The three of them ran up and down the surf line and played for a while. Then they went for a swim in the pool before they parted ways.

Edward was the first to hear the dogs barking on their way back from the beach. "Here come the dogs," he said. "I hope they are cleaner than Tar was, when he came in from the marsh." Then he told Kristina and Shanna to go outside and pump water in the large tub, and wash and dry the dogs before allowing them to enter the cottage. Before the girls could get outside, Tar ran up on the front porch and pulled the screen door open, and both dogs bolted inside the front room. Covered in mud and sand, they ran throughout the house as Kristina, Shanna, and Edward chased after them, laughing their heads off.

Beth screamed as the dogs crashed through the house and jumped across the beds she had just made with clean linens. Eventually the girls were able to push Tar and Cocoa outside, but not before they trashed the cottage. Beth was furious. "I don't know who is worse—the dogs, you girls, or your father!" she said to Kristina.

"Well, it *was* funny, Mom," Kristina replied. She and Shanna were laughing so hard that soon Beth got tickled herself.

"Well, maybe a little," Beth replied, "but now you girls can clean up the dogs, and your father can help me put this cottage back in order. The linens have to be stripped off the beds, washed and replaced, and this cottage must be cleaned from top to bottom before we can retire for the night. Now, how funny is *that*?"

Edward, Kristina, and Shanna looked at one another, and Edward shrugged. "We might as well get started," he told the girls. They did just as Beth had commanded and were finally able to get into bed just before midnight. Kristina drifted off to sleep, planning how she would convince her father to help her get close to Barnacle and regain his trust.

The next day, the girls went to the station to talk to Barney. They found him out at the boathouse splicing an eye on the end of the sand anchor strap. "Well, good morning," Barney said to them. "What are you girls up to today? Wait, let me guess. I'll bet it has to do with a very large chestnut horse now living in Cedar Hammock with Old Hazel. Am I right?"

"Yes," replied Kristina. "Will you please help me contact Hazel so that I can find Barnacle?"

"You can come with me to the store in Clarks, where Hazel trades. She comes to town about twice a month, on Thursdays," Barney told them.

"That's tomorrow!" Shanna said.

"That's right," Barney replied. "Keeper Daniels sends the wagon in for supplies every Thursday. He likes the mosquito smokes she makes."

The next day, Kristina and Shanna rode to Clarks with Barney to pick up supplies from the store and talk to Hazel. As they arrived, Hazel was pulling away with her wagon, until Kristina asked her about Barnacle. Hazel told her that Barnacle was fine, living in the lower Cedar Hammock meadows. "He comes around with his mare and colt about twice a day, for food and water. He moves them around a lot, and they sleep in a different location each night. If you girls want to come to the hammock, I could use some help for a week. You will have to work while you are there, but I'll help you with Barnacle. Right now I have to go because I am already late for a meeting with Aaron Hooper to trade a few mosquito smokes for some salt mullet. I'll be back in town this same time next week, and if you want to come with me, be here and be ready." With that said, Hazel turned her horse and wagon south.

Barney and the girls loaded the supplies and headed back to Northard Woods to the station. Kristina and Shanna said good-bye to Barney and thanked him for his help. The next thing they needed was permission to spend a week with Hazel. When Beth heard this, her reply was quick. "Absolutely not," she said. "There is no way in this world you are going to spend a week with that woman, by yourself, in that marsh."

"Where's Dad?" Kristina asked.

"He's gone clamming with Jason. They should be coming back soon, but don't think the two of you are going to gang up on me and change my mind about this. It is just not going to happen! You will have to come up with a better plan if you want my support on this matter," Beth told Kristina.

"We'll see what Daddy has to say about it when he gets home," Kristina said to her mother.

Shanna hurried home. Her family was fixing to go to Manteo to visit Stan. He had finished his training and was ready to be assigned to a station, and they would be attending his assignment ceremony.

❦16❦

TRIP WITHOUT PERMISSION

As soon as Edward walked in the door, Kristina started working on him, begging her father to let her spend a week with Hazel. He told her that he would discuss the situation with Beth, and that they would reach a decision together. Then Kristina started pleading with him to talk to her mother right away.

"We will have to wait until the Grays return from Manteo so that Stan or Shanna can go with you. You can't expect us to allow you to go by yourself," her father told her.

"But that won't be until next week!" Kristina protested.

"Then it will have to be next week," Edward replied.

"Where is Mom anyway?" Kristina asked.

"She went to the store, but she'll be back soon," he said.

The moment Beth came in the house, Kristina started in on her, but Beth said, "I told you: your father and I need to discuss this. There is no way you can go by yourself."

Kristina protested, "Barnacle will probably forget all about me by the time you and Dad let me go look for him!"

"Don't pout," Beth told her. "We will reach a decision soon."

Kristina went to bed but could not sleep. *There is no way I can wait a whole week*, she thought to herself. Soon she heard her father come in the cottage, and shortly thereafter she heard her parents talking about her trip to see Hazel to find Barnacle. Kristina knew they would not let her go until the Grays returned, which would be too long. She had to do something right away.

Kristina waited until there was complete silence in the cottage before she made her move. She packed a small bag with some extra clothes, then crept to the kitchen and gathered some food. As she was going out the door, Cocoa came up to her and began to whine. "Hush, Cocoa," she said. "You can come as long as you are quiet." Then Cocoa stopped whining and followed her out of the house.

Kristina and Cocoa made their way toward the beach, and as they passed the Grays' cottage, Tar started barking. Afraid that the ruckus would wake her parents, Kristina let Tar out of the pen. Then he stopped barking and ran to Cocoa. Kristina and the two dogs passed by the station and continued walking south, along the surf, toward Cedar Hammock. She knew it was about four miles to Clarks and another mile to the entrance of Cedar Hammock.

Arthur Gibbs and Lester Ambrose were making their way across the mouth of Cedar Hammock Channel, aiming to land their barge on the beach at Bay Landing. After they beached their barge, they would settle down for the night and begin their work the next day. Each summer, these two men would cross the Pamlico Sound to catch Banker ponies and take them back to the mainland to sell as farm labor animals. They would build a temporary holding pen until they rounded up enough animals to make a profit. Islanders were always allowed to check the stock to make sure none of the ponies belonged to them.

Kristina and the two dogs passed by Southard Woods about midnight. She could see the village lights from the beach. Daylight was breaking as they passed Clarks, and by the time they reached the edge of Cedar Hammock Marsh, it was fully light. Kristina knew she had to be careful of the floating marsh, keeping both dogs very close to her. She was making her way along a very soft, unstable path, and made a big mistake when she leaned on a small bush to keep her balance. Suddenly the water rushed in around her feet, and she began to sink. Kristina knew that she had to move, and move fast, so she took several quick steps. She was making headway across the marsh until she broke through the matted grasses and sank up to her knees. She began to struggle and was soon up to her waist in the muddy.

Kristina called the dogs, and both of them scampered back to her. As she supported her weight on them, they pulled her forward; soon she was able to crawl up on a small pod of grass in the middle of the floating marsh. Tar and Cocoa were half-swimming, half-walking around her, barking urges for her to follow them. Unsure what to do, Kristina jumped off the small grassy knoll and held on to both dogs. Cocoa and Tar pulled Kristina along, straight to the hand of Old Hazel.

"For land sakes, child, what in the world are you and these two mutts doing in the middle of this marsh at such an early hour?" she asked. Before Kristina could answer, Hazel said, "I bet it has to do with a stallion that lives around here."

"Yes," Kristina answered. "Have you seen him?"

"Hold on, child. Let me pull you out first. Then we can talk horses," she said, as she helped Kristina get to her feet.

"Please," Kristina said. "Have you seen Barnacle?"

"Look behind you," said Hazel, and when Kristina turned around, Barnacle and his family were standing just a few feet away. While Cocoa, Tar, and Barnacle were greeting one another, Kristina took a step toward them. The mare and colt quickly scampered back a few feet.

"Go very slow," Hazel told her. Kristina held her hand out to Barnacle, and he stepped toward her. Soon she wrapped her arms around his big neck, and he whinnied very softly to her. Kristina's eyes filled with tears; she did not want to let him go. "I will never leave you again."

"Better not make any promises you can't keep," Hazel told her. "He knows exactly what you are talking about, but he does not understand lying. Animals deal with facts and feelings that have direct effects on them and their everyday lives. He will stand by you forever, as long as you never trick him again." Soon the mare and colt joined them, and it turned into a very happy reunion.

"We have to get word to your mom and dad right away," Hazel told Kristina. "They are probably beside themselves with worry."

"No, please! We can't do that," Kristina pleaded, "because I came here without their permission."

"That's all the more reason to get into contact with them as soon as possible," Hazel told her. "We will get you cleaned up, get something to eat, and head up to Clarks right away. Barnacle and his new family will follow you now."

As soon as Edward and Beth woke up and found Kristina gone, they went to the station and told Keeper Daniels what had happened. "I know where she is, and so do you," the keeper told them. "She has gone to look for that horse! I suggest you hitch up a wagon, get Barney, and head for Old Hazel's place as soon as possible. That's where you'll find her."

When Barney came from his morning beach patrol, Keeper Daniels already had the wagon ready to roll. He told Barney to eat breakfast and get under way to Cedar Hammock to help Kristina's parents find their daughter. Just as they were getting into Barney's wagon, Beth said, "For heaven's sake, would you look at that!" A few yards from them, on the beach road, were Old Hazel and Kristina sitting in a wagon being pulled by Barnacle. Tar and Cocoa were in front of the wagon, and the mare and colt were following closely behind it. As they pulled up to the rental house, Beth shouted at Kristina, "You come in this house right now, young lady. We have a lot to talk about. You have scared the life out of me!"

"Please, Mom," Kristina cried. "Aren't you excited to see Barnacle and his new family? You and Dad should come out and meet them! We should invite Miss Hazel in and thank her for bringing us home."

"Of course, you are right, but you did scare us half to death," her mother said. "I will fix some lunch while you take care of the horses, and then you can tell me all about it. But don't think this is over," Beth reminded her. "We will finish this conversation later."

Kristina, Edward, Barney, and Hazel took the horses to the corral and fed, watered, and rubbed them down. "It's so nice to have Barnacle back," Kristina told them.

"Remember what I told you," Hazel said. "You must renew his trust daily, and never trick him again." Then they all went in the house and prepared for lunch while Cocoa and Tar whined at the door.

"You can bring the dogs in, but they must behave and had better not mess up this house!" Beth told Kristina.

Kristina opened the door and said, "Okay, you guys, you can come in, but you have to be good."

Tar and Cocoa walked in slowly with their tails between their legs, never taking their eyes off Beth. She gave the dogs a treat and scolded them again. "Don't you dare ramp and rave in this house again," she told them. "Tar, you're stuck with us until the Grays return," she said to the black Lab as she stroked his head. Tar wagged his tail, then Cocoa wagged hers.

"I could always take Tar back home," Barney told Beth.

"If you did, he would probably bark his fool head off all night, locked up alone in that pen. He'll be fine here with Cocoa," Beth said.

After lunch, Hazel thanked them and said she had to get back to the hammock. "We should be the ones to thank you. You brought our daughter back to us," Beth told Hazel. "Kristina did a foolish thing, going off to look for Barnacle without her father."

"She has very strong ties with that horse," Hazel replied.

When Hazel started to leave, Barnacle put up a fuss. "Stay here, big fellow," she told him as she stroked his head. When she started off again, Barnacle kicked the top two rails off the corral fence so that his mare and colt could join him, and they began to follow Hazel. As soon as she returned them to the corral and went back to her wagon, Barnacle jumped the fence. This time, he opened the gate with his mouth so that the mare and colt could escape. Each time Hazel tried to make them return to the corral, they ran off a little farther.

"They want to go back to the hammock with you," Edward told Hazel.

"Then I'm going, too," Kristina added.

"You most certainly are not," Beth told her.

"Then I will sneak off again tonight," she told her mother.

"I really don't see the harm in it," Edward added, "but you have to be invited first!"

"She's welcome," Hazel said, "but she will have to work to earn her keep. That means feeding all the animals and helping me make things to trade at the store."

"You let her do anything she wants," Beth said to Edward.

"It won't hurt a thing. She'll help Hazel, be close to Barnacle, and be happy," Edward assured his wife.

"Thank you, Daddy!" Kristina said as she hugged her father. "We'll come visit you on the weekend, if it's okay with Hazel."

"Of course," Hazel replied.

Kristina packed quickly and joined Hazel in the wagon. As they were leaving, the two dogs began to bark and cut up from inside the house. "I suppose you guys want to go, too," Beth said, and when she opened the door, they scampered after the wagon.

"Well, I hope you are proud of yourself," Beth said to her husband. "Our only child has gone off to live with a woman I just met today, who you have only been around one other time."

"Kristina will be perfectly fine," said Edward. "Hazel has turned out to be a very positive influence on her. I'm beginning to think that you and Kristina are a lot safer here than in Baltimore, especially when I'm away for long periods of time."

"Oh, no! Don't you even let that thought enter your mind," Beth told him as they watched Hazel's wagon disappear around the bend. "I realize that Kristina would be much happier living here rather than Baltimore, but the educational system is so limited here. I think she would be happy living on the moon if she could take Barnacle with her."

"You are forgetting that there are three horses to be considered now, instead of one," Edward remarked.

"Yes, I know," Beth replied. "Our small family has grown to include a chocolate Lab and three horses, but there is no way we can take them to live with us up north."

"No, but we could live here with them," Edward told her.

"I was afraid you might start thinking along those lines," Beth replied. "You would be away at sea most of the time, and we would be stuck here."

"That might not be such a bad thing. We will discuss this some more tomorrow," he told her, and they went into the house for the evening.

❧ 17 ☙

SEARCH FOR BANKER PONIES

Kristina was full of questions for Hazel as they made their way south to the Cedar Hammock Marsh. "How long do you think it will take Barnacle to fully trust me again?" she asked Hazel.

"It will not take very long, if you are straight with him," Hazel answered. "You can't fool or trick him anymore. You must always be truthful with him because animals don't understand the concept of lying."

"I will never trick or fool him again," Kristina replied.

Tar and Cocoa ran ahead of the wagon, searching through the grass along the way. The mare and colt brought up the rear and kept up with the wagon. Kristina said, "I am very happy this evening. I have the dogs, Barnacle, and his family, plus I get to spend time with you, learning more about animals."

"It's not going to be all fun and games," Hazel told her. "There is going to be a bit of work to it, too. You'll have to care for the animals and help me make a few things to trade at the store, in Clarks, for supplies."

"I am willing to work and do whatever you say, to care for Barnacle and his family," Kristina replied. "Just to be near them and spend time with them is enough for me."

All of a sudden, they became startled by a couple of pheasants that the dogs flushed from the marsh grass. "I've heard that sound more than a hundred times, I know," Hazel said, "but it still gives me a start every time a pheasant jumps near me." As she and Kristina entered the path to Cedar Hammock, the evening light was just beginning to fade.

Arthur Gibbs and Lester Ambrose woke up early the next morning and noticed their vessel was listing a bit. "What's going on?" Arthur asked.

"All the water is gone, and we are resting on bare sand," Lester replied. Arthur joined Lester on the top deck and looked over the side. Sure enough, they were resting on bare sand.

"What happened to all the water?" asked Arthur.

"I think it's this hard southeast wind that has caused it to run off," Lester replied.

"Well, then, even if we are able to round up some of these Banker ponies, we'll have to wait until the wind shifts and the water comes back in before we can get back across that sound," Arthur responded. "We can get started on the containment corral in the clearing and pile up the brush to create a lead path to the corral gate."

The men unloaded their brush-cutting tools and began their work. They finished up around noon, after having built a corral that would hold up to fifty horses. They piled up and fastened brush to form a long guiding path to the corral gate, and then went back to the barge to eat lunch and plan their search for the Banker ponies.

After lunch the two men off-loaded their horses and turned north along the shoreline, toward the village of Clarks. They intended to talk to the local residents about the location of the wild Banker herd. As they neared the village, they crossed over to the beach and rode along the surf line for the last couple of miles.

The Raven was leading a group of Banker ponies to the south to graze in the Cedar Hammock Meadows when he spotted the two men riding toward them. He stopped and sniffed the air but could not pick up their scent because they were downwind of him. Most of the riders they met would give them plenty of room and go around them, but these two were headed straight for the herd.

The Raven pawed the ground and snorted loudly to alert the remainder of the herd. Then all the ponies stopped to watch the approaching riders. The

Raven moved the herd to the right to see what the riders would do, and when the riders turned in the same direction, that was enough for the Raven. Then he took off in a gallop and called for the others to follow. He went around to the rear and began to nip at the slower-moving horses to move them faster. Soon the entire herd was galloping away at full speed.

Arthur and Lester gave chase and followed the ponies across the island, to the end of the marsh and out into the sound. The Raven and his herd quickly outran them and disappeared from view, around a long point of marsh sticking way out from the shore.

"Now what do we do?" Lester asked Arthur as they lost sight of the ponies.

"We will follow their tracks," Arthur replied. "They'll go back to the shore sooner or later, and be easy to follow."

Barnacle and his family were grazing in Cedar Hammock Meadow, and Kristina was nearby, playing with the dogs in the tall grass. Barnacle raised his head and sniffed the air. He could smell horses off to the north, but they were too far away to determine their direction. Cocoa and Tar smelled them soon after and began to howl, bark, and pace back and forth.

"What in the world is wrong with you foolish dogs?" Kristina asked them. "There's nothing in this grass." Suddenly, the pounding of hooves grew louder and louder, coming out of the sound from the north. Barnacle bolted toward the sound, with Tar and Cocoa at his heels, and the mare and colt close behind. Kristina tried to follow but was soon left behind, trying to deal with the tall marsh grass. She knew there was no way she could keep up after she lost sight of them altogether.

Barnacle and the dogs saw the herd of horses approaching and raced out on the hard sand to head them off. The Raven did not stop, even though he recognized Barnacle. Barnacle caught up to him and was eventually able to slow him down and stop the herd. All of the ponies were covered with sweat and gasping for breath.

The Raven was very nervous, pacing back and forth. Then Barnacle saw the riders and knew by their position that they were chasing the herd. The riders were making a direct path toward them. The Raven and Barnacle approached each other and began to whinny, as if they were talking, while the dogs ran around, barking loudly. Soon Barnacle and his family joined the Raven's herd, along with Tar and Cocoa. They headed south toward Cedar Hammock Island and crossed back over to the shore, leaving lots of easy-to-follow tracks.

Kristina could hear the horses running through the marsh. She could also hear Tar and Cocoa barking to the north. The sounds led her to believe that the animals were headed toward Hazel's shack. However, their tracks continued past Hazel's, toward the beach. Too tired to continue, Kristina returned to Hazel's and told her what had happened.

"There is a very good reason for them to race off like that and leave you behind," Hazel told Kristina. "Something's up with them. They feel threatened. Let's saddle a couple of ponies and follow them."

As Kristina and Hazel crossed the tracks, they ran into Arthur and Lester, who asked them if they had seen the Banker ponies. Hazel and Kristina quickly realized why the ponies were in such a panic and traveling so fast.

Hazel was not very cordial to the men. "There ought to be a law to prevent you men from chasing and terrorizing these Banker ponies the way you do," she told them.

"We are only trying to make a living," one of the men replied.

"We offer the ponies nice homes and plenty of food, and we take good care of them on the mainland," the other man replied.

"Yes, and they are made to live a life of slavery as farm labor animals after they have roamed these hills and lived a life of freedom. We are following the horses because three of the Banker ponies running with that herd belong to this young girl. We can't stop you from coming along, but we will not help you trap any of them, and we expect you to cut her ponies out of the herd if you catch them," Hazel stated. The men agreed, and all four of them followed the tracks toward the beach.

When Barnacle and the Raven reached the beach, they led the herd into the ocean and swam out to the second bar, where they could easily wade. The Raven took about a dozen young stallions and split off to the south, and Barnacle headed the rest of the ponies north. They traveled along the outside sandbar for about a mile. Then they crossed over to the sound in a single file and took off in an easy gallop. The unusually low tide allowed them to travel on packed sand, and Barnacle did not bring the ponies ashore until they reached the safety of the New Inlet area.

The Raven took his small herd about one hundred yards south before bringing them ashore. Then they settled in the soft beach sand and waited. The Raven did not stand up until he saw the four riders approaching from the west. When the men got within fifty yards, the Raven stirred the ponies, and they galloped away farther south along the surf line. When the two men gave chase, Hazel told Kristina to stay put.

"But we must follow them," Kristina replied.

Then Hazel asked a question. "Did you see Barnacle or your dogs with that herd?"

"No," Kristina replied.

"Stay still for a minute and listen," Hazel told her. Then, in a few seconds, Hazel asked, "Do you hear the faint barking of your dogs up to the north?"

"I sure do," Kristina said. She and Hazel both agreed that Barnacle and the Raven had probably split up, protecting the herd from the dangerous men by taunting them in the opposite direction.

Arthur and Lester were surprised that the Raven allowed them to drive the ponies along the brush borders and straight into their corral. "That was too easy, almost like they wanted to be caught," Arthur told Lester.

"That's okay with me," Lester responded. "We have an amazing black stallion and about a dozen good-looking young stallions in this bunch. Quite a haul, I would say!"

"We might as well return to Cedar Hammock," Hazel told Kristina. "Those Bankers have such a start on us, there's no way we can catch up to them before dark."

Kristina replied, "It sounds like they are making good time. I don't hear the dogs anymore."

"The animals will return home when the danger has passed," Hazel assured Kristina. Then Kristina went to bed with the animals on her mind, hoping and praying they were all safe.

Barnacle bedded his herd in the New Inlet Meadows, putting the lead mare and two flank stallions in charge before he turned south. His mare and colt tried to follow, but Barnacle made them return to the herd. Then he motioned for Cocoa and Tar to accompany him, and they turned south once more.

Just before dark, Barnacle and the dogs arrived at the Chicamacomico Station. Barney saw them drinking from the water trough and mentioned it to Keeper Daniels.

"Those three often move around together," Keeper Daniels told Barney.

"Yes, they do," Barney replied, "but that mare and colt weren't with them. Don't you think that's odd?"

"Not really," was the keeper's reply.

"Well, maybe not," Barney mumbled and went on about his duties.

Kristina was awakened by something scratching on Hazel's door. She got out of bed and found Cocoa and Tar on the front porch and Barnacle standing in the front yard. When Kristina asked them what they had been up to, the dogs whined and Barnacle pawed the ground. Barnacle ran off a short distance and then returned, bobbing his head. "You want me to come with you, is that it?" she asked, and Barnacle bobbed his head again.

Kristina slipped her clothes on; then she climbed on Barnacle's back, and they took off. Barnacle headed out in the sound to take advantage of the low water and hard sand. The two dogs followed closely, and soon they entered the Bay Landing area from the west. Kristina could see the sailing barge, and then she spotted the corral containing the horses.

"I see what you are up to," she told Barnacle. "You want to free the Raven and the stallions." Then she told the dogs to be very quiet as they approached the corral. Kristina very quietly slipped the corral gate open, and very quietly the Raven and the stallions walked outside the fence.

Arthur and Lester were standing on the deck of their barge when, much to their amazement, they saw all of the horses they had caught galloping away in the moonlight, followed by two dogs and a young girl with long blonde hair riding a large chestnut stallion.

❧18❧

The Escape

Hazel woke up to the sound of horses. She also heard dogs barking in the distance, approaching from the south. She checked the room where Kristina was supposed to be sleeping, but Kristina was not in her bed. *Just as I thought*, Hazel said to herself. *They are up to something.* When she went out on her front porch, she saw Barnacle, Kristina, and the two dogs coming up the path. "Where have you been, and what have you been up to?"

"We set the Banker ponies free from the corral where those men had them contained," Kristina shouted excitedly.

"Where are they now?" asked Hazel.

"The Raven is leading them up the sound side to the safety of New Inlet Meadows until those men are gone," Kristina replied.

"Those men will come looking for the herd again tomorrow," Hazel said.

"By the pace those ponies were making up the sound, with the water as low as it is, they'll never find them," Kristina answered.

Hazel changed the subject. "We have to go to Clarks tomorrow to trade for supplies. I have three boxes of fig preserves, five boxes of bayberry candles, and some assorted whistles and wooden toys for the store shelves. By the way, we will probably see those herders on the way to the store. Do you think they saw you when you let the ponies out of their corral?"

"I don't know," replied Kristina. "It was kind of dark when we were running away."

"I had no trouble seeing you tonight when you were approaching in the moonlight," Hazel said. "We'll just have to wait and see. The dogs will be okay on the porch, but go ahead and put Barnacle in the corral with the rest of the stock. Then come on in the house and rest until morning."

Arthur and Lester were up very early the next morning, looking for the herd of Banker ponies. Hazel spotted the men and pointed them out to Kristina. "There they are, to the east of us, riding along the surf line, headed north," she said.

"I see them," Kristina replied. "They're looking for tracks, but the last high tide has washed them away by now."

The men turned their wagon toward Hazel and Kristina, and as they approached, Hazel told Kristina to be cordial. "Answer their questions, but do not volunteer any information to them," she said. Hazel stopped her wagon when the two men rode up to her side.

"Where is the large chestnut stallion that normally pulls your wagon?" they asked Hazel.

"Oh, that one," she said. "He's around here somewhere, roaming free with the Banker ponies. If he belongs to anyone, it would be this young girl right here."

"Yes, we know. She and that stallion set loose the ponies we caught yesterday," Arthur replied. "We're not asking you to help us, but please don't hinder us. We are planning to sell the ponies we catch and use the money to help our families."

"Hinder you?" Hazel snapped. "If it were up to me, I would run you off these beaches. Why don't you just work like other folks and stop trapping these Banker ponies? These horses are born free and are accustomed to freedom. They are sleek and slender, built for running, not working—and they don't make very good farm labor animals. You need stocky workhorses."

"Just stay out of our way, and we will keep our distance from you," replied one of the men as they turned to leave.

"You have to be smarter than a Banker before you can catch one," Hazel told them. Then the two men sneered in disgust and rode away.

"Those men will not be very successful at catching Banker ponies," Hazel told Kristina. "You have to win a Banker over with trust by being kind and helpful to them. Once they allow your friendship, then and only then will they share their lives with you. Always remember that they can't be won over with force, and that you will never fully own them." Just before they arrived at the end of the village, Barnacle, Cocoa, and Tar came out to join them. They had been moving parallel to Hazel and Kristina, hidden by the brush line on the sound side.

Hazel stopped the wagon in front of the store, and she and Kristina began off-loading their goods for trading. On their way back to Cedar Hammock, Barnacle and the dogs took the sound-side trail, staying hidden by the brush, while Kristina and Hazel took the regular mid-island trail, which was wider and easier to travel by wagon.

When Barnacle returned to Hazel's shack, he refused to go into the corral for the night. Kristina stroked his large head and said, "What have you got on your mind, boy?" In response to her question, Barnacle ran toward the sound. He stopped for a few seconds and looked back at Kristina before he took off to the north, along the shore side, followed by Cocoa and Tar. Kristina called the dogs to come back. They hesitated, but then quickly decided to keep up with Barnacle and were soon out of sight. Then Kristina ran into the house to tell Hazel what had just happened.

"He's going to check on his family," Hazel replied. "The dogs are very close to Barnacle, and they are all very good friends. They'll be back, just as soon as Barnacle thinks it is safe to return."

Barnacle, Cocoa, and Tar entered the New Inlet Meadows just as the southeast wind shifted to the southwest. Then they headed for the oak tree grove where Barnacle had left his family. The colt ran over and bumped against him a few times, then romped off with Tar and Cocoa. All of the ponies were very glad to see Barnacle and welcomed him back. Shortly after the greetings, Barnacle went to snuggle with his mare.

The next morning, Barnacle and his family headed to the beach at a medium lope to begin their return trip southward. Barnacle loved to travel along the beach in the surf line. Besides that, offshore travel through the sound was no longer an option, due to the return of the sound water from the southwest wind.

Jason was on watch in the Chicamacomico Station tower and yelled down to Barney, "Here comes Barnacle, down the beach, with his family and the dogs," he said. "Stan's home for a few days and has been looking for Tar. He'll be glad to know I saw him today." Edward had already informed Jason that the dogs were with Kristina, down at Old Hazel's.

"They're not stopping! There they go. They just ran by!" Jason exclaimed.

The horses did not stop until they neared the west entrance of Cedar Hammock Marsh. Hazel was the first to see them coming. "There's what you've been waiting to see," she told Kristina. Soon, both dogs ran up to her, wagging their tails and rubbing on her. Barnacle lowered his head so that she could pet him, too, as his mare and colt approached with caution. Soon Kristina was able to greet and stroke all of them together.

For the next few days, Kristina and Hazel went about their work, making things to trade at the store. In the evenings, when the work was finished, they would spend time with the animals. Jason and Stan had taken Tar home, and his presence was surely missed.

One afternoon as Kristina and Cocoa were relaxing in the meadows with Barnacle and his family, Cocoa began barking and running around in the tall grass. "What is wrong with you, Cocoa?" she asked the dog. "There's nothing in this grass." When Kristina went to see what was making Cocoa so nervous, she saw Arthur and Lester running back to their horses. She watched them as they mounted and rode away. Then she ran quickly to tell Hazel what she had seen.

"They were spying on you, trying to find out about the Banker herd," Hazel told her.

The next day, Arthur and Lester approached Kristina down by the sound side while she was baling dried seaweed for the stalls. "We saw you let the ponies out of our corral," Lester told her. "We're sure you know where the Bankers have gone, and we want you to tell us where they are. Your ponies will not be bothered. We just want to find the herd. It will soon be time for us to leave. If we go home empty-handed, it will be a wasted trip and we will not make any money."

Kristina responded, "I will not help you enslave the Bankers to a life of farm labor. They live a free life here."

Just then Hazel appeared and asked the men what they were doing there, uninvited. "I don't have any say about the way you chase the Banker ponies on open ground, but this is my place and I do have a say here—so you had better be on your way before I return to the shack for my double-barrel. You'll move then."

"We were just on our way," Arthur said.

"Good," answered Hazel.

The next day, Hazel, Kristina, and Barnacle took the wagon to the beach to collect some firewood. The mare and colt tried to come along, but Barnacle made them stay behind in the safety of the Cedar Hammock meadows. Cocoa ran ahead of the wagon, barking and checking out each grass lump they passed. It wasn't long before they returned to Hazel's cottage with a wagon full of wood.

Later, while Kristina was stacking the wood, Cocoa came running out of the marsh, barking loudly, and started nipping at her shoes. "Stop that, Cocoa," Kristina scolded the dog, but to no avail. Suddenly, Barnacle came galloping from the tall grass. He ran down the path a short distance and then returned to Kristina, pawing the ground and bobbing his head.

"They want you to follow them. Something is wrong," Hazel told her. "Let me get a pony from the corral."

When Hazel was mounted, Kristina hopped up on Barnacle's back, and they took off with Cocoa in the lead. They followed the animals to the Bay Landing area, where they stopped and dismounted. Then they crept down to the clearing, where Arthur and Lester had their bargelike vessel anchored.

"So that's it," Hazel said. There, in a corral on the flat deck of the barge, was Barnacle's mare and colt.

Cocoa began to whimper. "Quiet!" Kristina told her. Barnacle suddenly darted out into the open and Kristina started to follow him, but Hazel stopped her.

"Look at that," Arthur said to Lester. "There's that big chestnut stallion. He sure would bring a good price back home. Let's see what we can do to round him up."

The mare and colt began to whimper when the men lowered the ramp. Barnacle boarded the barge, and when Lester opened the corral gate, Barnacle went inside. Kristina could stand no more. She ran to the end of the marsh and shouted, "Those are my horses. You let them go!"

Arthur yelled back, "You wouldn't tell us where the Bankers were, so we're taking what we can get!"

"We'll be back with more help!" Hazel warned them.

"We'll be gone by then," Lester hollered back. Then he told Arthur to chop the anchor rope.

Arthur chopped the rope in half, and the barge started pulling away with one end of the rope dangling from the deck. Kristina went from being depressed to thrilled when she saw more rope drop from the side of the barge and fall into the water. She took off, as fast as she could run. When Kristina was finally able to grab the rope, she hung on tightly, even though Hazel was yelling for her to let go. The last thing Hazel saw in the fading light was the barge, sailing away with Barnacle and his family trapped aboard; Kristina, being dragged through the water clinging to an anchor rope; and Cocoa, swimming as fast as she could, right behind her.

❧19❧

THE STOWAWAYS

Kristina was holding onto the rope with both hands as she was being dragged behind the sailing barge. Cocoa was swimming behind her, just out of reach, and Kristina wondered if she should risk letting go of the rope with one arm to grasp the dog. She knew that, if the men were at the front of the vessel, they would soon have to make a short tack in order to turnaround. In this case, there would be some slack in the rope to help her reach the dog.

Kristina's thoughts were right. As soon as the barge reached deeper water and was a good distance from shore, the vessel turned and headed into the wind. The large sail flapped as it shifted to the opposite side. The barge slowly responded to the opposite tack and turned bow first into the wind, providing enough slack on the rope for Kristina to grab Cocoa. Eventually they were able to climb just above the waterline and cling to the side of the loading ramp. Then they crawled under a shelf-arm containing the raising and lowering rope, where they could not be seen from the deck of the barge.

Arthur yelled to Lester, "You better go check on that girl and her dog. I lost sight of them when we made our tack to turn around. Go ahead and raise the ramp, and secure it for sailing so that we can raise the jib and increase our speed."

Lester walked to the front of the vessel and looked over the side. All he saw was the loose end of the rope curving around and dragging by the side of the barge. "No sign of them here. They must have let go," he yelled back to Arthur. "I'll go raise and secure the ramp," he hollered.

Lester hooked the block and tackle to the ramp and raised it. He hooked the eye of the securing rope to each side of the cleats securing the ramp and released tension on the block and tackle. Then he raised the jib, and the vessel began to pick up speed.

Cocoa began to whimper when Kristina climbed to the top rail, using the ramp hinges and chocks as hand- and footholds. "Quiet!" she cautioned the dog. "I will help you." Then she grabbed Cocoa by the scruff of the neck and pulled her to the deck. From there, they crawled over and hid behind a large wooden box containing the block and tackle, and more coils of rope.

The deck of the barge was dark. The only light came from one lantern, which was fastened to the gate of the corral, casting long shadows in all directions. Kristina rested for a short time, and then she and Cocoa began to crawl toward the corral, along the port side, among the shadows. When they reached the corral fence, they slid under the lower rail and stopped. A large section of light was between them and the stall where the horses were, and Kristina did not want to be seen.

How are we going to cross that section of light? Kristina thought to herself. At that instant, Barnacle came out of the stall and sat on the deck, casting a large shadow all the way to the corral enclosure. Kristina mumbled silently, "Sometimes it's like he knows what I'm thinking, even before it enters my mind." Then she and Cocoa crossed over Barnacle's shadow and lay down on the pine straw with him, his mare, and his colt. Finally they were together and could plan their escape.

"Better go check on the horses," Arthur told Lester, "and make sure the back of that shelter is protected. We'll be very close to Long Shoal Point on our southward tack, and it gets choppy in that channel." Then Lester took the lantern from its perch, walked to the front of the shelter, and looked in. Kristina and Cocoa had covered themselves with pine straw and were hiding behind Barnacle.

"They're fine," Lester called to Arthur. "They're all settled down, and the colt is asleep."

When Arthur turned the vessel southward, the mainsail shifted and grabbed the wind. Lester adjusted the jib, and they took off on a southward tack.

"This direction will bring us close to Long Shoal Point," Arthur said. "I turned just a bit early on the northern tack, so I'll need to turn up even sooner down to the south to keep us from running aground," he told Lester. "If we get too far south, we won't be able to clear Long Shoal when we turn up."

"Well, I have to trust you," Lester told him. "You are the better navigator. You got us over to the beach, and it's up to you to get us back."

"We don't have very much to show for the time we spent there," Arthur said.

"I know," answered Lester, "but that big chestnut will bring a good price. He's not like those other Banker ponies. He is much smarter, larger, faster, and stronger than the others."

"If we are able to sell all three of them, I will be very happy and surprised," replied Arthur as they sailed along a southward tack, headed for Long Shoal.

Hazel was beside herself. The vision of Kristina hanging on to the rope, with Cocoa swimming after her, was all she could visualize in her mind as she hurried to Clarks to summon help. *What in the world am I going to tell that girl's parents?* Hazel thought as she hurried the horse to Aaron Hooper's house. By the time she got there, everyone was asleep, so Hazel banged on the door. "Aaron, wake up! It's me, Hazel, and it's a matter of life and death!"

Aaron came outside and said, "What in the world is the matter with you, Hazel? You're banging so hard, you could wake up the dead! Calm down and tell me what's happened." After Hazel told him the whole story about Kristina, he told her to go in the house and rest. "I'll ride my fastest horse to the Chicamacomico Station to see Keeper Daniels. He'll know what to do." Then Aaron woke his wife and told her what was going on. "I'll need you to stay here with Hazel while I ride for help."

Aaron reached the station just about daylight, and Keeper Daniels was having coffee in the galley. He told the keeper that Kristina was in danger and quickly explained the situation exactly as Hazel had explained it to him.

"Take your time and don't leave anything out. Every detail is important," Keeper Daniels assured Aaron. When he had heard the entire story, the keeper said, "First we will have to tell Kristina's parents, which will be tough. Then we must form an extensive search pattern to cover that part of the sound."

Aaron and Keeper Daniels found Edward sitting on the front porch of his cottage. He greeted them and asked if they wanted some coffee.

"No, thanks," replied Keeper Daniels. "I'm afraid we have bad news for you." Then Aaron repeated the story to Edward as Hazel had told it to him.

"Oh, good *Lord*!" exclaimed Edward, "How will I tell her mother? She didn't want to let Kristina go in the first place."

"I don't envy you that job," Keeper Daniels told Edward. "Aaron and I will be over at the station organizing a search. Join us when you can, and I'll ask a couple of surfmen to send their wives over to be with Beth." As he and Aaron left, Edward went into the house. When he told Beth about Kristina, she collapsed into his arms, and as she came around, he was wiping her face with a cool, damp cloth.

"You're telling me that the last time Hazel saw Kristina, she was being dragged through the water by a barge, holding onto a rope?" Beth asked.

"That's what they told me," Edward responded.

"Well, let me tell *you* something, Edward. You get out in that sound, and don't you return without my baby. Do you hear me?" Beth demanded.

"Will you be alright while I join the search?" Edward asked her quietly.

"I'll be fine," Beth said. "Just get out there and find her and bring her home." Then Edward went to join Aaron and Keeper Daniels, just as soon as the ladies arrived to sit with his wife.

"I'll inform Little Kinnakeet Station and Gull Shoal Station of the circumstances and coordinate the search from here," Keeper Daniels said. "We'll use the sound sprit sailboats from all three stations. Chicamacomico will cover this area, Gull Shoals will take the center, and Little Kinnakeet will cover the south. Aaron, I want you to organize some smaller boats from each village to fill in the gaps between station boats." With that, Aaron and Edward left the station to begin the search. On their way out, Aaron said, "Edward, you can either crew with me, or I will loan you my sixteen-foot sprit sailor, and we can find someone with sound experience to crew with you."

"I would like to have a boat," Edward responded.

"Then I'll get my brother, Seth, to crew with you," Aaron replied. "We'll get some fishermen from the three villages to fill in the gaps between the station boats and help find Kristina."

Hazel was waiting at Aaron's house in Clarks and was beside herself by the time he and Edward arrived. "What took you so long?" she asked them. "I was here before first light, and now it's almost noon!" Promptly, both men began to fill Hazel in on the search plans.

"Well, I'm either going with you or Edward," Hazel exclaimed. "Take your choice."

"Hazel, you would be better off—" Aaron began, but was interrupted.

"Stop right there. You either take me, or I will take my own boat by myself," Hazel told Aaron emphatically.

"Alright, Hazel, you can come with me. You and I will tack north until we meet up with Jason and Barney," he said. "Edward and Seth can take my other boat and head south until they meet up with Clyde Gray and Jim Scarborough." Soon they parted ways to go search for Kristina.

The wind had breezed up quite a bit from the southwest since Arthur and Lester began their tack to clear Long Shoal. They entered the open water and had smooth sailing for the rest of their trip. Arthur could see the breakers on the end of Long Shoal Point as they neared the edge of the channel.

"I'm sure we can make a good tack and slip by that point, but we have to be ready," Arthur told Lester. "Be ready with that jib, and when I holler, shift it quick and let it out quick. That big line of thunderstorms to the left of the point is bearing down on us hard."

The first thunderstorm hit as they were entering the shallow end of the point. "I can't see a thing," Arthur yelled as he and Lester became engulfed in blinding rain and howling winds. Suddenly, a downburst of wind rocked them to the left, ripping the jib line from Lester's hand. The boat slammed hard, stern first, onto the end of the point, crushing the rudder. Without the rudder, Arthur and Lester were at the mercy of the elements. The rushing tide coming through the channel carried them, end for end, to the windward side of the shoal.

The next thunderstorm hit stronger than the first, bringing more blinding rain and fierce winds. The men could not see anything, and they took cover in the wheelhouse to ride out the storm. After it passed, they found themselves completely grounded, on the center of the point, about fifty yards from the channel. The vessel had a severe crack at the mid-ship line and was being torn apart by the pounding, wind-driven waves.

"We need to make a decision soon before the barge breaks up completely," Arthur told Lester. "Right now, we have enough water on the leeside of the boat to lower the sprit sailor, but we had better do it soon before another storm hits and drives us farther up onto the shoal."

"How about the horses?" Lester asked.

"There's not enough time to worry with them," answered Arthur.

"At least let me open up the gate so that they can get off the barge if they need to," Lester said.

"Okay, but hurry," Arthur replied.

After Lester opened the gate, they had just enough time to lower the sprit sailor, raise sail, and make it to deep water before the next storm hit. Arthur turned around and looked back through the blinding rain, then pointed to the barge. "Look, Lester," he said. "It's that girl and her dog on the deck with those horses!"

Lester looked toward the barge. "You just imagined it. I can't see a thing," he said.

"Well, maybe you're right," Arthur replied. "Anyway, it's too late to worry about it now."

The two men had a struggle on their hands, trying to navigate the small sprit sailboat in such adverse weather conditions. They headed downwind, away from the barge, and sailed across the shoal. Then they entered the channel and made a northward tack around the point to open water. The strong southwest wind was causing waves to crash over the bow of the boat. The water ran out the scuppers, but everything was awash on the small deck.

"Well," Arthur said to Lester, "that old woman got her wish."

"What in the world are you talking about?" Lester asked.

"She said if it was up to her, we would have to find a different type of work and leave the Banker ponies alone to run free. It looks like we are out of the horse-trading business with the loss of our barge," Arthur replied.

The men watched as the barge broke into two pieces. The front half, carrying the horses, floated across the shoal to deep water. "I just hope those horses make it back to shore," Lester said.

"They're Banker ponies. They are a hearty lot," Arthur told him.

"But the colt is so small and fragile," Lester replied as he watched the barge and Long Shoal fade in the distance.

❧20❧

Lost in the Sound

The current of Long Shoal Channel carried the front half of the barge out into deep water. The weight of the loading ramp kept the broken end of the barge a few feet above the crashing waves as it drifted around in circles to the northeast. Trapped in the shallows of Long Shoal, the rear half of the barge was being battered to pieces by the pounding waves.

Kristina walked toward the broken end of the barge to see if water was coming in. Barnacle started to follow her, but the combined weight of both of them caused the end of the barge to dip below the surface and take on water. "No, Barnacle, go back!" Kristina shouted as she ran back herself. Slowly the open end of the barge rose back up above the water.

"We have to stay on this end or we will sink," Kristina told the animals. As she spoke, a large piece of decking broke away from the barge and floated alongside them for a while, then drifted out of sight. The wind and current, running up the center of the sound, carried them northward toward Oregon Inlet. They drifted all night, and by daylight they were way past the search area.

It was past noon when the boats began their search, covering the sound from Kinnakeet village to Northard Woods until nightfall. Keeper Daniels traveled down to Gull Station to discuss the day's search results with the leaders from each search party. On the first day, no one had seen any signs of the bargelike vessel. "We will return for the next few days until we have some answers," the keeper told the men.

Hazel was not satisfied, and she informed Aaron that she would be taking her own boat out the next day.

"Hazel, you should go with me," Aaron said.

"You can find someone else to crew with you," she told him. "My boat is smaller and much faster, and I can cover more area by myself."

The next day, Hazel set out from the creek behind her shack, long before any of the other searchers were out of bed. She knew a vessel as large as the barge would have to make a long tack to the north in order to clear Long Shoal, so she decided to search Long Shoal Point.

Beth was at Chicamacomico Station when Keeper Daniels and Edward returned from Gull Shoal Station with the news of the first half-day search. She groaned and burst into tears when they told her that no sign of the barge had been found. "We won't stop searching until we find them," Keeper Daniels reassured her.

"I hate the thought of her being out in that sound at night," Beth said. "This is your fault," she turned to Edward. "It was your idea to let her go to Cedar Hammock."

"I know," Edward responded. "If I had it in my power to change things, I surely would. I should have listened to you. Instead, I let Kristina's happiness sway my judgment for her safety. Now she may be lost, and there is absolutely nothing I can do about it." Then Edward collapsed into one of the galley chairs, placed his head in his hands, and began to weep.

Beth came over and put her arms around his shoulders. "I could have protested more," she said, choking back tears.

"We will find her, I promise," the keeper told them. "Try to stay strong, and don't give up hope."

As the barge section approached Oregon Inlet, it looked as though Kristina and the animals would drift out into the ocean. Then Kristina spotted a small island near the main channel, with a hunting shack on it, and she decided it was time to jump off the barge with the animals and swim for the island. Cocoa would follow her, and she was sure the mare and colt would follow Barnacle into the water.

Due to the way the tide was running, Kristina had to time their jump just right. Barnacle would have to jump first because he was the strongest swimmer. Kristina knew she might have to push the mare and colt into the water, if they refused to go, so she went to the rigging box and got a long piece of rope. She tied it around Barnacle's neck, then to the mare, and at last but not least to the colt. Then she tied a loop in the end to hold on to herself.

Kristina let the ramp down to the surface of the water, and when she called Barnacle, he walked to the end of the ramp. "Get ready, boy," she told him as they waited for the barge to swing toward the island. "Now, boy, jump!" she shouted, and Barnacle plunged into the water. The mare hesitated to follow Barnacle, but the rope came tight, pulling her off the ramp. Then Kristina pushed the colt into the water, and she jumped in, too, yelling for Cocoa to follow, which she did.

Barnacle was serious about this rescue, and he swam with all his might to reach the last point of sand sticking out in the channel. He was finally able to gain his footing just before the inlet widened into deep, fast-moving water. When Kristina and the animals were swept past him by the rushing tide, Barnacle had to dig his hooves into the sand and pull very hard to drag them out of the strong current and onto the shore. "I'm sure glad we were tied around your neck," Kristina told Barnacle. Then Barnacle pulled the rope tight and forced them to move higher up onto the beach. Cocoa was already on shore, barking joyously. After they rested for a minute, Kristina untied the rope, and they headed toward the hunting shack.

Hazel set her sail for a very long tack to the north, in order to be in the Long Shoal area at the end of her southward tack. By noontime, she could make out the breakers on the outer rim of Long Shoal Point. The wind had shifted some and was now due west, causing the water to run off and expose the shoal. When Hazel got closer, she saw some debris piled up on the middle of the shoal. She sailed to the lee side of the point, took down her sail, and paddled into the shallow water. Then she anchored the boat and went to inspect the debris.

Hazel knew right away that the debris was from the barge that she and Kristina had seen at the Bay Landing. She recognized the wheelhouse window frames and the ladder that led from the deck to the upper level. Other parts of the barge were strewn up and down the shoal, yet there was no sign of life as far as she could see in any direction.

Hazel was overcome with emotion. What in the world was she to do? How would she be able to face Kristina's parents? They had entrusted their only daughter to her care, to help Kristina gain new experiences, restore her relationship with Barnacle, and gain a better understanding of animals. She would never be able to live with herself if Kristina was not found alive.

Hazel sailed her boat up and down the shoal until every inch of it had been covered several times. Then she turned her small boat to the east with a heavy heart and very bad news. She was almost to Gull Island when she noticed two larger station boats to the north.

Keeper Daniels recognized Hazel as she sailed up to them. He was meeting with the Gull Shoal Station keeper, near Scott's Reef, to discuss the search pattern. "What are you doing out here alone?" he asked Hazel.

"That is of no importance now," was her reply. "I have some bad news," she said, as she choked back the tears. She told both keepers that she had seen the barge on Long Shoal Point, but no life. "Maybe this is not important," she began, but was cut short by Keeper Daniels.

"At this point, everything is important," the keeper assured her.

Hazel continued. "It did not seem to me like there was enough debris on the shoal to account for that whole barge. I believe part of the barge could have floated off."

"That's important!" said Keeper Daniels. "They could still be floating around out there, which is all the more reason we need to expand the search farther north."

"If I could only believe that," Hazel sighed.

"Well, there's a good chance that's exactly what happened," the keeper said. "I trust your judgment, and if you feel like part of the barge is missing, we will search until we find it. For now, let's go back to shore and share the new information you have given us."

The search crews met at Gull Station to share the results of the day's search efforts. Everyone had come up empty, with the exception of Hazel, so Keeper Daniels asked her to share her experiences and thoughts with the rest of the group. Afterward, everyone agreed that there was still hope and that the search should continue. Then Edward returned to Northard Woods to tell his wife.

"Another night out there, hopefully floating on debris, in that sound, all by herself!" sobbed Beth.

"Don't you think it's strange that neither Barnacle nor Cocoa have been found?" Edward asked Beth.

"They're probably all at the bottom of the sound," Beth said as she wiped her eyes.

"That's possible," said Edward, "but it's also possible that they're together, looking out for each other, until they can be rescued or make it home on their own."

"Oh, I pray you are right," Beth cried.

Cocoa was the first to reach the hunting camp and the first to find fresh water. A large wooden container, built on a low stand, held rainwater that ran off the roof of the camp. "Good girl! You found us some water!" said Kristina. Cocoa wagged her tail while she drank, and then the horses took a turn. Kristina found a seashell and washed it out, then drank some water herself.

When the horses walked over to graze on the saltwater grass near the camp, Kristina said, "Well, that's good for you three! Now I have to find something for me and Cocoa to eat. Then I have to figure out how we're going to get across this inlet so that we can go home."

The cabin door did not have a lock. Instead, there was a button, which Kristina easily turned to the side, and the door opened. Inside, she found a lantern and matches, and very soon Kristina had the shack lit up and was able to check it out.

A small woodstove sat in the corner of the shack, and dried beans, salted meat, and a few canned goods were on the counter. "We're in luck," she told Cocoa, and the dog wagged her tail and whined in response. "We need to find some wood for the stove so that we can fix something to eat," and out the door they went.

While Barnacle and his family were still grazing, Kristina started a fire in the stove and cooked a large pot of beans. Then she and Cocoa had a supper of dried meat and bean soup. After they ate, Kristina gathered up a bunch of dried seaweed and made the horses a huge bed on the lee side of the camp. She and Cocoa returned to the shack and settled in for the night. Kristina slept in the small built-in bunk, and Cocoa slept on the floor by her side.

Hazel tossed and turned in her bed at Cedar Hammock but could not fall asleep. She felt strongly that Kristina and the animals were out there somewhere, and she was determined to find them. Hazel had spent many hours out in the sound and knew how strong the currents flowed north toward the inlets. Based on her gut feeling, Hazel decided to take her boat and sail past the new search areas. It would take more than a day to complete this trip, so she would have to plan accordingly. Someone would have to look after her stock for a few days, and there were not many people she trusted with her personal property.

Norman Scarborough came to Hazel's mind. She knew he could be trusted and would gladly stop by each day to care for her animals. She contacted Norman and told him of her plans. "Don't tell any of the others what I'm up to," she made him promise. "I'll only be gone three or four days, long enough to check the area from New Inlet north to Roanoke Island. Then I'll be back."

After Norman agreed to take care of her animals, Hazel hurried home to make ready for her trip. Long before first light, she sailed out of the small creek behind her shack and headed her small boat north, with a fair wind from the south. Hazel knew that by daybreak the other searchers would be resuming their search efforts, too. In order to keep from being seen, she headed far away from the shore.

❧21❧

The Search

Hazel had sailed past all three villages and was already out past the reef before first light. She was leaving Southard Channel, coming up on Old House Channel, when she saw the first sail. Hazel watched the sail fade in the distance and figured that if she could no longer see their sail, chances were pretty good that they could no longer see hers either. Hazel did not turn shoreward until she could see the breakers on the bar at New Inlet. The keeper's plan was for the search pattern to extend as far north as New Inlet, so Hazel decided she would cover the area from New Inlet on up to Oregon Inlet.

As Hazel made her way toward the mouth of Oregon Inlet, she noticed something worrisome. A large line of thunderstorms was approaching from the northwest. The sky was very dark behind the storms, and it looked like a shift of wind was coming. *If only I can make it to the lee of the inside islands before the wind shifts*, she thought.

Hazel made it to the large island just as the first storm struck. She was able to pull up inside a small creek and anchor near some cedar trees for cover. The sail flapped in the wind, so Hazel lowered it and used it for cover from the rain. Then, suddenly, the wind shifted to the northwest and started blowing at twenty-five to thirty knots. As the temperature dropped a good fifteen degrees, Hazel huddled in the bottom of her small sailing skiff and did all she could to keep herself and her supplies dry.

Due to bad weather conditions, the sound search had to be called off at midmorning. It was almost impossible for the search crews to navigate the boats in the heavy winds, which were gusting above fifty knots at times. Instead, Keeper Daniels organized a shoreside search, from New Inlet south to Northard Woods. With the wind from the west, as it had been for a while, Keeper Daniels was sure that, if Kristina was still on the barge, she would have drifted near shore by now. He sent two riders to the New Inlet area to work south, and two riders from Northard Woods to work north. He instructed the men to search the entire shoreline and report directly back to him. Then Keeper Daniels sent for Edward to come to the station.

When Edward arrived at the station, Keeper Daniels was on the porch waiting for him. "If my men come up empty with this shore search, I don't know what else to do," the keeper told Edward. "We've covered the entire sound. By now, they should have drifted to shore. There's no need to cover the areas we've already searched, and in my opinion, we need to expand to the north even more."

"I have to come up with something to tell Beth so that she won't lose all hope of finding Kristina," Edward answered.

"I will accompany you to your cottage just as soon as I have something to report from the shore search, and we will discuss the results with Beth then," the keeper told Edward.

Jason and Barney had been assigned the north end of the shore search. They stopped at a freshwater pond to rest their horses and get a drink when Barney said, "What is that?"

"What are you talking about?" asked Jason.

"Up there! See it? Out on the end of that marshy point," Barney said as he pointed in the direction of the object. The sun was just beginning to break through the clouds.

"I don't know. It's too far away to tell," said Jason as he shaded his eyes with his hand. "Let's ride up and take a closer look."

Soon, Jason and Barney were staring down at part of the decking from a large vessel. "We need to report this to Keeper Daniels right away," Jason said. Then they turned their horses south and arrived at the Chicamacomico Station near dark. Keeper Daniels was delighted with their news and hurried off to see Beth and Edward. He found Edward sitting in a rocking chair on his front porch, staring straight ahead. Edward never even noticed Keeper Daniels until the keeper spoke to him.

"Where is Beth?" the keeper asked.

"Asleep, finally," Edward said. "We had to send for the doctor from the cape. He gave her a sedative, and she's sleeping for the first time since this whole thing began. When she's awake, she just sits in that front room, holding Kristina's picture, and stares out the window toward the sound. Yesterday Beth said she heard Cocoa barking, and when I looked, there was nothing there. I am at my wit's end."

"I have some news for you, Edward," said Keeper Daniels. "Jason and Barney found a piece of the barge decking way up past New Inlet. Most likely, the section of barge carrying Kristina has drifted up there as well," he told Edward.

"That could mean almost anything," Edward replied.

"You're right," the keeper agreed, "but it could also mean that Kristina is still waiting to be rescued."

"'Bits and pieces, this and that, could, may, perhaps.' I'm tired," Edward said. "We've been searching for three days now. I am not going to wake Beth for this. She has got to get some rest."

"Well, I just wanted to let you know what Jason and Barney saw and fill you in on the results of our shore search," replied Keeper Daniels.

"We appreciate your efforts and the time you have spent looking for her, but it's been too long now for us to be very optimistic," Edward said.

"I have to go to Gull Station to discuss today's search efforts with the rest of the group. The wind is supposed to moderate around midnight, so we'll move the patterns farther to the north for the next few days," the keeper said as he walked off the porch.

After the wind fell out, Hazel rose from under her shelter and decided to make sail before daylight. With a clear sky and a lighter breeze from the northeast, she could tack short and make it to Oregon Inlet by first light.

As Hazel approached the Oregon Inlet channel, she thought she smelled smoke, and then she saw it, coming out of the chimney of a hunting camp. *How odd*, she thought to herself. *The waterfowl won't be here for several months. No one should be at the camp during this time of the year*, she concluded. Hazel pulled her skiff onto the island, not far from the camp, and before she could get out of the skiff, Cocoa jumped on top of her.

"Praise be!" she said. "I have never been so glad to see a dog before!" Then she saw Barnacle and, finally, Kristina standing in the doorway of the camp. Kristina ran up to Hazel, and they hugged for a very long time. "Oh, I am so very glad to see you!" Hazel said. "The last time I saw you, you were being dragged through the water with that fool dog swimming after you and me screaming for you to let go of that rope! How in the world did you get way up here?"

"Come in, and I will tell you," Kristina answered. "We can finish off the food Cocoa and I cooked last night, and then figure out how we are going to cross that inlet so that we can go home."

"I have an idea about that," Hazel replied. "The wind is light northeast. In a few hours, the tide will be coming in, and we can make our move then."

Hazel and Kristina waited until the tide started running strong in the inlet. Then they loaded the sailboat and started across the inlet. The mare was tied to one side of the boat, and the colt was tied to the other, with Barnacle and Cocoa swimming at their sides. The incoming tide carried them quite a ways out into the sound, but they finally made it to the south side of the inlet. Then they regrouped and made plans to return to Northard Woods. Hazel, Kristina, and Cocoa would sail south, to New Inlet, and let the horses follow them along the shore.

When Hazel and Kristina beached the boat at New Inlet, Kristina said, "I think we should send Barnacle on home with a pouch around his neck and a note to let everyone know we are alright."

"That's a very good idea," Hazel agreed. "He's fast and will be there in a flash. We can explain in the note that we're sailing back and should be home just after nightfall."

Kristina fitted the small pouch around Barnacle's neck and said, "Take this message to Mom, boy." With no further instruction, Barnacle reared up, turned, and took to the south. Cocoa chased after him until Kristina hollered for her to come back. When the dog began to whine, Kristina said, "Oh, alright, go ahead." Then Cocoa raced out of sight to catch up with Barnacle. The colt and mare began to put up such a fuss that Hazel told Kristina, "You might as well let them go, too!"

"But it's so far," Kristina said.

"They'll be fine. They'll get home long before we do," Hazel assured her.

"Okay, go," Kristina told the horses. Then the mare and colt ran after Cocoa and were soon out of sight.

"Now we need to get going ourselves if we are to make it home by nightfall," Hazel told Kristina.

Back at the station, Keeper Daniels listened to the search results very carefully before he spoke. Then he asked if anyone had seen Old Hazel, but not a soul raised a hand. "No one has seen her," the keeper stated, "which is very strange. She has attended every one of these follow-up meetings to exchange information about the search with us. I'll stop by and check on her on my way back to the station.

"Alright, boys, for the next couple of days, these follow-up meetings will be here at this station," the keeper said. "We'll extend the search patterns north to Oregon Inlet starting tomorrow. Let's get a good night's rest so that we can get an early start in the morning."

On the way back to Northard Woods, Keeper Daniels stopped by Cedar Hammock in search of Hazel. He was surprised to see Norman Scarborough coming out of the path leading to her shack. "Have you seen Hazel?" the keeper asked him.

"When are you asking about?" Norman replied.

"The very last time you saw her," said the keeper.

"It wasn't today," Norman said. "She made me promise . . . ," he started.

"I don't care what she made you promise! Give me the straight of it," Keeper Daniels demanded.

"I saw her yesterday, before the blow. I'm looking after her animals. She hasn't returned yet," Norman said.

"Why didn't you say so in the first place?" yelled the keeper.

"Because I promised," was Norman's reluctant response.

"Hand your promise! Now I have another missing person on my hands!" scowled the keeper. "Norman, I could skin you for not coming to me before now," he said, as he turned his horse north. Before going on to the station, the keeper stopped to see Edward and Beth. As he approached their cottage, he saw Edward sitting in a rocking chair on the front porch.

"How is Beth?" the keeper asked.

"She just sits in that big chair, staring toward the beach," Edward replied.

"Can we join her? I have news that may concern both of you," Keeper Daniels said.

"Sure. We can go in the house, but she won't respond. Beth doesn't make any attempt at conversation, and she won't allow you to make any noise. She's waiting to hear Cocoa's bark when she comes running home," Edward told the keeper. The two of them went inside the house, and when Keeper Daniels began to speak about Kristina, Beth put a finger up to her lips and made a hushing sound to quiet him.

"Listen for the dog," she said. "She'll be along any time now."

Keeper Daniels began again. "I would like for you to listen to me for a minute," he started, but Beth cut him off.

"Listen! I can hear her now," Beth told them.

"You know? I think I do hear a dog barking, very faintly in the distance," Edward said.

"You hear it because you want to hear it," said the keeper. "Your minds are playing tricks on you."

"No, listen!" Beth said, as the barking grew louder. "It's Cocoa! I knew she would come!" Suddenly the barking was joined by the pounding of a running horse. Coming up the path from the beach, in a dead run, were Barnacle and Cocoa!

Barnacle did not stop. He jumped the fence and came straight to the edge of the porch. Cocoa stopped outside the fence and howled until Edward opened the gate and let her in. She ran up to Beth on the porch and circled her several times; then she ran to Barnacle. "I am really glad to see you!" Beth exclaimed to the animals. "Now where is my baby? I know you know where she is. Take us to her, *please*." At that moment, the mare and colt came running from the beach and begged to be let inside the fence.

Barnacle came to Beth and put his head down so she could reach it. When she began to stroke his head and talk to him, he turned sideways and pressed the rubber pouch against her face. "What is this?" she said as she looked at the small canvas pouch that had scratched her cheek.

"It looks like some type of canvas bag," Edward said.

"Someone tied it around Barnacle's neck," added Keeper Daniels.

"I am going to look inside to see if anything is in it," replied Beth. Then she put her hand inside the pouch and pulled out the note. Her hands trembled as she read the message. Then she exclaimed, "Kristina is alright! She and Hazel are on their way home!"

Edward and Beth clung together and wept. Keeper Daniels placed his arms around both of them, patting them on their backs and hugging them. Then he said, "I must go and spread the joyous news." He jumped off the porch and started running toward the station.

It was getting dark as Hazel and Kristina sailed out of Old House Channel and entered the mouth of Southard Channel. They would soon make their last tack shoreward, to the mouth of Northard Woods Harbor. "The mouth of Northard Woods Harbor is going to be especially shallow, with all the tide gone, due to this northeast wind," Hazel told Kristina. "The lights of the dwellings will be coming into view after this last bend, which will help us make out the location of the harbor, but I'm worried about crossing that muddy shoal near the entrance. After this day, I am a bit tired, and I don't feel much like getting over the side and pulling." As they rounded the last point of the marsh, Hazel said, "Sakes alive, would you look at that!"

The harbor—from the entrance all the way up to the basin—was aglow with light. People were standing shoulder to shoulder, holding lanterns along both sides of the harbor, causing the entire area to be lit up as bright as day.

"Look at all those people," Kristina said.

"And all those lanterns!" added Hazel.

As they paddled into the harbor, everyone was shouting and waving. Cocoa was at the end of the dock, barking and wagging her tail. Beth, Edward, and Keeper Daniels were eagerly waiting on the dock, and Barnacle and his family were standing on the hill behind the dock.

⚹22⚹

LIFESAVING DUTIES

Everyone was extremely happy that Kristina, Hazel, and the animals were safe. Keeper Daniels decided to declare a holiday and throw a huge celebration at the station, and the end of the summer would be a perfect time for a party. He asked all of the station keepers to get the word out to the villages and invite everyone far and wide to attend. The party would begin on a Friday, last all weekend, and end up late Sunday evening.

Everyone brought their favorite types of food and beverages to share. Games were arranged for older folks and young alike. The celebration was attended by all the station crews and residents in the entire area. Of course, Hazel, Kristina, and the animals were the guests of honor and were greeted and congratulated by all who attended. Each time one group moved away and another group approached, Kristina and Hazel would tell about their entire adventure again. Keeper Daniels, Edward, and Beth thanked and praised all those who were involved in the search process.

On Sunday evening the party ended in church services. The minister's last prayer included thanking the Lord for watching over everyone and bringing those who were lost safely home to their loved ones.

On their way back to the cottage, Beth said, "Your father and I have something we would like to talk to you about, Kristina. It includes Barnacle and your future here at Northard Woods. You know I would like for you to come back to Baltimore with us to finish your education. Even so, the local school administration approached your father, and they would like to offer you a position as an elementary teacher in the school system here. Barnacle has also been offered a position as lead stallion with the lifesaving service. He'll have to be trained, and Keeper Daniels is hoping you can help. Your father and I have discussed the situation at length and have come to the conclusion that you're mature enough to decide what you want to do. If you decide to stay, I will be disappointed, but I will respect your decision."

Kristina was delighted and asked, "You're good with this, Dad?"

"If it's really what you want, and it makes you happy, I will also support your decision," her father answered.

"I would like to discuss this with Hazel and Keeper Daniels before I make my final decision," Kristina responded.

"You can have all the time you need, Kristina. This is a very important point in your life, and you need to give it a lot of thought," her father assured her.

Kristina replied, "As far as the school job is concerned, I would love to remain here and teach elementary education! I'll give you a final answer in a couple of days, after I have spoken to Hazel and Keeper Daniels about Barnacle's training." Kristina was excited about the news and thought about being a schoolteacher all the way back home. She helped off-load the party supplies, said goodnight, and went straight to bed.

Early the next morning, Kristina saddled Barnacle and headed for the station to discuss Barnacle's potential lifesaving training and responsibilities with Keeper Daniels. As she started out, the mare and colt put up a fuss to go with her, so she told them to come on. Cocoa took the lead, as usual, stopping to checking each clump of grass along the way.

"Look yonder," Keeper Daniels said to Barney and Jason as they were feeding the stock at the corral. As Kristina and Barnacle approached them, the keeper said, "That's a fine-looking horse you've got there!"

"He is also a very smart horse!" Kristina replied. "He is able to sense danger, almost before it occurs."

"He will be a very valuable asset to our service after he has received the proper training. I want to talk to you about the training process," Keeper Daniels told Kristina.

"The mare, colt, and Cocoa are Barnacle's constant companions. The animals are very hard to separate, which could cause problems during the training process," Kristina informed the keeper, with concern in her tone.

"That's where you come in," the keeper said. "The animals will be able to accompany Barnacle almost everywhere he goes, so long as you are able to maintain control and keep them at a safe distance."

"I think I can do that, if they can stay within eyesight of each other," she replied.

"Barnacle is very strong and will be especially helpful if we need to use the surfboat for rescues located outside the range of the shot-line, fired from the black powder cannon. He gets along well with other horses and will make an excellent lead stallion to pull the surf boat wagon. Plus, he likes Barney and Jason and will do well on mounted beach patrols," stated the keeper.

"I'm not so sure Barnacle is ready for such a commitment," Kristina told the keeper. "He is a free spirit and likes to roam the marshes of Cedar Hammock. Most of the time, he likes to roam with just his family. He loves to run in the surf with Cocoa and Tar, his two favorite canine friends, and during certain times of the year he likes to run with the Raven and the Banker ponies. It's nearing the end of the summer, and I have to make an important decision myself. I really think Barnacle should remain a free spirit and be able to seek his own type of happiness."

"Is that your final word?" asked the keeper. "After all, he does belong to you."

"I think that is my final word," Kristina said. "If there's one thing I've learned from Hazel, the animals are our friends, and we should share our lives with them, not own them. Barnacle fought so very hard to save us when we were in danger, and to ensure his own freedom. I don't have the heart to take it away from him at this point."

"You and Old Hazel," replied Keeper Daniels. "Next thing you know, you'll be making bayberry candles and reciting chants."

They both laughed, and Kristina said, "I think we'll return to Cedar Hammock, where we all have time to think and consider our future plans. Barnacle and his family can roam the meadows and marshes with Cocoa for the remainder of the summer. Hazel and I will have time to relax and finish up the things we started before those stinkin' horse thieves showed up and threw us off track."

"Be safe and stay out of scrapes, and stop by the station to see us from time to time," said Keeper Daniels.

"You know we will," said Kristina. Then they headed toward the surf line, with the colt and Cocoa running ahead, while the mare walked quietly beside Barnacle and Kristina.

"Now there is a sight," the keeper said to Jason and Barney. "A big chestnut stallion, a small mare and colt, a brown dog, and a young girl, all sharing the same outlook on life, and they are completely satisfied to experience it together."

"Yes, that group is truly a rarity," answered Barney as the friends disappeared from sight.

When they reached the surf line, Kristina wanted Barnacle to be able to run freely up and down the beach with his friends, so she took off his saddle and placed it on a washed-up hatch cover. Barnacle took off, galloping north with his small group behind him and Cocoa nipping at his heels. Then Kristina sat down on the hatch cover to wait for their return.

The horses disappeared from Kristina's sight as they moved farther up the beach. Barnacle led them to a meadow where they grazed on new saltwater grass shoots, while Cocoa sniffed for fiddler crabs and dug up their holes. There was a freshwater pond near them, so they all took a drink.

Suddenly Barnacle lifted his head and sniffed the air, and then Cocoa started sniffing and whining. In the distance, they could hear the sound of horses approaching. Shortly, the Raven and a large herd of Banker ponies came into view. Barnacle ran toward the surf line to get their attention, and when the Raven saw Barnacle, he stopped his herd and trotted over to him. They greeted each other and then moved the Raven's ponies to the pond for a drink.

As Kristina was relaxing, Cocoa ran up and jumped on her. "What is the matter with you, girl?" she said to the dog. Then she said, "Oh, I see," when she noticed all the horses coming down the beach toward her. *Boy, that's a fine-looking bunch of Banker ponies. It's no wonder the men from the mainland are so interested in them,* Kristina thought to herself.

Barnacle, the mare, colt, and Cocoa came right up to Kristina, but the Raven and the remainder of the herd stopped a short distance away. "What's wrong, fellow, don't you remember me?" she asked. The Raven cocked his head, pawed the ground, and made a whining sound. "I'm the one who helped you escape from the barge and a life of farm labor," Kristina told the horse. Then the Raven circled her, easing up even closer. As he looked Kristina square in the eye, a more relaxed sound came from his throat.

"So maybe you do remember me," she said. Slowly, the Raven bobbed his head. As he began to walk away, the rest of the Bankers circled Kristina and followed behind him. When Barnacle called to the horses, they all stopped, and many of them answered him, including the Raven. Barnacle trotted over and nuzzled several of the mares, then looked back at Kristina and whinnied to her.

"You want to roam with them for a spell, don't you, boy?" Kristina said. Then Barnacle walked back over to her and stopped so that she could put the saddle on him. As they began to move in the direction of the cottage, Kristina was puzzled at how the group of Bankers remained stationary until she and Barnacle passed, then fell in behind them. "I see now," she said to Barnacle. "Your friends are going to follow you home and wait for you, aren't they?" Barnacle responded by bobbing his head up and down in agreement.

Beth was sitting in the porch swing when she saw them approaching. "Edward," she said, "you have to come see this. Here comes your daughter, followed by almost every horse on this island!"

Edward stepped off the porch and opened the gate. Cocoa was the first to enter the corral, followed by Barnacle and Kristina, then the mare and colt and all the other ponies. "I'll have to put out a lot of extra hay and feed for your guests," Edward told Kristina.

"I don't think they'll be staying very long," she said, as the Raven paced back and forth near the gate. "The Raven seems very nervous."

Just before dark, Hazel came up in her wagon. "For land's sakes, child! You have caught every Banker pony for miles around, even the feared large black one that leads the herd!" she said to Kristina.

"They haven't been caught," Kristina responded. "They are Barnacle's invited guests, but probably for just one night. The black one seems to be so nervous."

"Maybe you've learned something about animals after all," the old woman said.

"I had a very good teacher," Kristina replied. "Where are you off to now, at such a late hour?"

"I have an order of bayberry candles and mosquito smokes for the store here at Northard Woods," Hazel answered.

"When you are finished with your delivery, why don't you settle here for the night?" Kristina asked Hazel. "You can help me calm the Raven, and just maybe the ponies will stay for the night. I'd like for you to be here anyway, when I talk to my parents about returning to Cedar Hammock for a few days, to consider my future plans. They have indicated that they'll support whatever decision I make, and I'm thinking it might be time to make my home here instead of the city. I believe I will be much happier living here."

"Okay. I'll return as soon as my delivery is complete," Hazel answered, and she headed for the shore.

After Hazel returned, she and Kristina talked to the Raven until he seemed ready to calm down for the night. He finally stopped pacing and settled down near Barnacle and a group of mares. The colt and mare were lying as close to Barnacle as they could get. At last, Cocoa, Hazel, and Kristina went inside the cottage.

"You can wash up for supper," Beth told Hazel and Kristina. "It's almost ready, and we will eat in just a little while." Shortly, they sat down at the table, graced the food, and ate their meal. When they were finished, Kristina started the conversation by saying, "I want to take Barnacle, his family, and Cocoa back to Cedar Hammock with Hazel to relax and consider my plans for the future."

❧ 23 ❧

THE BANANA BOAT

Beth cleared the table and suggested that everyone move to the front sitting room for coffee and sweets and resume the conversation until bedtime. Edward started by addressing Hazel. "Beth and I have not thanked you properly for finding our daughter and her animals and returning them home safely."

"To tell you the truth, we all looked out for each other," Hazel replied. "When I found that wreckage out on Long Shoal, I almost lost all hope of finding any survivors, but when Barney and Jason found portions of the barge up near New Inlet, I knew part of it must have drifted north with the southwest wind."

"How did you know where to find them?" Edward asked.

"I didn't know until I saw smoke coming from a hunting cabin at Oregon Inlet and went to check it out. When I pulled my skiff ashore, Cocoa almost knocked me out of my boat! That's when I knew!" Hazel answered. "Kristina was organized and had a plan of her own for returning home. I'm amazed that she was able to keep those animals together and safe." Then Hazel changed the subject. "When I came by your place this afternoon and saw all those Banker ponies, I was truly amazed!"

"That was easy," Kristina told Hazel. "Barnacle invited them over, and they followed us home! I'm going out to check on them before I go to bed, and I'll let them out of the corral in the morning. Barnacle wants to spend time with the ponies, roaming the marshes of Cedar Hammock, and if it's okay with you,

I would like to bring Cocoa and finish up our work at your place. I still need time to think about my future plans and put my mother's mind at ease."

The next morning, after a big breakfast, Edward opened the corral gate and all the horses walked out, followed by Kristina and Hazel in Hazel's wagon. "I'll be back for the weekend, Mom," Kristina hollered. Then they disappeared around the bend in the road and headed toward the beach, with Cocoa up front in her usual position, barking and running ahead of the group.

"Look at that," Barney said to the other surfmen as they prepared for morning drills. "I didn't realize there were so many Banker ponies around."

"And look who's bringing up the rear," Jason said. "I believe that girl would rather spend time with animals instead of humans."

"That's the influence of Old Hazel rubbing off on her. She spends most of her time in Cedar Hammock Marsh with Hazel and those horses," Barney added.

When Hazel and Kristina got to the beach, the Banker ponies were anxious to take off for a run. Barnacle trotted over to Kristina and hesitated until she said, "Go on, boy. You can go with them if you want to." Then he rejoined the ponies and they took off, out of sight, and headed south. *Most likely to Cedar Hammock*, Kristina thought to herself.

"Look, there's a vessel within sight," Hazel told Kristina, pointing to a sail on the horizon, "and it looks like it's headed this way."

Keeper Daniels was in the tower and saw the vessel, too. He watched it strike sail and anchor outside the outer bar, about five hundred yards off the beach. Then he called for his crew to ready the wagon with the station boat and be prepared for a possible rescue. When the station crew arrived at the beach, they watched the vessel's crew lower a longboat into the ocean and start rowing shoreward.

"Hold fast, men!" shouted Keeper Daniels. "We will render assistance as needed. I'm wondering what has happened to the vessel. The wind has been light and the sea fairly calm for the past few days."

When the longboat reached the shore, the men aboard pulled it up onto the sand with the help of a few men from the station. Then one of them asked who was in charge.

"That would be me," responded Keeper Daniels. "I am the head man in charge at Chicamacomico Lifesaving Station."

The man introduced himself and stated his problem. "My name is Joseph Harper." He pointed to the vessel offshore and continued. "I am the captain of the *Mary E. Worth*, out of Boston, with a cargo of molasses, bananas, and rum. We have some busted timbers just below the waterline as a result of grounding hard near the Florida Straits in a northeast storm."

"How can we be of service to you and your crew?" inquired Keeper Daniels.

"How well do you folks like bananas?" asked the captain.

"We like them fine," replied Keeper Daniels.

"We need to lighten our load as much as possible so we can raise the cracked timbers above the waterline and caulk the cracks. You can have all the bananas you want," the captain said. "Otherwise we will have to throw them overboard."

Keeper Daniels and the crew made several trips to the vessel and returned each time with a boatload of bananas. When the villagers heard the news, they came to the beach with their wagons and took the bananas home. Kristina and Hazel took a few bunches for themselves and headed down the beach to Cedar Hammock.

Barnacle and the other ponies were already back in the Cedar Hammock meadows, enjoying the sweet saltwater grasses growing there. They romped, played, and galloped around for the rest of the day, then returned to the safety of the marsh for the night. As they bedded down, a severe thunderstorm came up from the west. The storm contained very little rain, but had severe lightning and thunder activity, with random strikes to the southeast. Barnacle was the first to smell smoke. He woke the Raven, then he woke his mare and colt, and together they woke the other horses.

Fueled by the dry grass and a brisk southeast breeze, the fire was spreading rapidly and was headed straight for the Cedar Hammock Marsh. The Raven and Barnacle tried to move the herd north to get around the advancing fire, but they were cut off and forced to retreat to the south end of the Cedar Hammock bog. The horses had just enough room to cross the bog in single file as they followed Barnacle from one grass lump to another, trying to stay ahead of the fire. The smoke burned their eyes, and at times the flames licked at their heels, but Barnacle managed to lead the ponies to the end of the bog, to the short grass.

The southeast wind was also allowing for shallow waters. The horses galloped out onto the shoals in the sound, away from the advancing smoke, where they were finally able to catch their breath. Shortly they took off after Barnacle in search of the closest freshwater pond. Desperate for water, the horses drank as the fire burned to the end of the marsh and turned north, toward the village of Clarks.

Barnacle knew he had to head north and warn the people. The mare and colt started to follow him, but he made them return to the herd, where they would remain under the watchful eye of the Raven until his return. Then he cut across the marsh, ahead of the fire, and headed for Hazel's shack.

Kristina was awakened by Cocoa's bark. "Be quiet, girl! You'll wake Hazel," she said, but Cocoa would not stop barking and jumping and trying to get out the door.

"What's wrong with your dog?" asked Hazel.

"I don't know," Kristina replied. At that moment, both of them heard Barnacle neighing just outside the door. "Something's wrong," Kristina said. She went outside to find Barnacle kicking up a fuss. He was snorting and pawing the ground, rearing up on his hind legs, running back and forth along the path leading to the sound.

"Both those animals sense something," Hazel said. Then she and Kristina became aware at the same time that the whole marsh to the west of them was aglow. "The lightning must have started a marsh fire," Hazel said, "and it's burning in the direction of Clarks. We must get help now, before the fire jumps those two creeks south of the village," she insisted. "Get Barnacle and go wake Aaron Hooper. Tell him to alert his brothers and meet us at the creek with a wagon and skiff. Then we'll have all the help we need to keep the fire isolated and away from the village. Cocoa's barking will wake the dead, so take her with you, and I'll be there just as soon as I can get there."

Kristina jumped on Barnacle's back and they galloped out of the marsh, toward the village, with Cocoa in the lead, yapping her head off. When they reached Aaron Hooper's cottage, Cocoa barked while Kristina banged on the door. Finally, Aaron answered. "This had better be good if you're waking me up at this hour."

"The whole marsh is on fire, and it's headed in this direction!" Kristina exclaimed.

"Oh, Lord," Aaron said. "We need to wake my brothers right away." Then he ran next door to both of their cottages, telling them to get up and why. On their way to get a wagon and skiff, Aaron yelled out to a few other men and alerted them to the approaching fire. He instructed Kristina to hitch Barnacle to the wagon and tow the skiff down to the creek, south of the village. Then he told his brothers to go into the village and get as many blankets as they could gather. They soon returned to the creek with heaps of blankets and a few more men.

Aaron spaced the men along the creek and told them to wet the blankets and beat out the fire if it jumped the creek. Then he instructed Kristina to drive the wagon down into the creek so that the skiff would sink and fill with water. "We'll need the water in the skiff to keep the blankets wet if the fire spreads to the open ground," Aaron said.

Once the skiff was full of water, Kristina said, "Come on, Barnacle. Pull, boy!" Then Barnacle hauled the wagon out of the creek, according to her instructions. Aaron then told Kristina to drive the wagon along the bank and down to the end of the creek.

The men on the creek side were able to smother any fire if it jumped the creek, but the men out on the open ground were not having as much success. The fire had spread to the meadows and had burned past Barnacle and Kristina several times, but they continued forward, keeping the skiff close to the men so that they could wet their blankets and fight the fire. Hazel showed up with her wagon, carrying another skiff full of water, and as more villagers arrived, they joined the group to fight the fire. Covered with sweat, cinders, and soot, they were eventually able to extinguish the fire due to their combined efforts.

"We should head for the large freshwater pond near the church and wash off," Hazel told Kristina. "Bring Barnacle so we can cool him off and clean him as well." By the time they finished with their baths, it was making daylight, and they were delighted when some of the women from the village came with coffee, food, and cool, fresh water. Everyone relaxed a bit, ate sandwiches, and drank coffee, and Kristina fed Cocoa half of a sandwich.

"You can come to my house and rest before you go back to the hammock," Aaron told Hazel and Kristina. "Your horses can stay in my corral, where there is plenty of food for them, and the two of you can get some sleep. We all deserve some rest, and we are all thankful to you ladies for alerting us to the fire."

"It was Barnacle who woke us and alerted us to the fire," Kristina told Aaron.

"That Barnacle has always had a knack for sensing danger and helping folks," said Aaron. "He is truly an exceptional horse, and you are very lucky to own such an animal."

"Oh, I don't own Barnacle! He's just one of my best friends," Kristina said, and Hazel looked at her and smiled.

❧24❧

BLACKBERRY PIES AND OYSTERS

Hazel and Kristina accepted Aaron Hooper's offer to rest at his home before heading back to Cedar Hammock. They had worked very hard, along with the other villagers, to extinguish the fire and protect their village. After they rested, fed, and rubbed down the horses, they left for Cedar Hammock. When they arrived at Hazel's, Barnacle did not want to go inside the corral. Instead, he pawed the ground and backed up.

"He doesn't want to go in there," Kristina said to Hazel.

"Not only that, but I think he wants you to let his colt and mare out to join him," Hazel responded. "He wants to go find his Banker friends and roam the marshes for a few days. Go ahead and open the gate so that they can join him."

When the gate opened, the mare and colt ran over to Barnacle, rubbed noses, bobbed their heads, and then ran a short distance down the path before stopping to look back. When Kristina waved her hand and told them to go on, they turned on their heels and were gone in a flash.

Barnacle, along with his mare and colt, stopped often to listen for the sound of ponies and finally found their tracks headed southward. They followed the tracks all the way to the center of the Cedar Hammock Marsh, where there was plenty of fresh water and saltwater grass all around. The Raven and a couple of the older stallions were keeping a watchful eye on the surrounding area for any sign of danger to the herd. Meanwhile, the mares were sunning in the soft grasses, and their colts were playing in the muddy pools. When his mare and colt went to join their friends, Barnacle galloped off to join the rest of the herd.

The ponies enjoyed the remainder of the summer season in the Cedar Hammock marshes, knowing that it would soon be time for them to move farther south to begin the fall season. Barnacle returned to Hazel's house with his mare and his almost-grown stallion colt. When Hazel saw them coming up the path from the sound side, she opened the corral gate for them, and they went into the corral. Then she gave them some hay, oats, and fresh water. Later Kristina rubbed them down, and Hazel trimmed and checked their hooves for cracks.

"We have finished our work here for the summer," Hazel told Kristina, "and I feel good about your understanding of animals and the relationships you have developed with them. You have important things to discuss with your parents, so we will go to Northard Woods in the morning. We'll take all the wares we've created and sell them for the supplies I need."

The next morning, Hazel and Kristina hitched Barnacle up to the wagon and loaded it with all the candles, mosquito smokes, freshly canned jellies, figs, and other assorted things they had made. Then they left for Clarks to make their trade at Mr. Midgett's store. Mr. Midgett credited Hazel's account and told her she could pick her supplies up on her way back home. Then she and Kristina headed for Northard Woods to see Kristina's parents. When they arrived, Beth and Edward were sitting on the front porch.

"What a nice surprise! I already have a meal prepared," Beth exclaimed. "You two come on in the house, and let's eat. Then we can settle down and talk."

"I'll put the wagon and horses away and be in soon," Kristina replied as she unhitched Barnacle. Then she led all three horses into the corral. As she stroked Barnacle's head, Kristina wondered how her mother would react to her plans for the future. Then she patted Cocoa's head and said, "Come on, girl, let's go face the music." When they went inside, Beth told Kristina to wash up and join them at the table. Cocoa checked her bowl.

"Don't worry, Cocoa. I didn't forget you," Beth said.

After supper, Beth said, "Well, Kristina? What have you decided?"

"I think you know the answer to that," Kristina replied.

"Your father and I have anticipated your answer and have decided that I will stay here with you for a year while you try out your new job. Your father has several trips this fall, but says he should be home by Thanksgiving, depending on the weather. He's leaving for Baltimore in just a few days," Beth said, with a pouty face, and continued. "You have a meeting with the school board on Monday, so next week is going to be a busy one for all of us."

"Well, I'm glad this is all settled," Edward said. "Now maybe we can just relax and visit for a while, and enjoy the evening."

"I really didn't think it would be this easy," Kristina said with a puzzled look on her face.

"We just want you to be happy," Beth told her daughter, "and you are happy living on this island, close to Barnacle."

"I just didn't think the two of you would give in so easily," Kristina said, "especially you, Mother!"

"Well, you are grown now," Beth said. "Your father and I agree that you should have something to say about your own future."

Edward spoke up. "I think you and your mother are much safer here than you are in Baltimore, and when I have to sail, I'll feel much better knowing you are here among friends."

After two days passed, Kristina and Beth saw Edward off at the landing. "I will write to you before I leave port," the sea captain said as he hugged them good-bye. Then he boarded the *Sea Mullet* and headed out in time to catch the *Coastal Rambler* to Elizabeth City. From there, he would catch a larger vessel to Baltimore.

"Thanksgiving is a long time off," Kristina told her mother.

"It will be here before you know it," her mother replied. When Barnacle turned the wagon toward the cottage, Cocoa jumped in and started licking Kristina on the hand.

"She's really going to miss Daddy," Kristina said. "He plays with her so much when he is here."

"Your father spoils Cocoa rotten," replied Beth, "giving her pork chops, steak, and chicken the way he does!"

"That's because he really loves her," said Kristina.

"Your father brushes and feeds those horses every day and gives them lots of treats. I can't keep fruit in the house because he gives it all to your horses."

"He really loves them, too," Kristina replied with a smile.

Beth changed the subject. "Let's stop by Zack's Place and see if they turned ice cream last night," she said. Then Barnacle turned the wagon in the appropriate direction.

"That horse really understands everything you say to him," Beth said. She and Kristina laughed when Barnacle bobbed his head in agreement and made a snorting sound from deep within his throat.

Keeper Daniels and Barney were sitting on the porch eating ice cream when Beth and Kristina arrived at Zack's Place. "Well, hello!" said Barney. "I know you eat ice cream," he kidded Kristina, "but how about the rest of your crew?"

"Mom and Cocoa like it, but the horses prefer apples," she responded.

Then Barney asked, "Do you two know how funny it looks to see your wagon coming up with those ponies always following behind you?"

"And the dog between us," Beth said. "She especially loves the ice cream cones!"

"You are a sight to be seen," Barney said.

"I'm sure that's true," Beth replied, "but we are all doing just fine, and we would like to enjoy some ice cream before returning to the cottage."

"By the way," Keeper Daniels asked Kristina, "do you think Old Hazel has any bayberry candles left? They make the tack room smell so much better, especially if Leonard Etheridge has been in there smoking those infernal cigars."

"Mom and I are going to visit Hazel in a few days, before I start teaching, and if she has any candles left, I'll bring some back for you," Kristina assured him. Then she and her mother went into the store to buy ice cream and apples. They returned to the porch, where the horses ate the apples, and Cocoa gulped ice cream from Beth's hands.

"Look how your dog just swallows that ice cream! She'll get a brain freeze if you're not careful!" said Barney.

"She always gulps it like that," Beth said, as Cocoa licked her mouth and begged for more. When Beth and Kristina finished their treats, they hopped up in their wagon and said good-bye to Barney and the keeper.

"Don't forget my candles!" Keeper Daniels yelled after them.

"I won't!" Kristina called back over her shoulder, as she and her group rolled away.

"Don't you think it's very strange that they never have reins attached to that horse? Kristina just tells him where to go and he goes there," said Barney.

"He's always done that, even when she rides him," answered the keeper. "She just climbs up on his back, with no saddle or bridle, and tells him where to go, and he goes there!"

Early the next morning, Beth and Kristina got up early and headed for Cedar Hammock to visit Hazel. Beth had never been to Cedar Hammock before and was excited about the trip. She was amazed at the manner in which Barnacle led them through the floating marsh and delivered them safely to Hazel's front porch.

Hazel greeted them as they approached. "How are y'all doing today?" she asked.

"Fine," Kristina answered. "Before I forget it, do you have any bayberry candles left? Keeper Daniels wants some for the station, to get rid of cigar odor."

"Yes, and you can take him some when you go home," Hazel told her. Then she said, "I'm surprised to see you here, Beth! Welcome to Cedar Hammock!"

"I wanted to see where you live," Beth told Hazel. "This place is all my daughter talks about, and how you live a life of harmony with nature and animals. This is something I just had to see for myself. I hope you don't mind!"

"Certainly not!" answered Hazel. "I am mighty pleased to have you here. I have a pot of lima beans on the stove, with sausage and fresh-baked bread, and enough for all," she insisted. Then she told Kristina to go ahead and let Barnacle loose. "The corral gate stays open, so the stock can go and come as they please, and there is always plenty of food in there for them. Cocoa can share the sausage with us."

After they ate the meal and were relaxing on the front porch, Hazel asked

Beth what she would like to do for the day. "My work is all done for now, and I have some free time. If you like, we can explore the creeks and marshes, and I'll show you what the hammock has to offer," she told Beth.

"You decide," Kristina told Hazel. "Show us what you think is most important. You're the expert here, and it's Mom's first trip."

"Alrighty then," Hazel said. "First, we'll catch a few oysters from the south creek for roasting. Perhaps we can find a soft crab or two for frying. Then we'll gather some bayberries, in case I have to make more candles soon. After that, we'll check the hills for a few late-season blackberries, for some homemade tarts."

"It sounds like an exciting afternoon," Beth said.

Hazel asked Kristina to get the two yard rakes they had rigged with chicken wire during the summer. "We can use them to catch us some oysters," she said, "and as soon as I get my hip boots and a container for the berries, we can get under way."

As Hazel, Beth, and Kristina entered the creek and started oystering, Barnacle and his group joined them. Kristina spoke to Barnacle and said, "I want you to stay behind us, boy, and keep Cocoa back there with you, so you guys don't stir up the mud. Otherwise, we won't be able to see the oysters." As instructed, Barnacle held the ponies at bay, and Cocoa walked quietly beside him, just exactly as she had heard to do.

Once all three ladies had filled their buckets with oysters, they carried them to shore, and then they went bayberry hunting. Hazel described the candle-making process to Beth as they gathered a few limbs from the bayberry trees, then they continued on to the beach hills for their blackberries. When they returned to Hazel's shack, they built a large fire in her block grill and roasted the oysters. Hazel placed two blackberry pies in the oven, and soon the ladies were enjoying the rewards of their efforts.

"Is it true what some say about sweets and seafood? That if you eat them together, you'll get sick?" asked Beth.

"Just don't overeat! That's what makes folks sick," Hazel answered. Then they heard a bloodcurdling scream arise from the marsh.

❧ 25 ❧

Old Scratchum

Edward arrived in Baltimore a few days before he had to ship out to the South American coast for a load of coffee. He was ready to get this trip under way. His company had put him in command of the *Aletia*, a four-master, only four years old. He wrote his family a letter to inform them about his new vessel and upcoming trip, and mailed it the day before he left Baltimore.

Edward and his crew sailed out of Baltimore and headed down the coast without incident. However, as they neared the Florida Straits they ran into heavy weather. A violent early-season hurricane was making its way up the coast, and the *Aletia* ran right into its path.

It would take awhile for the terrible news to get back to Northard Woods. The telegram at the post office could not be released until Beth and Kristina returned from Cedar Hammock. The telegram said that three vessels had been lost in the storm, and that the *Aletia* was listed as missing, with all hands presumably lost.

"What in the world was that horrible noise?" Beth asked Hazel as they all three reacted to the unnerving scream coming from the marsh.

"I'm not really sure," Hazel replied. "It sounded like Old Scratchum!"

"Say that again," Kristina said.

"Years ago, my sister Hattie told me of an old wild hog that lived south of us. The hog had been a domestic pet of an old man who once lived in the Noache Marsh and would follow the old fellow wherever he went. When the old man died, the hog refused to leave his graveside for weeks on end. Many of the old man's friends tried to coax the hog with food and water, but it refused all help and remained on guard, chasing away anyone who came near the grave."

Hazel told the story about how two young Clarks boys had tried to catch Old Scratchum with a snare one time. "They trapped him by the hind leg, but the hog was too much for them, and before they could disentangle him, he chewed off his own hind foot to get free," she told them. "The wound became infected, and the hog got meaner. He finally left the old man's grave, but he never left Noache Marsh. He would chase away everyone who came near and try to gore them with his tusks.

"Legend has it that the wild hog had mange, open sores all over his body, and an infection that affected his brain," Hazel continued. "The villagers named him Old Scratchum, and folks say he wasn't fit for man nor beast. I've only heard that noise once before." Just then, another scream rang out, interrupting the still of the night.

"What do we do?" asked Kristina.

"Stay inside until he leaves!" Hazel answered.

"What about the horses?" Kristina replied.

"They can take care of themselves," Hazel said.

"Well, I'm worried about the colt, and I'm going out to find him," Kristina replied.

"Don't you dare go out of this house with that thing out there," Beth told Kristina. "You could be injured or even killed by a wild hog!"

"Mom, it's only an animal, not much larger than Cocoa," Kristina said.

Cocoa was standing behind Kristina, with her hair standing straight up on her back and a low growl coming from deep inside her throat. When she heard her name, she wagged her tail a little, but the growl continued.

"Your dog senses the danger," Hazel told Kristina. "If you must go, take this lantern. Go straight to the gate, close it, and call your horses. Stay inside the protection of the corral, and when the horses come, let them inside, and close the gate immediately. Leave the dog inside. Your mother can hold her, and I'll stand on the porch with my gun, just in case."

Kristina slowly opened the door, stepped outside, and walked over to close and latch the gate. When she went to the corner of the corral to call the horses, she heard a rustle in the bush, and Barnacle appeared in the path. "Come here," Kristina said, as she opened the gate for him. Then Barnacle came to her, but he grabbed her shirtsleeve and pulled her through the gate to the outside of the corral. "No, Barnacle! We must go inside," she told her horse. All of a sudden, Kristina smelled a horrible stench, and out of the corner of her eye she caught sight of a horrible creature charging straight for her.

The crazed hog rammed headlong into the half-open gate, knocking Kristina off her feet, but she got up quickly and closed and latched the gate. The hog rammed the gate several times, but the latch held. Then he found a place under the fence, where there was a little room between the bottom rail and the ground, and he started digging. He only stopped digging long enough to try and crawl under the fence, and when he could not fit, he dug some more.

Cocoa was barking and jumping around, and it was all Beth could do to hold her back. Barnacle was pacing back and forth, snorting, and pawing the ground. Just as the hog was about to crawl under the fence, Cocoa broke away from Beth and ran straight to the wild hog. Cocoa tried to pull the hog by the tail into the corral, but the hog was too strong for her. The beast managed to get loose, but not before Cocoa's teeth stripped the skin off his tail. Then the hog charged Kristina again. She opened the gate and tried to run, but the hog slammed the gate into her back, knocking her headfirst to the ground, and was upon her before she could stand up. The odor almost took Kristina's breath. It was like nothing she had ever smelled before.

Cocoa charged the hog and grabbed it by the neck, trying to pull it away from Kristina, but the hog swung around and threw Cocoa off her feet. Then the dog sprang back and faced the hog head-on. The beast charged Cocoa and caught her under the chest with its tusk, then threw the dog up into the air. Cocoa hit the ground, stunned, severely gored, and bleeding. As the vicious beast turned to face Kristina again, Barnacle kicked the hog in the side and knocked it off its feet, giving Kristina time to run to the house. Then Barnacle placed himself between the boar and the injured dog, facing it as it stood up.

"We have to get Cocoa," Kristina cried out. "She's bleeding badly!"

"Not until that hog leaves," Beth said to her.

"Barnacle will help us," said Kristina. "He'll keep the hog away until we get her."

Hazel got a blanket. "Come on. We can use this," she said, and they headed outside to rescue Cocoa.

"Keep that hog off us," Hazel told Barnacle. As instructed, Barnacle circled around and protected Kristina and Hazel until they got Cocoa back into the house. When Barnacle was sure they were safe, he called to the mare and colt, and the three of them disappeared in the marsh.

"Cocoa is hurt badly," Kristina said as she rubbed the dog's head.

"Let's get her cleaned up so that we can see how deep the gashes are," said Hazel. "She has stopped bleeding but is covered with dirt. We need to clean her off so that we can treat her wounds."

As they cleaned up Cocoa, they realized her skin was hardly broken. "She's a very lucky dog," Hazel said. "She has some bad scratches, but she'll be fine."

"Cocoa was so very brave. She was willing to give her life to save mine," Kristina told Hazel. Then Cocoa looked up at Kristina and weakly wagged her tail as Hazel dressed her wounds.

The next morning, everything was clear. The wild hog was gone, and the only evidence of the attack was the torn-up ground and damaged gate. After breakfast, Beth, Hazel, Kristina, and Cocoa got in the wagon. Then Kristina said, "Home, boy," and they took off, with the mare and colt close behind. As they passed the village of Clarks, Aaron Hooper met them on the road.

"Well, I see y'all are still traveling together. Could you tell me one thing?" he asked. "How does that horse know where to take you?"

"He understands whatever Kristina tells him," Beth said. "She just asks him to take us where we want to go."

"Where is your brown dog?" Aaron asked.

"She's riding in the back," answered Hazel. "She tangled with Old Scratchum last night."

"I thought he was farther south, in Noache Marsh," said Aaron.

"Normally he is, but he decided to pay us a visit last night," Hazel replied.

"Was the dog the only one hurt?" asked Aaron.

"Yes, and amazingly enough, she only got scratched. I think she's pretty sore from where the hog tossed her up. She landed pretty hard," Hazel said.

"All of you are very lucky," said Aaron. "Two boys from Little Kinnakeet got tangled up with him not too long ago and were badly gored by his tusks. Their wounds got infected, and one of them nearly lost a leg before an antibiotic was finally effective. I hate to harm animals, but that one needs to be put down before he kills someone. Folks have tried to get a good shot at him, but he always seems to attack and vanish before anyone can get a bead on him. It's like he has some sort of magical power or something." Then Aaron said, "Oh, by the way, Beth, I saw Mrs. Scarborough yesterday. She said there's a telegram for you at the post office."

"Thank you for telling us," Beth said as they bid good-bye and went their separate ways.

After they returned to their cottage and unloaded everything, Kristina told her mother she would ride Barnacle over to the post office for the telegram. "I'll bet it's from Daddy," she said.

"I think your father would have written us a letter instead of sending a telegram. It's probably from the shipping company, meant for Edward," said Beth.

"At any rate, I'll be back soon," Kristina replied. Then she hopped on Barnacle's back and told him to go to the post office, and the mare and colt followed them.

Cocoa whined and tried to stand. "Not this time, girl," Beth said to the dog. "You have to take it easy for a while."

"I think I should be getting back to the hammock," Hazel said to Beth.

"Nonsense," Beth answered. "You can stay with us and get an early start in the morning. Kristina will be back soon, and we will fix something to eat. Let's sit on the porch and wait for her."

As soon as Kristina came into view, Beth and Hazel knew something was wrong. Kristina was not on Barnacle's back. Instead she was walking beside him, and as they neared the porch, Kristina burst into tears and ran to her mother. "What in the world—" Beth began, but before she could finish her sentence, Kristina cried out, "Daddy and his crew are missing! His ship has gone down. He's gone!" she said.

Hazel had to grab Beth to keep her from collapsing on the porch. Then she eased Beth down into the closest chair and told Kristina to let her see the telegram.

Kristina and her mother embraced and were sobbing as Hazel read the telegram. "It says that they're missing. That means there's still hope," Hazel said. "Your father is an excellent sea captain, and he knows the sea very well. If anyone can survive a hurricane, your daddy can." After she helped Kristina and Beth into the cottage, she went out to check on the horses. When she returned, Kristina and Beth were huddled on the couch together, still crying. Cocoa had crawled over to Kristina and was licking her hand, as if she knew something was wrong.

"All is not lost," Hazel said to them. "Don't despair. Keep your faith. Contact the shipping company and see if they have any current information about the vessel. Ask about their last confirmed location or any wireless transmissions received from them. I have to return to the hammock in the morning, but I'll be right back to help you any way I can. And before I go, I'll contact Mrs. Gray and ask her to look in on you until I get back. I am going to stop by the station to inform Keeper Daniels of the situation and see if he knows how we can gain more information. There might be something the lifesaving service can do to help."

Hazel wasn't gone long, and she returned with homemade soup. She encouraged Beth and Kristina to eat something, but both of them politely refused the food and fell asleep together on the couch. Hazel covered them with a blanket and settled down in a nearby chair. Then Cocoa settled between the couch and the chair and fell asleep, too.

As the sun was shining through the curtains the next morning, Cocoa woke Hazel with a low growl coming from deep within her throat. "What do you hear, girl?" Hazel asked the dog. Then she opened the door and saw people walking toward their cottage, as well as several wagons headed in her direction. "Beth, you and Kristina had better wake up. You're about to have company," she said, in an effort to hastily rouse the two.

"Oh, Lord," Beth said. "Not today. Who in the world is coming?" she asked.

"It looks like about half the island," Hazel responded.

Beth and Kristina went to the door and saw the people coming from all directions. Mrs. Gray was the first to reach them. She set two baskets of food on the table, then hugged Beth and said, "We'll take care of you, and we will get through this together."

Keeper Daniels was next. He embraced Beth and Kristina and said, "When you get squared away later this morning, come to the station. We will use all resources available to gather information about Edward."

"All these people," Beth said.

"Don't worry about them," said the keeper. "They care about you and your daughter and are willing to do anything to help in your time of need."

The villagers brought food and comfort until late in the afternoon, willing to do whatever they could to help ease their fears. Then Mrs. Scarborough came up in a wagon and yelled, "I have a letter for you, from Edward!"

❧26❧

Missing Father

Barnacle was confused the next morning when he woke up and the corral gate was closed. The rope that held the gate in place was still looped over the gatepost. Normally, Kristina would have already propped the gate open to allow her horses to come and go as they pleased. Barnacle knew that he and his young stallions could easily jump the fence, but his mare could not clear the top rail and would have to wait until someone came to let her out. Barnacle didn't know what was wrong, but he knew something was not right, especially when no one came out to water or feed them.

When Barnacle saw the Raven and a large group of Banker ponies moving south between the corral and the station, Barnacle called out to him. The Raven then turned and brought his entire herd of ponies up to the corral gate. He and Barnacle exchanged glances and nods, and then the Raven nudged the rope off the post with his mouth and nose; then he pushed the gate open. Barnacle called for his family, and they joined the horses outside the gate and took off for the beach.

When Kristina woke up, Hazel said, "I watched the Raven open the gate this morning and let Barnacle and his family out of the corral. They have joined the Banker herd and are making their way toward the beach.

"Oh, my goodness!" Kristina exclaimed. "I neglected to release them for their beach run. I don't feel like doing much of anything until we find out more about Daddy. Mom and I were excited at first about the letter Mrs. Scarborough brought yesterday, but as you know, it was dated before Dad left Baltimore. Mom and I may have to go to Baltimore before this is over. If so, I'm hoping you'll watch after Barnacle and his family until I can return. I'm also hoping you can help me figure out a way to explain it to Barnacle if I have to leave."

Hazel assured Kristina that the horses would be fine. "I'll make sure they have enough food and water in the corral, and I'll leave the gate open so that they can come and go as they see fit. They need some time to roam with their friends, and thankfully there are no horse trappers around right now. And as far as leaving Barnacle is concerned, it won't be hard to explain to him. You have a good relationship with him now, and Barnacle has confidence in you again," Hazel assured Kristina.

"I sure hope you are right," Kristina told Hazel, "because I never want to hurt Barnacle again."

"The first time you left Barnacle, you and Stan tricked him. This time, all you have to do is tell him you are leaving and that he will be staying at the hammock with me," she explained. "If you do have to leave, we'll see you off at the landing, and I am sure that Barnacle will believe everything you tell him."

"Thank you, Hazel. That's exactly what I will do, if I have to go," Kristina replied.

After the hurricane swamped four vessels in the Florida Straits, including the *Aletia*, it turned seaward and passed to the east of Bermuda, having little effect on the East Coast. The *Aletia* had been a bit luckier than the rest of the vessels. She had broken up on an outer bar, very close to the southwest tip of Cuba, and most of the crew was able to make it to shore during the night, including Edward. Having landed in an unpopulated area, they had no way of getting a message to the mainland until first light.

Kristina and Beth went to the station to see Keeper Daniels. He had already sent a wireless message to the Currituck Beach Lifesaving Station about the missing vessel and crew. The message was relayed to the Virginia Capes Lifesaving Station, then on to the shipping company in Baltimore. "We should have a reply in about an hour," the keeper told them. When the reply came from Edward's company in Baltimore, the information was the same. The *Aletia* was still listed as missing, along with her crew, somewhere near the Florida Straits.

"We already knew that from the telegram," Beth said. "I think we should go to Baltimore to be close to the shipping company, just in case more news comes in about your father," she told Kristina. "You still have some time before your teaching begins, and we have a few things up there to take care of, no matter how things turn out," Beth said. Then she went back to the cottage to pack her things.

When Kristina came inside, her mother said, "If at all possible, I would like to leave in the morning. Captain Mansfield and the *Coastal Rambler* will be leaving here around nine o'clock, and we must catch the *Sea Mullet* by eight o'clock to begin our trip," Beth said.

Kristina understood immediately and told her mother that she needed to find Barnacle before they left so that she could explain the situation to him.

"He'll be back before dark," Beth said. "He always is."

Just ahead of dusk, Barnacle and his family came galloping in from the beach. Kristina and Hazel went out to meet them and let them in the gate. Then Kristina put her arms around Barnacle's big neck and began to talk to him. She explained that she had to go find out what had happened to her dad. Barnacle remained completely still and made soft whinnying sounds until Kristina tried to go in the house. Then he blocked her way. "I have to go in, Barnacle," she told him, but he would not let her pass.

"Stay with the horses tonight," Hazel told Kristina. "I'll explain to your mother and get you some blankets. Barnacle understood everything you just told him, and he wants to spend as much time as possible with you before you leave."

Kristina slept in the stall with her head resting on Barnacle's big neck. The mare bedded down close by, and the overgrown colt slept with his head in Kristina's lap. The next morning Beth woke everyone up early. Kristina and Hazel loaded the wagon and hitched Barnacle to it. Cocoa was able to walk to the wagon, but Kristina had to help her in. "You're going to stay with Hazel while we're gone, girl," she told Cocoa. Then she said, "To the landing, Barnacle," and they headed to the landing with the mare and colt following closely behind.

Beth and Kristina loaded their luggage onto the *Sea Mullet*, and Kristina hugged the mare and colt good-bye. Then she hugged Cocoa. "You be a good girl and take care of Hazel," she told the dog. Next Kristina hugged Hazel and thanked her for being the best friend anyone could ever have. Finally she went over to Barnacle, and he lowered his big head so that she could hug him, too. "Watch over everyone for me, boy. I'll be back as soon as I can," she told Barnacle as big tears ran down her face. Then she and her mother boarded the *Sea Mullet*.

"Don't worry about your animals," Hazel told her. "I'll take good care of them for you."

"I know you will," Kristina replied as she waved good-bye.

Standing on both sides of the shore were their many friends, waving good-bye and shouting well wishes. "Hurry back! God bless you! Hope everything turns out alright!" they shouted as the *Sea Mullet* pulled away from Northard Woods.

Back on the shore Cocoa stood up in the wagon and began making a pitiful yelping sound. The mare stood and stared out at the *Sea Mullet*, and the colt whinnied and circled the wagon. Barnacle lowered his head and made a soft moaning sound as large tears dripped off the end of his nose. The villagers remained very still and watched Kristina as she waved constantly until the *Sea Mullet* was completely out of sight.

"Okay, it's back to the hammock for us," Hazel said. "Let's go, boy." Slowly, Barnacle turned and headed for the landing road, stopping a couple of times to look back. "She'll be back soon, and that's a promise."

It was dark when Hazel and the animals got back to Cedar Hammock. She put the horses in the stall and rubbed them down, and then she fed and watered them. "Come on, girl. Let's go in the house," Hazel told Cocoa, but instead Cocoa limped slowly into the stall with the horses. "So you want to stay with them tonight, is that it?" When Cocoa looked up at her with sad eyes, she said, "Oh, alright then. Stay here and I'll be right back."

Hazel returned to the stall with a few blankets, and they all settled down for the night. The horses huddled together, and she and Cocoa bedded down in the blankets on the straw. Then Hazel blew out the lantern and faded off to sleep. She was soon awakened by Cocoa's whimpering and crying. The dog was moving her legs as if she was running, and Hazel had to shake her awake. "You're just dreaming, girl," Hazel said. "Go back to sleep." Then Cocoa licked her hand, yawned, and closed her eyes.

The next morning, Barnacle was pacing and acting very nervously. "What's the matter, boy?" Hazel asked him as she fed and watered the horses. Barnacle ate in a hurry, and then he wanted to be let out of the corral. When Hazel opened the gate, he galloped out and called for the mare and colt to follow. Cocoa began to bark and whine, and Hazel said, "Go on, if you think you can. You won't be happy here waiting for them to come back."

Barnacle slowed down and waited for Cocoa to join them. She was still sore from fighting with the wild hog and could only trot. Barnacle led the way across the floating marsh and out to the beach trail, and they headed up the beach toward the Chicamacomico Station as fast as Cocoa could run.

"Look over yonder," Barney said to Jason. "Here comes the Cedar Hammock crew of Barnacle, the mare, the colt, and Cocoa. Everyone except Hazel."

"Wonder where they're going?" Jason said.

"It looks as if they are coming here," Barney replied. "Better call Keeper Daniels to see what he makes of it."

When Keeper Daniels arrived at the boathouse, Barnacle was waiting for him. "Well, Mr. Barnacle, what can we do for you this morning?" the keeper asked the horse. When Barnacle walked over to the corral gate, Keeper Daniels opened it, and all three horses walked into the corral. "So, you want to join us after all," the keeper said. Then he told Barney and Jason to get word to Hazel that Barnacle was in Chicamacomico. "Otherwise, she'll spend half the night looking for them," the keeper said.

Barney and Jason saddled up and headed toward the hammock to see Hazel. When they told her about the horses, her response was to tell Keeper Daniels that she would come up and get the animals the next day. However, on the following day, when she arrived at the station, Barnacle would not budge from the corral.

"You can leave the horses here if you want," Keeper Daniels told Hazel. "We'll take care of them and feed them good. Heck, we'll even feed the dog and look after her, too!" Keeper Daniels said with a grin.

"Well, I guess they are just as well off here as they would be at the hammock," Hazel replied. "If they give you any trouble, notify me, and I will come for them," she said before leaving the station.

"That is a very smart horse, and he is up to something," Keeper Daniels told the station crew. "There's a reason he wants to hang around here with his family."

The next day, as the station crew readied their gear for morning drills, Barnacle started making a fuss. As soon as Barney opened the gate to the corral, Barnacle walked over to the beach cart and backed up to the harness.

"He wants to be hitched to the beach cart!" Jason said.

"Well, hitch him up, but no bridle or bit," the keeper said sternly.

"How will you control him?" Barney asked.

"He'll go where we tell him," the keeper answered.

"Sure he will," said Jason sarcastically. "That works for Kristina, but what makes you think it'll work for us?"

"You'll see," Keeper Daniels replied. Then he said, "Hey, Barnacle, are you ready to be in the lifesaving business again?" Barnacle made a low whinnying sound from deep within his throat, and the keeper said, "Okay, then, it's off to the drill field for you!" Then Barnacle took off with the beach cart—with Cocoa by his side and his family close behind him.

"I still can't figure out what he's up to," the keeper told the men.

"Maybe he knows we have the wireless and is sure this is the first place Kristina will contact with any news about her father," kidded Barney, as he winked at the keeper.

"No way," said Jason. "He's not that smart!"

"How do you suppose Barnacle expects to receive the news?" asked Keeper Daniels. "Does he think we will tell him, or does he expect to wait in the tack room to hear the transmissions?" he kidded back.

❧27❧

Shipwrecked in Cuba

Just after daylight, on the morning after their shipwreck, Edward and three members of his crew came out of the jungle on the southwestern tip of Cuba. The beach was bare as far as the eye could see in all directions. The men decided to walk toward the east, since the beach would be easier to navigate than the dense jungle.

They came to a clearing full of tall plants in long rows. "I think that's sugar cane," Edward told the other two. Suddenly, three armed men came out of the jungle and took them hostage. "Hands up!" they were told, and then they were blindfolded.

"Where are you taking us?" Edward asked.

"You'll see," the tallest man told them. After what seemed like hours of hiking in the jungle, their blindfolds were removed. That's when they found themselves standing in a large room, facing a very fat, bearded man.

"Where are we, and why have you brought us here?" asked Edward.

"If any questions are to be asked, they will be asked by me," the man told them. "Now," he said, "who are you, and how did you get here?"

Edward told the man their names and the story of how they were wrecked. The man identified himself as Julio Garcia, and he told Edward that he and his men were on a government-owned sugar plantation, accessible by boat only or by walking across miles of dense jungle. Mr. Garcia continued, "This is a top-secret location. Our business here is very private and has to do with the security of our nation. How do I know you are not spies for the United States?" he asked.

"Well," Edward answered, "I can show you the remains of our ship, if you like."

Mr. Garcia replied, "We will go there in the morning. We have a load of cane to move down the coast, and you will be our guests until our government officials decide what will become of you."

That night, after they were fed, Edward and his shipmates were locked in a small storage shed and could see nothing but the moonlight through a small hole in the thatched roof. "There's our means of escape!" Edward exclaimed. Later, all three men climbed up the door and crawled along a ceiling beam to the hole above them. Then they pivoted out onto the roof, slid to the ground, and remained very still for a few moments.

"Now what?" one of the crewmen asked Edward.

"Now we find the beach and a small boat and sail out of here. Let's listen for the ocean and head in that direction," Edward told them.

Soon they were walking along the surf line, and they came across a protected cove with three small sailboats and a seventy-foot clipper vessel docked inside. They could see men walking on the deck of the large vessel. Edward reminded his shipmates to be very careful and quiet as they eased off the shore and swam to one of the smaller boats. Concealed by the shadow of the moon, they pushed the boat far enough away from shore to raise the masts and make sail. Navigating by the moon, they headed south and then turned toward the west, putting them about ninety miles from the coast of Florida. Edward hoped they could reach the shipping channel of the Florida Straits and be picked up by a larger vessel.

When daylight came, all they could see was ocean. There was no sign of land or sail in any direction. The small boat was not made for open ocean sailing and was taking on water from the choppy seas. There was nothing in the boat to scoop the water, so the men used their hands as bailers. However, they were unable to keep up with the incoming water and were in danger of swamping. Then a large wave completely filled the boat with water. Edward and his mates clung to the frame as the boat rolled onto its left side and turned bottom up. They were at the mercy of the currents in the Florida Straits. With no life jackets, they lashed themselves together with rope and drifted toward the Florida Keys.

When Kristina and Beth arrived in Baltimore, they headed straight for the shipping office and soon became discouraged when they learned that no additional information had arrived regarding Edward. "I have to make a decision," Kristina told her mother, "which is to stay here with you for the winter and help you settle things or go back to Northard Woods and become a schoolteacher. I really would like to find out more about Daddy, because I don't think I can keep my mind on teaching as long as he is missing."

Kristina continued, "Daddy is a very good sea captain, and he knows the ocean well. If anyone can survive under adverse conditions, my daddy can. I'm going to send a message to Hazel and ask her to explain my situation to the local school board. I'll also ask her to explain it to Barnacle," Kristina said.

"Do you really think Hazel can make Barnacle understand things?" asked Beth.

"Oh, I know she can. I know that for a fact! She's the one who taught me to communicate with Barnacle," replied Kristina. Then she told her mother she had made her decision. "I will remain here with you for a while, until we have some type of closure about Daddy and decide what we are going to do. As horrible as it may seem, we must hope for the best but prepare for the worst." Then they both burst into tears and hugged each other.

On her way to the station, Hazel stopped by the post office and found a letter from Kristina in her box. She decided not to open the letter until she arrived at the station so that she could share it with Keeper Daniels. "She's not coming back right away," Hazel said, "and she wants me to explain it to the school board and to Barnacle." Then she asked the keeper, "Could you possibly talk to the school board members for me?"

"I'll be glad to," Keeper Daniels replied.

"And I'll take care of the explanation to the animals," Hazel said. "I'm sure I can get Barnacle to understand, and the rest will follow his lead."

"The animals will be fine here at the station with us," the keeper told her.

"For some reason, Barnacle seems happier here, helping you and the crew, rather than being back at the hammock," Hazel said. "I don't know why he chooses to stay here and work over leading a life of leisure and wandering free, but right now, that seems to be his plan."

"It's as if he knows something or is expecting something that will involve his presence here. He stays within eyesight of this corral and is constantly watching the surf line," the keeper said.

"Well, I'm off to talk to him, as Kristina requested," Hazel replied, "and I'll be back in a few days."

The northeast wind pushed Edward and his shipmates southwest into the Florida Straits, with currents like a raging river. The Dominican Channel and the Gulf of Mexico narrowed at the straits and joined with the Gulfstream currents. Edward knew these currents flowed north, parallel to the Atlantic East Coast, coming closest to land near Cape Hatteras, North Carolina, which was hundreds of miles from their current location. He also knew that the Labrador currents and the Gulfstream currents met there and created some of the most treacherous waters to navigate on the entire East Coast. They had no food, and their only fresh water was supplied by an occasional rain shower. Edward knew they could not survive by drifting on the overturned boat. Many odds were against them if they tried to drift too far, including the treacherous Diamond Shoals.

"We must right this boat and figure out a way to paddle!" Edward said. Then all three of the men got on one side and managed to roll the boat over. They swam beside it, scooping water out with their hands, and were finally able to raise the gunnels above the surface of the water and climb inside the boat. They pulled a couple of boards from one of the seats and paddled with the wind, across the current, for five days and nights. Finally, on the sixth night, at about midnight, they saw a faint glimmer of light, far off to the west.

The men paddled the entire next day as the sight of land renewed their strength. Late in the afternoon, just as it was making dark, they climbed onto the shore and collapsed on the beach. From the sight of palm trees, Edward knew they were somewhere on the east coast of Florida. Then the three men crawled up into the tall grass and fell asleep for the first time in days.

At the station, Barnacle was making such a fuss that he woke Barney and Jason from their sleep through an open window in the crew's quarters. "Do you hear that fool horse, Jason?" asked Barney.

"Yes, I hear him," replied Jason. "One of us should see to him before he wakes the keeper."

"Alright, I'll go," Barney said, and walked out to the corral.

Barnacle had already jumped the fence and was trying to raise the rope latch to release the mare and colt. When Barney propped the gate open, the horses took off toward the beach with Barnacle in the lead, followed by the mare, the colt, and then the barking dog. "Hush, you fool dog, before you wake the rest of the men!" Barney fussed at Cocoa.

When Barney returned to the crew's quarters, Keeper Daniels said, "You and Jason have to come up with a better plan to deal with that horse at night."

Then Barney said to the keeper, "That horse works hard all day, but he insists on early beach visits before daylight, as if he's looking for someone or something."

"Well, you and Jason need to follow him and see what he is doing on the beach so early in the morning," replied Keeper Daniels.

"Yes, sir. You're right. I never thought of that," Barney replied.

The very next morning, Barney followed the horses to the beach. He stayed far enough behind them so that they wouldn't know he was on their trail. As he peeked at them from the top of a large sand hill, he saw the small mare standing in the surf, looking out to sea, as if she was waiting for something. Cocoa and the colt were romping and playing in the sand. However, Barney did not see Barnacle anywhere.

"Where in the world is that horse?" Barney said aloud. At that moment, he heard something behind him and turned to see Barnacle's big brown eyes glaring at him. The stallion snorted and nudged Barney hard with his nose, causing him to tumble down the face of the sand dune. Barney quickly got to his feet and gave chase, but Barnacle took off to the south along with his buddies and was soon out of sight.

It was making daylight when Barney got back to the station, and he was shaking his shirt off when Jason walked out onto the front porch. "What in the world happened to you?" Jason asked. When Barney told him about the horse nudge, they both had a good laugh. "Maybe he thought you were a spy," Jason said.

"Oh, I think he was just playing with me! I could swear he was laughing as he galloped away," Barney replied.

"How does a horse laugh?" Jason asked.

"You know that snorting, snickering sound he makes?" said Barney.

Keeper Daniels walked out onto the porch, and Jason told him about Barney being pushed down a sand hill. "All you have to do is tell him you want to go with them," said Keeper Daniels, "and he'll walk along with you. I've seen Kristina and Hazel talking to him hundreds of times. Just the other day, Hazel told Barnacle that Kristina would be gone longer than she had planned, and he took in every word. I saw it with my own eyes. When she was finished, Barnacle bobbed his head up and down to let her know he understood."

"Talking to a horse? How silly is that?" said Barney.

"About as silly as a horse sneaking up behind you and pushing you down a sand hill, I reckon," said the keeper. They all had a good laugh, and Barney told Keeper Daniels he would try his method the next time. Then they parted ways to get ready for a day of lifesaving drills.

Barnacle was already at the boathouse, waiting for them when they arrived. He walked over to the beach cart and allowed them to hitch him up, and then he headed toward the drill field. He stopped at the make-ready marker, where they unhitched him, and then he walked to the surfline and stared far offshore.

❦28❧

SAFE IN GEORGIA

After a night of restless sleep and still uncertain of their whereabouts, Edward and his shipmates awoke to a sunny day. However, all they saw in both directions was deserted beach. "We must find water and something to eat," Edward told the men. Then he suggested that they walk north, toward some palm trees in the distance. When they did, they found some coconuts and a pond of fresh water.

The men drank the water coming from the higher rocks and washed themselves under the small waterfall. They used the rocks to open the coconuts, and after a meal of coconut and water they continued their walk up the surf line. As they rounded a bend in the beach, they saw several fishermen pulling their nets up onto the shore, and several wagons were parked close by. "I think we're saved!" Edward exclaimed. "Let's find out where we are!"

Edward identified himself to the fishermen and introduced his mates. They discussed the hardships of their recent experience, including the shipwreck, their days at sea with no food or water, and being captured in Cuba. The fishermen had heard about the missing ships and crews since the hurricane and agreed to take Edward and his shipmates to a nearby seaport town as soon as they finished their day's work. The three sailors helped the fishermen with their nets, and it was just about dark when they arrived at the small seaport town. From there they would go to the Savannah River Lifesaving Station and send a wire up the coast, first to their families, and then to the shipping company in Baltimore.

It was a late October afternoon, on the third day of a rainy northeaster, when the wireless communication officer at Chicamacomico summoned Keeper Daniels to the tack room. A broken message about Captain Edward and the *Aletia* was being relayed up the beach by the Creeds Hill Station. Keeper Daniels told the officer to contact the cape and Big Kinnakeet Stations immediately for a cleaner transmission. When they received the complete message, the two men were astonished. "Relay this on up the line as soon as possible," Keeper Daniels instructed the officer.

It was mid-morning when Kristina and Beth heard the knock on the door at their apartment in Baltimore. Kristina opened the door, and when she saw the messenger from the shipping company, her heart sank as she immediately assumed the worst. When the young man noticed the expression on her face, he said, "Miss, I have good news for you. Your father is alive and safe."

Tears of amazement streamed down Kristina's face. She could hardly read the message to her mother. "Daddy is safe! He and three shipmates are in Georgia and are making their way up the coast. He expects to be in Chicama-comico by Thanksgiving!" Kristina exclaimed. "We must get ready to go back home! Oh, what a joyous reunion!"

Beth was overjoyed. "I think we can finish our business here in a few days and begin our trip back to the island by next weekend," she replied.

Edward arranged a working passage aboard a three-mast schooner, hauling a full cargo of salt crystals and rough-cut lumber from the Savannah River to the port of Charleston. When he and his shipmates arrived in Charleston, Edward contacted a longtime friend whom he and his family had visited many times—the very plantation where Kristina had met Barnacle. After hearing about Edward's experience at sea, his friend asked the men to come inland and rest for a few days, but they graciously declined, explaining that they were all very anxious to get back home as soon as possible.

The next day, Edward's friend arranged northward passage for them aboard the *Lucy May*. The vessel was carrying a load of cotton to Baltimore and would only be making one short stop in Beaufort, so that the captain could pick up a couple of hundred pounds of shad roe. From Beaufort, Edward would arrange a one-way working trip to Ocracoke, and then catch the *Coastal Rambler* to Chicamacomico. His shipmates would continue on to Baltimore, aboard the *Lucy May*.

One week before Thanksgiving, Edward returned to Northard Woods. Beth, Kristina, and all of their friends, including the animals, were waiting for him at the harbor. The reunion was filled with joy, with lots of hugs, tears, and thankfulness. When Edward and his family returned to their cottage, Beth and Kristina clung to him and Cocoa curled up near his feet as close as she could get. "You missed me, didn't you, girl?" Edward said to the dog.

For the rest of the day, Edward rested in his home with his wife and daughter, thankful for his blessings. Later that evening, the people of the village brought containers of food to the cottage, and everyone ate and shared fellowship until late that night. Finally, the minister suggested that folks return home so that Edward and his family could get their rest, and then he said a closing prayer. Before dismissal, Keeper Daniels announced the big feed being planned for Thanksgiving and told everybody they were invited.

The word soon spread about the Thanksgiving get-together. Almost everyone attending would bring plenty of food to the gathering. Keeper Daniels was concerned about having enough seats for everyone at the station, so he decided to change the location to the Northard Woods schoolhouse. Since the weather was unseasonably warm, it would be an all-day affair, with games and outdoor activities. The school had playground equipment for the smaller children to enjoy, as well as a baseball diamond and horseshoe pits for the older kids and adults.

When the big day arrived, folks came from near and far. They enjoyed the outside activities and shared a big midday meal. Later they gathered inside the schoolhouse to tell stories and sing songs. During story time, Edward was asked to tell of his shipwreck adventure and quest of returning home. Kristina told the story of how Barnacle came to live in Chicamacomico. Norman Scarborough told many of his hunting stories, and Hazel told stories of her relationships with animals. She encouraged everyone to extend understanding and assistance toward them, especially during harsh winter weather. At the end of the day, the Thanksgiving feed was a big success, enjoyed by all who attended.

The very next day, Keeper Daniels, Barney, and Jason were having a cup of coffee on the eastward porch of the station when Jason noticed clouds racing from the southwest toward the northeast. "Look at that," he said. "I think we're in for a blow."

"Let's go inside and see if the wireless operator has received an update on the weather," said the keeper. The weather report was just coming in as they entered the tack room.

"We are in for an early winter storm," the operator told them. "The wind will increase tonight from the southwest—to gale force by morning and storm force by midday tomorrow. It will blow steady, seventy to eighty miles per hour, with possible gusts to ninety from the southwest before tomorrow evening. Then the wind will shift to the northwest as the center of the storm passes to the west. They are calling for heavy rain on the coast and snow inland, to the point of blizzard conditions."

"We have to contact the Gull Shoal and Pea Island Stations to make sure they have received this weather information," Keeper Daniels insisted. Then he told Barney and Jason to organize the crew and send them out to Clarks, Southard Woods, and Northard Woods to inform everybody of the upcoming extreme weather.

Edward walked out onto the porch of the cottage as Barney reached the front gate on horseback. "We've received a storm warning transmission," said Barney. "Heavy weather is headed this way today and into tomorrow, and if you have anything that might possibly blow around and cause damage, you need to secure it. Store some water and make sure you have batteries and candles ready." Then he told Edward to pass the word, and he galloped off.

Edward took the rocking chairs inside and went to the corral to tend to the horses. The mare and colt were still sleeping, but Barnacle was gone. Edward returned to the house to ask Kristina if she knew where Barnacle might be, and he discovered that Cocoa was also missing from her normal spot on the rug beside Kristina's bed. Then Edward woke his daughter and questioned her about Barnacle.

"He's in the corral, as far as I know," Kristina responded.

"Well, how about Cocoa? Have you seen her?" Edward asked.

"I had to let her outside, just before daylight, to keep her from waking you and Mom," Kristina answered.

"Well, then, Barnacle and Cocoa are most likely at the beach together. I'll walk over and check the surf," her father said.

When Edward topped the dune, the sea was already building. He could hear its roar above the strengthening southwest wind. As he neared the surf he saw Barnacle standing beside the ocean, staring out at the growing waves, and Cocoa was sitting on the sand beside him. When Edward called to them, Cocoa ran up and jumped on him with her wet paws, but Barnacle just stared offshore and would not move. "Come on, guys. Let's go home before this storm hits," Edward told them. After much coaxing, Barnacle finally gave in and started following Cocoa toward the dune. Then they both turned around and ran back to the surf line.

Edward left the beach and walked back to the cottage. Beth had fixed the morning meal and told Edward to sit down and eat.

"No time," he answered. "That fool horse won't come home from the beach, and bad weather is on its way. I have to get Kristina up so she can get Barnacle to the corral before the storm hits," he told Beth.

In a few minutes, Kristina and Edward went to the beach and found Barnacle and Cocoa in the same spot where Edward had left them. With all their coaxing, neither Kristina nor Edward could get Barnacle to return to the corral, and Cocoa wasn't budging either. "We have to get Hazel as fast as we can," Kristina told her father. Then they headed to the station to tell Keeper Daniels about the situation.

Jason was just getting ready to go to Clarks to advise folks about the weather when Kristina and her father arrived at the station. Keeper Daniels told Jason to go quickly to inform Hazel about the storm, bring her back to Chicamacomico, and meet them on the beach.

When Hazel and Jason arrived at the beach, Hazel walked up to Barnacle, placed a pair of blinders over his eyes, and gently tugged on his neck. When he lowered his head she whispered something in his ear, and Barnacle instantly turned and began to follow her back toward the corral. Cocoa gladly ran ahead to lead the way.

"What in the world did you tell him?" Kristina asked.

"I told him it was alright, and that we couldn't help them until the sea calms."

"Help who?" asked Keeper Daniels.

"Whoever's out there in trouble," answered Hazel.

"How do you know someone is out there?" asked the keeper.

"I don't know, but Barnacle knows. I just told him that the sea is too rough, and there is no way we can help them until it calms down some," answered Hazel.

"You mean to tell me that Barnacle understood everything you said?" asked Keeper Daniels.

"I don't know it for a fact," Hazel answered, "but he's headed home, and for the moment our problem is solved. Now I suggest we ready ourselves for the upcoming weather."

❧ 29 ❧

WRECK OF THE *LUCY MAY*

"We need to hurry," Keeper Daniels told the group as they started back to the village.

"Yes, I agree," Hazel said as she swung her leg over the saddle. "Barnacle will follow you now," she told Kristina. "I have to get back to the hammock to care for my stock," she said, and galloped away.

Keeper Daniels instructed the rest of the group to put the storm blinds on the windows, get extra food, and batten down "anything that will blow," he said. When they parted ways to prepare for the storm, Kristina and Edward led Barnacle and Cocoa into the corral. They placed the heavy hatch boards on the second level and spread hay over them so that the horses could escape any rising water, and then they headed for the house. Cocoa didn't want to come inside with them because she wanted to stay outside with the horses.

"Come on, Cocoa," Kristina said.

Cocoa came to the corral door, hung her head, and started back inside the corral, but Kristina said, "Oh, no, you don't. You're going in the cottage with us." Kristina grasped Cocoa by the scruff of the neck and began to drag her until Edward came over, picked up the dog, and carried her to the cottage. When they got inside, Cocoa stayed by the door and began to howl, bark, and whimper.

After enough annoyance, Kristina said, "My lands, I reckon, Cocoa," and escorted the dog back to the corral. Cocoa ran to the second level and curled up in the hay with the horses. "You think you're a horse, don't you?" Kristina asked the dog. Cocoa replied with a sharp *yap* of approval and started licking the colt's nose.

A high-pressure system, stalled off the Virginia capes, was holding the storm at bay until it weakened and drifted out to sea. Then the storm center took a more easterly course and entered the lower Pamlico Sound. It traveled northward, attacking the inland with storm-force winds and heavy snow, leading to whiteout conditions. Blowing sand and blinding rain covered the entire coastal area, from the lower portions of North Carolina to the upper Jersey shore.

Many coastal structures suffered severe damage, and some were even washed off their foundations. Large inland cities were brought to a standstill, covered with two to three feet of heavy, wet snow. Violent weather conditions were experienced for about three days, until the storm center followed the high-pressure system out to sea.

In Chicamacomico, the wind had blown seventy-five to eighty miles an hour from the southwest. The sound water had completely covered the island, and every item that was not tied down either blew or washed away. Several boats had broken free of their moorings and were floating around in the village. By the second day, the wind shifted to the southeast, pulling the sound water completely away from the coast and flooding many inland cities and villages. On the third day, as the storm moved past, the wind shifted to the northeast and blew gale force once again, returning a surge of sound water across the island to mix with the ocean over-wash.

The next day dawned a clear, cloudless sky. The wind was still blowing from the northeast about fifteen to twenty miles per hour. The ocean tide had not completely run off, so Kristina and her father waded in knee-deep water to let the horses out of the corral. The mare and colt were on the upper hay bed, safe and dry, but Barnacle and Cocoa were nowhere to be seen.

"Where in the world could they have gone?" Kristina asked her dad. Then they saw the horse and dog coming from the beach, south of the station. Only the tops of the randomly spaced hills were above water. Barnacle waded, and

Cocoa swam from one hilltop to another. If Barnacle got too far ahead, Cocoa yelped, and he would stop to wait for her. Just before they crossed the cart path, Barnacle stepped in a deep hole and plunged under water. He came up, snorting and blowing, then he swam across the deep section and waited for Cocoa.

"When did those two become such good friends, and where have they been in this weather?" asked Beth as she came out onto the porch.

"Barnacle's been acting funny, just staring offshore, even before the storm," Kristina answered her mother. "He went to the beach again this morning, and Miss Curiosity-Plus was right there beside him. Cocoa involves herself in everything that involves Barnacle."

"Oh, look at how clear and blue the sky is today," Beth said. "There isn't a cloud to be seen anywhere. Don't you think that's funny?" she asked Edward.

"Not really," Edward answered. "A strong storm center moves in a counter-clockwise direction through the air, similar to a whirlpool in water, and sucks all the clouds out with it as it moves away. When this occurs, it leaves a very deep, dark blue sky. In the absence of clouds, there is no white contrast."

"Interesting," Beth said. "Now, what about Barnacle staring offshore? What do you think he's looking for?"

"Hazel thinks he can sense that someone is in trouble out there, and he wants to help them," said Kristina.

"Then maybe you and your father should check the beach when the water subsides," her mother replied.

Edward replied, "I'm sure the lifesaving service will continue their patrols as soon as the sea gets down a bit."

"Yes, that's true," Beth said, "but a few sets of extra eyes won't hurt a thing. Besides, it will get the two of you out of the house so that I can do some post-storm cleanup." She smiled as she reminded Kristina and Edward that they were in charge of cleaning the yard.

The next morning, almost all the water was gone. Only small puddles were visible here and there. Edward and Kristina came out of the cottage to bright sunshine and a light east wind. The ocean was still very rough, and they could hear the constant roar of waves crashing on the offshore bar and beach. When they looked inside the barn, they found the colt and mare still asleep, but Barnacle and Cocoa had already scampered off.

"I know where they are," said Kristina. Then she and her father walked over to the beach, and sure enough, Barnacle and Cocoa were standing at the surf line. Barnacle was staring offshore, moving his head back and forth, as if looking for something, and Cocoa was standing right beside him, watching his every move.

"Dad, what are all those white bundles strewn along the beach?" Kristina asked her father.

"Oh, Lord, they look like bales of cotton," Edward exclaimed. Then he said, "The vessel I was traveling on from Charleston to Beaufort was transporting a load of cotton. I suspect the crew either threw it overboard to stay afloat, or else the *Lucy May* has been swamped and gone down. I would have been aboard her, had I not been coming here to see you and your mother."

As they were counting their blessings, Jason rode up on horseback. He had just finished his patrol southward to meet the surfman from Gull Shoal Station. "The surfman reported seeing something very odd and out of place," Jason told them. "He said there's an unopened case of pickled shad roe about a mile outside of Clarks, lashed between two bales of cotton!"

"That confirms my suspicions," Edward replied. "I know for a fact that the *Lucy May* has either gone down or is in serious trouble." Then he told Jason that the only reason the *Lucy May* had stopped in Beaufort on its way back to Baltimore was for the captain to pick up a mess of shad roe for himself.

Barnacle moved slowly up the beach while Cocoa ran back and forth, barking and spinning around in all directions. "What does that dog want?" Edward asked.

"She wants us to follow them," Kristina answered.

Kristina, Edward, and Jason followed Barnacle and Cocoa about two miles up the beach. Then Barnacle stopped, reared up on his hind legs, and began spinning around and pawing the ground. Cocoa was barking and jumping around, too.

Jason had a glass with him and began to scan offshore. Then he said, "I think I see something. It's small. Definitely not a ship, but I'm not sure what it is."

"Let me see your glass," Edward said. "Where are you looking?"

"Off to the left, way out on the horizon," Jason replied.

"I see it now," said Edward. "It's just a small speck, drifting toward the south at a good rate."

"I'll go back to the station and tell Barney," Jason told them. "He has tower duty this morning, and we can take a look with a more powerful glass. I'll be right back," and he took off. He did return quickly, with Keeper Daniels and Barney by his side. They were on horseback, followed by the surfboat on a wagon, being drawn by two large horses. Keeper Daniels instructed them to take the boat down the beach about two miles and launch it there.

On their first attempt to launch the surfboat through the shore break, a big wave caught the boat and turned it bottom up, pitching all the surfmen into the ocean. They had to gather their oars and right the boat to get the water out of the scuppers. The surfboats were decked over, with water outlet areas above the waterline. Even when large waves broke onto the boats, the water would run out the scupper areas.

"Back in the boat!" yelled Keeper Daniels.

The crew scrambled aboard, grabbed their oars, and began to pull. They were almost through the shore break when a wave turned them completely sideways. "Pull men, pull!" yelled the keeper from the back of the boat.

They met the next wave straight on and barely made it over the top before the wave crashed on the beach. Then the surfboat slammed over the crest of the wave and settled in the calmer water between the shore break and the outer bar. The keeper said, "Okay, men. We've got to get past the outside bar. Now, pull to the south. It looks like there's an outlet at the end of this bar."

The surfboat shot through the outlet, propelled by the water as it rushed toward the only opening in the bar for about two miles. Once they got outside the bar to deeper water, all they could see was white water. Keeper Daniels wiped his glass and scanned the distance, looking for the floating object. Then he looked back at the beach. He had asked Edward to give them ranges from shore by waving his arms. That way, they could reach the object on the shortest course possible.

Edward was waving his arms up and down, in a northeasterly direction, to let the keeper know they were still south of the object. Then Keeper Daniels yelled, "Pull straight away, boys!" Before long, the crew could see the object as it crested the waves, and soon they were able to make out half a lifeboat—overturned but still afloat. When the crew arrived at the site, they found two unconscious men lashed to the wreckage and to each other. They immediately pulled the men aboard the surfboat and headed for shore.

"Check 'em out good," the keeper instructed Barney.

"They're still breathing," Barney replied, "but the larger man has a gash in the side of his head and is bleeding badly."

"Try to stop the bleeding with direct pressure, and wash their faces with fresh water from the water can," the keeper told Barney.

As soon as they reached the beach, the crew pulled the surfboat up onto the wagon and headed to the station.

❧30❧

The Offshore Rescue

When they arrived at the station, Keeper Daniels had the crew carry the victims inside. By then, one of them had gained consciousness and was soon able to give an account of the *Lucy May*. Keeper Daniels took down all the information he could in order to prepare his official report.

The *Lucy May* had been on an inward tack near the northwest point of Wimble Shoals when she bumped hard on the bottom several times. The master had ordered the tack short and switched the short jib, then headed the vessel seaward, hoping to get back into deeper water. When the *Lucy May* stopped bumping and was off the shoal, the crew discovered the badly bent rudder. The rudder damage made the vessel very difficult to maneuver, especially as she took a pounding from the strong northeast swell and forty-knot winds.

According to the rescued sailor, once the vessel reached deeper water, the master had ordered a seaward tack for one hour and then a turn toward the land. The master knew they would be able to clear the point of the shoals and sail north with just the short jib. However, he did not know that the vessel was sideslipping backward toward the shoal due to the bent rudder.

Keeper Daniels continued to write as the survivor recalled the events leading up to the rescue. "We could not believe our eyes when we saw the white water," the sailor said, "but it was too late. The *Lucy May* grounded hard and rolled on her side, coming to a jolting stop on the northwest point of

Wimble Shoals. She immediately started taking on water over the starboard side and broke into two pieces from the constant pounding waves. The master and one other crew member cleared the front half of the vessel and were last seen adrift in the sea, lashed to two cotton bales, with a large canister of pickled shad roe between them. Six of us tried to launch a lifeboat from the other half of the wreck, but it smashed against the vessel and was crushed. My mate and I were able to grab hold of a piece of the lifeboat when it resurfaced, but unfortunately the other men disappeared beneath the waves. Somehow we managed to cling to the piece of lifeboat until you came to our rescue," the sailor concluded gratefully.

After the rescue, Edward and Kristina helped the crew clean and stow away the gear, and then they headed home.

"Where's the horse and dog?" Kristina asked her father.

"I don't see them anywhere," Edward responded. Then they heard Cocoa barking in the distance. "It sounds like they've gone back to the beach."

"What in the world for?" Kristina asked.

"I don't know, but I'll get a lantern and we'll go investigate," her father told her.

"I think we should go back and talk to Keeper Daniels," Kristina suggested, "and tell him that Barnacle and Cocoa are acting suspicious." Then she and her father headed to the station in search of the keeper. The cook informed them that Keeper Daniels, Jason, and Barney were out in the boathouse, checking the gear for the next day's drilling.

"Do you hear that dog barking out toward the beach?" Edward asked the keeper.

"Yes," the keeper said. "Dogs bark all the time."

"But that's Cocoa. She and Barnacle are acting really strange," Kristina insisted.

"So what does that mean?" asked the keeper.

"Maybe nothing, but we think we should investigate," Edward replied.

"Alright," Keeper Daniels agreed. "Let's get going." Then he told Jason and Barney to grab a couple of lanterns and come on. At the beach they found

Cocoa swimming about a hundred yards offshore, out near the first bar, but Barnacle was nowhere to be seen.

"Where is that horse?" Kristina said.

"I see him," Barney replied, then pointed. "He's out past the second bar, caught in the tide, swimming south." Kristina could barely make out Barnacle's head in the moonlight, bobbing between the waves. Cocoa was swimming parallel to him, closer to the beach.

"Barnacle has something in his mouth," Jason said, "and it looks like a piece of rope."

"It *is* a piece of rope," replied Keeper Daniels, "and he's dragging something behind him." They watched as Barnacle turned and swam across the bar. Then Cocoa grabbed the rope and began to help pull the object toward the beach. It turned out to be a life ring, with a man's head sticking through the middle, just above the surface of the water.

"He's still breathing," Barney shouted as he and Jason pulled the man up on the sand. Then Barney, Jason, and Keeper Daniels carried the man back to the station to warm and revive him. He was very weak, and he kept passing out from exhaustion.

"We'll have to let him rest until he can give us an account of his experience," said Keeper Daniels. "We'll try to get more information from him tomorrow, when he is stronger." Then the keeper said, "How in the world did Barnacle know that man was out there?"

"He just seems to know things like that," responded Kristina.

"Where is Barnacle now?" asked Edward.

Everyone looked around for Barnacle but he was gone, and so was Cocoa. Kristina and Keeper Daniels ran back to the beach, and sure enough, Barnacle was standing in the surf, with Cocoa sitting next to him in the sand.

"Let's go home, fellow," Kristina told Barnacle. "There's nothing more we can do to help anyone tonight."

"Help who?" asked the keeper.

"Whoever Barnacle thinks is still out there in need of our help," Kristina replied.

Barnacle finally turned and followed Kristina until they started past the station corral. Then he stopped at the gate. "No, Barnacle, you have to come home with us," Kristina said, but the big stallion wouldn't budge. When Barney opened the station corral gate, Barnacle walked right in, followed by Cocoa.

"He wants to stay in our corral!" Keeper Daniels said, delighted. "I think he finally wants to join the lifesaving service!"

The following morning, before first light, Keeper Daniels was banging on Edward's door, so Edward invited him in for coffee. "No time," responded the keeper. "That Barnacle and your dog are missing again this morning. When I went out to feed the stock earlier, they were nowhere to be seen. It looks like the horse jumped the fence and the dog dug under. In any event, they're both gone again. The sailor they rescued yesterday was the cabin boy on the *Lucy May*. He came around early this morning and told us that there are more men still trapped on the wreckage."

Completely exhausted and barely able to talk, the cabin boy explained to Keeper Daniels that, after the *Lucy May* broke in half, the bow portion had washed up high on the middle of the shoals and had grounded above the wash. The boy had left the men waving and scrambling around on the deck when he decided to paddle the life ring toward the shore for help. He explained how he had been pushed to the north by the south wind, and back to the south by the north wind. He had yelled at the top of his lungs when he saw the lights from the village, hoping the sound would carry shoreward.

"Maybe Barnacle heard him shouting," Keeper Daniels told Edward.

"So what are your plans now?" Edward asked the keeper.

"That's where you come in," Keeper Daniels told Edward. "I need your help during this rescue. I'll be taking the entire station crew to the shoals with me, except for the cook, and I'd like for you to man the station until some other surfmen arrive from the Gull Shoal and New Inlet Stations. Wimble Shoals is about eleven miles due east of us, and it will take a lot of rowing and sailing to get there. We have three nearly-drowned men recovering at the station, and the cook will take care of them. But there are other duties that will require extra hands, and I'm hoping you can stay here until the other surfmen arrive."

"I'll be glad to help in any manner I can," Edward responded.

Keeper Daniels continued, "I'd like for you to man the wireless, since you know how it works. Perhaps your daughter can monitor the beach, with Barnacle and her dog. I'm sure they would love that. If Barnacle could walk on water, he would already be out on those shoals, assisting with the rescue."

"I believe he's considering trying to swim there now," Edward said, laughing.

"You're probably right," said the keeper. "Barnacle is obsessed with lifesaving and helping sailors in peril."

"He's obsessed with helping people in general, especially if he senses danger," Edward replied. Then he assured Keeper Daniels that he and Kristina would be at the station within the hour, and that he would be glad to help the cook until the Gull Shoal and New Inlet surfmen arrived at the station.

When Edward and Kristina arrived at the boathouse, the station crew had readied the surfboat, hitched up the horses, and were loading the gear for a long sail out to Wimble Shoals. Edward and Kristina followed the crew to the beach and found Barnacle and Cocoa in the water near the surf line. Barnacle was standing perfectly still, staring offshore.

"He knows they're out there and wants to try and help them," Kristina said.

"You're absolutely right," Edward replied.

The wind had fallen off considerably and had shifted to the northwest. The sea had also calmed, and conditions looked good for the long sail to Wimble Shoals. "We'll be gone for hours, maybe even overnight," Keeper Daniels said as his crew launched the surfboat. Then he told Edward to be on the lookout for their lantern when darkness came. "Place a lantern in the tower and one on the long pole, here on the beach," the keeper instructed. "You can ask some of the village folks to relieve you, if necessary, and we will return as soon as possible, one way or the other." Then Keeper Daniels thanked Edward for his help.

"Good luck!" Edward hollered.

"We'll need it," the keeper yelled back as they made their way over the first bar. The crew raised the sail when they cleared the second bar, and soon the boat was just a small white speck on the horizon.

The men from Gull Shoal Station arrived at the Chicamacomico Station first, followed by the men from New Inlet. Edward relayed the keeper's orders to the replacement surfmen and gave them their assignments. The surfmen prepared the beach with a small canvas lean-to for shelter and a tall lantern pole for light. They used a pulley to raise the lantern to the top of the pole, once it was lit. Then one of the surfmen went to man the tower while another took over the wireless. Edward walked back to the beach to join Barnacle and Cocoa at the water's edge.

Keeper Daniels began his first tack in a due northeast direction. With a fair wind behind them, they would make good time on their trip out to the shoals. The wind breezed steadily from the northwest, and occasionally the surfboat took on water over the stern, washing the feet of the surfmen before running out the scuppers. They sailed steadily along and were soon out of sight of the glass through which Kristina had been watching them.

By mid-afternoon, the surfmen could see the white water of Wimble Shoals. At the very northern end of the shoals, they saw two tiny bumps on the horizon. Soon, Keeper Daniels brought the surfboat as close as he could to the backside of the wreck, in the lee. From there, they saw two men waving from a broken piece of the vessel, about five hundred yards away.

Keeper Daniels ordered the sail struck, and the man-the-oars order was given. The surfmen would have to hold the boat in place, in deep water, while a float attached to a single pulley block was sent out to the wreck. This maneuver was tried several times, but the lifesaving crew kept getting swept off the shoals by heavy cross currents each time they got about halfway to the wreck. Then they moved the surfboat to the north point of the shoals and tried to drift the float with the current, but the wind carried them off-course in the deep water before they could reach the shoals. It was finally decided that one surfman, attached to a separate line, would have to take the pulley to the wreck. Barney quickly volunteered for the task.

The surfboat got as close to the back of the shoal as possible. Then Barney jumped over the side and swam toward the wreck. He soon reached shallow water, where he was able to stand. The water was only about chest-high, but the sand was very soft. With each step he took, Barney sank past his knees in the loose gravel, making it extremely difficult to move ahead. Finally he came to a section of the bar where the bottom was much harder, but the water was neck deep and his feet barely touched the bottom when the waves came. He tried to swim again, but the strong current swept him off the bar, back into the deep water, and the surfmen had to pull him back into the boat.

"We have to move the boat back up to the north end of the shoals and place Barney to the east side of that rip," said Keeper Daniels. As the crew rowed the surfboat almost parallel with the wreck, Barney jumped overboard and swam to the edge of the bar. Fighting the wind drift he was able to stand and make his way toward the wreck until he got about fifty yards away, and the current swept him off his feet again. This time, Keeper Daniels was ready, and he ordered the surfboat rowed farther to the west. At last the line came tight and the boat pulled Barney within a few yards of the wreck, where he could holler to the shipwrecked men.

Barney asked the men how many were left aboard and if anyone was injured. One of the men yelled back.

"Six," he hollered. "A few minor cuts, nothing serious."

Barney knew he couldn't get any closer to the victims because of the wash around the wreck, so he told them to throw a line up tide of him. Soon Barney made the connection, and after the pulley block was tied to the wreck, he signaled the surfboat. Then Keeper Daniels moved the surfboat back to the lee side of the shoals, and the crew tied the breeches buoy to the hawser and pulled it to the wreck. They repeated the process until the sixth man was safely aboard the surfboat. Then Barney cut the hawser and allowed himself to be pulled off the shoal so that his crew could pull him back to the surfboat.

The rescued men told the crew that their captain and first mate had fashioned a float and had launched off the shoal from the other half of the wreck early that morning. "Maybe we will come across them on the way in," said Keeper Daniels. Then the crew rowed the boat past the north point of the shoals, raised the sail, and made their first tack to the southwest.

"I just hope we will be able to spot the lantern in the tower," Keeper Daniels said as the sun began to go down.

❧31❧

The Guiding Light

It was getting dark. The station was properly manned, and they had kept their promise to Keeper Daniels. It was time to collect their animals and go home, so Edward and Kristina went to the beach to get Barnacle and Cocoa.

"Where are those two?" Kristina asked her father.

"I hear Cocoa barking very faintly to the south of us," Edward answered. Then they began walking down the beach toward the sound of the barking dog. The farther they went, the louder the barking became, until they could see Barnacle and Cocoa in the fading light, as well as something awash in the surf beside them.

"Oh, Daddy! That looks like a body!" exclaimed Kristina.

Edward strained his eyes. Indeed, the object did resemble a body, lying motionless in the surf. Barnacle was standing over it, and Cocoa was running around and around it, barking, as if trying to revive it. Edward told Kristina to remain a few feet away while he took a closer look, and he was relieved when he saw the dead porpoise. "You can come over now," he said to Kristina. "It's a very bloated, badly decomposed porpoise, and it looks like it's been dead for a while."

Edward and Kristina had a hard time getting the animals to leave the beach. Barnacle just stared at the bloated porpoise, while Cocoa tried her best to roll on it. Kristina frowned when her father told her that dogs like to get the smell of rotting tissue on them because they think it makes them smell good. "Your mother will not let that dog in the house tonight," said Edward.

Kristina spoke to her horse. "If you come, Cocoa will follow you," she said, so Barnacle started up the beach. Cocoa remained with the rotting porpoise for a few minutes and then ran past them, stinking to high heaven.

"You're sleeping in the barn tonight, old girl," Edward said to the dog. Cocoa responded by jumping up on him and smearing him with stink. "Get away, you stinking mutt!" Edward yelled, but Cocoa jumped up and rubbed against him again. Edward swatted her on the butt, then pulled his hand back and smelled it. Kristina laughed and Barnacle made a gurgling noise in his throat when Edward gagged and almost puked.

"Even Barnacle is laughing at you," Kristina said.

"This dog of yours smells like a rotten fish!" Edward said.

"Guess what, Daddy? So do you!" said Kristina. "Both of you could use a bath!"

"A bath? I think I'll have to shave that dog and burn my clothes to ever get rid of this aroma," he answered. They both laughed and continued on up the beach.

Before they took the path leading to their cottage, Edward and Kristina decided to check on the two surfmen who were manning the beach and lantern site. They asked if there were any new developments, or if they had heard any news from the station crew. There was no word, and now it was totally dark. The search lantern had been lit and hoisted to the top of the pole, and the tower lantern was glowing brightly from the window at the station. The wind had dropped off and shifted to a light breeze from the northeast, and the sea had calmed and glassed off a good bit. All they could do now was wait and hope.

Keeper Daniels and the crew on the surfboat sailed to the end of their first tack on their way back to the station. Barney had lit the boat lantern and raised it to the top of the mast. "I think it is dark enough now that the light can be been seen from a distance," he said.

"The wind has shifted to light out of the northeast," Keeper Daniels told the men. "We almost have a fair wind home," he said, feeling encouraged.

They made pretty good time. The keeper kept checking his compass and scanning the darkness for any sort of light, but all they could see was darkness. "If this wind falls out any more, we'll have to start rowing," he told the men.

"Listen, Captain! Do you hear that?" asked Barney.

"Hear what?" asked the keeper.

"I hear it, too," said Jason.

"Well, what does it sound like?" asked the keeper.

"Like some sort of very faint tapping or scratching sound. It sounds like it's coming from behind us, up to the north a little," said Barney.

"Strike sail and everyone quiet!" ordered the keeper. Then they heard a very faint cry for help, followed by a tapping noise. "Row toward that sound!" the keeper commanded the men. As they got closer, they saw a piece of wreckage lashed to cotton bales, with two men clinging to it. One of the men was halfway up on the wreckage, unconscious and bleeding from the side of his head.

"It's the captain and the mate," one of the men in the boat said. The larger man had pushed the injured man up onto the wreckage to keep his head above water, and the larger man himself had remained in the water, trying to paddle toward shore.

"Look! The captain is still clinging to his shad roe!" said the mate to the very welcome rescuers. The unconscious man's hand had a piece of rope tightly wrapped around it, which was tied to two containers bobbing behind them. "He's been out since he banged his head, but hasn't let loose of that rope the whole time!" said the mate. They loaded the injured captain into the surfboat first, and then the mate.

"What about these containers?" asked Barney. "We can't get the rope out of his hand!"

"We'll tow them along with us. I wouldn't have the heart to take them from him, after all he's been through," answered the keeper. "Alright, men, tie off the captain's roe containers, and let's make sail and head her home," barked the keeper.

Barnacle didn't want to leave the beach. He hesitated and resisted as Kristina tried to coax him along. Then Edward said, "I'll take this dog on home, give her a bath, and try to get rid of this rancid odor."

"We'll be along as soon as I can get Barnacle to come," Kristina told her father. Then she spoke to Barnacle. "We can come back tomorrow at first light, if you want." Then, slowly, they made their way toward the cottage.

Edward was having a tough time trying to bathe Cocoa out at the hand pump. She was doing her best to get away from him, so he tied her up in order to complete her bath. When he was finally finished, both he and Cocoa were soaking wet from head to toe. "I think I got all of the stink off of her," Edward said as the dog shook from head to tail.

"Cocoa, you're wetting me!" Kristina fussed. "You smell like a wet mop!"

"At least it's better than that rotten, fishy smell," said her father. "Now, to get it off of me," he said as he walked inside.

Kristina took Barnacle to the corral, but he wouldn't go inside. Instead, he looked in the direction of the beach. "I know you want to go back over there, and I might as well just let you go, because as soon as I turn my back, you'll go anyway," Kristina said. Then Barnacle made a satisfied *snort* sound and galloped off into the night, toward the beach.

"Where's Barnacle going at this time of night?" Beth asked as she came out onto the porch.

"He's on his way back to the beach. He thinks he's in charge of the lifesaving activities, and he has to be there," Kristina responded.

"How about your dog? Are you going to leave her tied up like that all night?" Beth asked.

"Only until she dries out a little," answered Kristina. "Dad had to bathe her. She rolled on a rotten porpoise."

As Kristina started into the house, Cocoa began to howl. "Hush, Cocoa," Kristina told the dog, but the howling increased and Cocoa began to pull hard on the rope that held her. "Oh, alright. I'll let you go, but you had better not roll in that porpoise again, or you're in for it!" As soon as she let Cocoa loose, the dog was gone in a flash, headed for the beach.

"Look over there," said one surfman to the other.

"What is that?" his companion asked.

"It's that horse and dog from the village. I wonder why they're just staring out into the darkness."

"The horse is always around when anyone is in danger, and the dog is always there to help him. They think they're in the lifesaving service," said the first surfman, and they both laughed. "I don't see a thing, do you?" he asked the other.

"No, but I'm sure they have a lantern lit at the top of the mast, even if they're rowing in this slack wind," answered the surfman.

Barnacle and Cocoa had settled on top of the nearest dune. Barnacle continued to scan the darkness while Cocoa settled near him, yawned, stretched, and faded off to sleep. The surfmen on the beach set up a watch rotation. One of them slept while the other scanned the horizon with a glass, looking for signs of light. The surfman in the tower was also on the lookout for any glimmer.

At about three o'clock, Barnacle began to make a fuss. He woke Cocoa, and she started barking, which woke up the sleeping surfman. "Do you see anything?" he asked the watchman.

"No, not a thing," the man replied.

"Well, evidently the horse thinks he sees something, and the dog is swearing to it," the surfman said. Then he headed to the station tower to find out if those men could see anything.

"Nothing yet," was the answer.

"Well, that horse is causing a ruckus over on the beach," the surfman said. "He sees or senses something."

"Wait a second," said the tower man. "I do see a small glimmer of light."

From offshore, the keeper and Barney spotted the light from the tower at about the same time. "Look to the southwest of us," Barney told the keeper. "There's a shore light."

"Yes, I see it," said Keeper Daniels as he turned his glass in the direction of the tiny, flickering light. "It's elevated a bit, and I'm pretty sure it's the tower lantern. Pull away, boys, hard to the southwest. We've got about five miles to go, I suspect."

It was nearly daylight when Barney and the keeper sighted the beach. The storm had left large waves that were breaking hollow and clean on the outside bar. "We have a load and not much freeboard," said Keeper Daniels. "We'll have to pick our chance carefully to get past this outside bar. If we're lucky we'll be able to catch one of these waves all the way to the beach, so when I give the word, I want you to row like you've never rowed before!"

⸙32⸙

OVERTURNED SURFBOAT

E dward was jarred awake by Barnacle's snorting and Cocoa's barking. When Edward walked outside, Barnacle was spinning around in circles, neighing. Cocoa was at the bottom of the steps with her chest touching the ground and her hind legs elevated, barking constantly. Then Barnacle started running back and forth between the gate and the porch.

"Alright, you two. I'll follow you, but first I need to wake Kristina. She'll never forgive me if we leave her," Edward told the animals.

Kristina got out of bed, and the four of them walked over to the beach. It was just turning daylight when they sighted the surfboat approaching the outer edge of the outside bar. The crew was rowing for all they were worth, trying to catch a huge wave as they crossed the bar. The wave rose up behind them and they tried to stay in front of it, but at the last second they were sucked up onto the crest.

The surfboat began to slide down the face, turning sharply to the right, before it rolled over and disappeared from sight into the tube of the wave. The boat turned over and over inside the large wave, tossing everyone and everything into the ocean. The men had life jackets on, and soon they all popped up into the top swash of the white water. The empty surfboat had righted itself and was way ahead of them, moving toward the beach.

Keeper Daniels yelled to Barney and Jason. "Get the injured man and the captain. I've got the other three, and we're fine," he said. Then he yelled to the rest of the crew and told them to swim toward the surfboat.

Barnacle and Cocoa took off from the beach and jumped into the ocean. They began swimming as fast as they could toward the men in the water. They swam past the inner bar, then the surfboat, and headed straight for the men who were floundering in the white water of the outer bar. When Keeper Daniels saw Barnacle, he shouted, "Over here, boy," as Barnacle swam toward him and the three sailors.

Keeper Daniels strapped the sailors to Barnacle and said, "Take 'em to the boat, boy." Upon command, Barnacle started swimming toward the surfboat. Jason grabbed Barnacle's tail as he swam by and hitched a ride to the surfboat, pulling the other injured sailor behind him. In the meantime, Cocoa was assisting Barney with the injured captain. The station crew members climbed into the surfboat first to help the victims into the boat. Keeper Daniels tied a rope around Barnacle's neck, then hoisted himself onto the surfboat and said, "Take us to the shore, boy."

Barnacle towed the surfboat to the beach as Cocoa swam beside him. When they reached the beach, everyone was there to help. The injured men were carried to the wagon first, followed by the other victims. Then a surfman took them to the station. The rest of the crew loaded the surfboat onto the wagon and headed back to the boathouse. Along the way, Keeper Daniels told Kristina that, if he could, he would recommend Barnacle for the Gold Lifesaving Medal. "So far as I know, it's only been awarded to men," he stated, "but if any animal ever deserved it, in my opinion, Barnacle does! He's truly a remarkable horse, absolutely obsessed with the well-being of mankind."

"I believe he's concerned with the well-being of all living things," Kristina added. "Even when I was a small child, he went everywhere with me. He always seemed to know when danger was near, and he protected us from harm. Somehow he always knows. Hazel thinks he's gifted, like some people are. He can visualize things before they actually happen."

After the gear was cleaned and stored, Keeper Daniels invited everyone for lunch at the station. During the meal he asked everyone to stay and discuss their individual parts in the save that had made the rescue a success. He wanted to be sure to include all the specifics in his official report to the lifesaving service, so he took very comprehensive notes, careful not to omit anything of importance.

Each man gave a personal account of his involvement in the operation, and when all were finished, the keeper asked Kristina if she would consider letting Barnacle officially join the lifesaving service as a patrol horse. He assured her that he could utilize Barnacle's talents in lifesaving activities without affecting their relationship.

"We won't have to change a thing or do anything differently," the keeper explained. Barnacle is at the beach with that dog every morning. All I have to do is assign a surfman to join him in our daily patrols, which will improve our beach coverage considerably. If you will agree, Barnacle will become a commissioned member of the Chicamacomico Lifesaving Service Beach Patrol System."

"How do I fit into this situation?" Kristina asked the keeper.

"I just want you to explain to Barnacle how his involvement will greatly improve our effectiveness," the keeper said.

"I'll consult Hazel and have an answer for you tomorrow," Kristina replied.

Early the next morning Kristina, Barnacle, and Cocoa went down to Cedar Hammock to see Hazel and get her opinion about Barnacle becoming part of the lifesaving service. Hazel listened to what Kristina had to say about the situation, and then she began to laugh. "What's so funny?" Kristina asked.

"You and that keeper think you have to ask Barnacle to be a part of the lifesaving service! In his mind, he's *in charge* of the lifesaving service, and all the surfmen work for him! You still don't realize the intelligence of this animal. He knows exactly what's going on all the time. You don't have to worry about telling him anything. Just always pay attention to him when he becomes excited, and try to figure out what he's saying to you. If you and that keeper will allow yourselves to follow Barnacle's lead, you'll not have to worry about many dangers that arise in everyday life." Then Hazel said, "I think you both have made a very good choice. Now all you have to do is follow Barnacle's lead!"

Kristina returned to the station in the afternoon and told Keeper Daniels what Hazel had said to her. "You know, I think she's right," the keeper said.

The very next morning, Barnacle and Cocoa headed for the beach just about daylight. Barney joined them on another mount, and they had a nice ride along the surf line. Barnacle took the trip to the south a couple of miles, then turned around and covered the same distance north. He stopped several times to scan the horizon and sniff the air, and when he was satisfied all was well, his crew returned to the station without incident.

And so it was. For the next few weeks, the conversation around the breakfast table at the station was buzzing about the newest beach patrol member and how he always conducted a very in-depth watch.

The weather was starting to turn cold as December approached. The holiday season was not far away, and the villagers were ready to celebrate. On the north end of the island, folks celebrated Christmas twice, once on the conventional date of December 25, and again on the first weekend in January. The Chicamacomico clan had adopted the week of January 6 to celebrate Old Christmas. Folks would decorate their dwellings and yards about two weeks before the twenty-fifth of December and leave the decorations in place until after the sixth of January.

For those who were new, Barney explained how the decorations were made from things that island living provided. Families would pack picnic lunches and take their sailing skiffs up and down the sound side, or they would hitch a horse up to their wagon and roam around in search of a Christmas tree of cedar or pine. This was always an outing of fun and excitement, especially for the little ones.

It was a warm, sunny day for December, and Barnacle had just returned from his beach patrol duties. When Kristina called for him, he came galloping up from the boathouse, with Cocoa was at his heels, barking and jumping around with excitement as usual. She ran up to Kristina and licked her hand.

"I don't have anything to eat," Kristina told Cocoa. "Mom will feed you before we leave. But I do have a surprise for you. We're going Christmas tree hunting today, and the Grays are going with us. Mom is packing lunch, and we're going to make a day of it! Mrs. Gray made her delicious fried chicken, Mom baked a ham, and we're going to do it up right! Stan is home for the holidays, so he'll be coming, too, along with your ol' buddy Tar." Then she spoke to Barnacle.

"Barnacle, you can bring your family along, too. It's about time we gave your son a name anyway. We're going to Cedar Hammock to look for a tree," she told her horse. "Hazel said there's a meadow there filled with some real nice ones. We'll get Hazel, Stan, and Shanna to help us come up with a name for your colt."

Edward and Beth loaded the wagon and hitched Barnacle. "Take us to the Grays', boy," Kristina said to Barnacle, and they were off. Cocoa ran out in front, barking and leading the way, and the mare and colt followed behind the wagon, on their way to meet up with the Grays. Along the way to Cedar Hammock, Tar joined Cocoa in checking every clump of grass and bush, sniffing as they went along, and Stan rode beside the wagon on his newly acquired Banker pony.

"I think it's truly amazing how Kristina asks Barnacle to take you folks to any destination and he just goes there, without the aid of a bridal or bit," said Mrs. Gray.

"That's not all," added Kristina. "Keeper Daniels trusts Barnacle's judgment and is so satisfied with his lifesaving skills that he made Barnacle an official member of the morning beach patrol! Barnacle is very special, and we have a very special relationship. He seems to be concerned about everyone he's around and tries his best to protect them from harm." Then everyone laughed when Kristina said, "I wonder if his talents include the ability to pick out nicely shaped Christmas trees?"

Hazel was waiting for them out near the wagon path so that they wouldn't try to cross the floating marsh. Then she led them farther south, to a meadow full of beautiful cedar trees. "This is the place I was telling you about," she explained. "We can stop the wagons in that clearing over there and set up our shade and table. Then we'll spread out our food. There's a freshwater pond for the horses, and grass just beyond that clump of bushes."

After their site was set up, Kristina, Shanna, and Hazel walked around the meadow looking at the trees. Kristina asked Hazel and Shanna to help her think of names for Barnacle's mare and colt.

"Well, there's always something special about each animal that will help you find a suitable name for them," Hazel answered. "Barnacle drifted in the sea so long, his name fits him perfectly. Cocoa and Tar are nicely named from their colors. Physical characteristics and mannerisms should also be carefully considered."

❧33❧

Christmas Celebration

Stan, Jason, Barney, and Edward took the wagon to the beach to pick up firewood so that they could roast the oysters Barney had caught. On their way out, Mrs. Gray asked them to gather shells, skate egg and conch shell cases, colored glass, pinecones, and anything else they thought would make nice Christmas decorations. Then she told Beth to save some eggs for the next few days. "We'll punch holes in the ends of 'em and get the insides out. Then we can paint the eggshells and make decorative balls to hang on our Christmas trees," she said.

After Kristina, Shanna, and Hazel returned from looking at trees, Hazel suggested that they all go to the clearing near the marsh and gather bayberries for candles, while the menfolk were gathering wood. Mrs. Gray suggested that they also collect some holly and yaupon berries to string together with needles and thread for more Christmas tree decorations. Then Hazel said, "I know just the place! Come on, and I'll show ya," she told them.

"We can all meet right back here, and the boys can build a fire. Then we'll have our midday meal and go pick out our Christmas trees," said Mrs. Gray, and they were off.

"Where did Barnacle and the dogs go?" asked Kristina.

"Where do you think?" answered Beth. "That beach is where Barnacle is, along with the dogs," she added.

The mare and colt followed behind Kristina and Shanna on their way to the marsh. "What did they do?" Shanna asked the ponies. "Leave you here when they went to the beach?" As Shanna stroked the mare's head, she answered with a low whinny and looked up at them with her big brown eyes. "Look," Shanna said. "Look how the mare's eyes twinkle when she looks at you."

"That's it!" said Kristina. "We'll name her Star! Her eyes twinkle like stars in the night sky!" she exclaimed. After they all agreed that Star was a fine name for the mare, Kristina said, "Now we need a name for the colt!"

Then Hazel said, "Give it some time and it will come, just as his mother's name did."

Coming from the beach, Barnacle, the dogs, and the guys were almost to the dividing line where the grass turns to sand when suddenly Old Scratchum appeared from the trees and stopped right in their path. Both dogs stopped and began to growl as the hair rose up on their backs.

"Here, Tar," Stan yelled. "You and Cocoa come get in the wagon. The last time Cocoa tangled with Old Scratchum, she didn't fair too well." Stan got out of the wagon and grabbed both dogs by their collars. He dragged them to the rear of the wagon, put them in it, and told them to stay. The dogs obeyed him and stayed put but continued to growl and hold their threatening postures. Old Scratchum stood his ground, too, pawing and scratching the dirt and shaking his head from side to side.

"I think he intends to charge the wagon," said Barney. When the crazy hog began his charge, Barnacle galloped in and kicked him in the side, sending Old Scratchum end over end. Before the beast recovered, Barnacle bit him on the back. Then Old Scratchum got to his feet and ran off into the safety of the bushes. As Barnacle maintained his stance between the wagon and the bushes, both dogs jumped out of the wagon and came to join him, barking ferociously. "Take that, Old Scratchum!" shouted Barney as they continued onward.

Stan called to the animals. "Come on," he said, "we still have a lot to do." The dogs obeyed, but Barnacle stood still until the wagon moved past him. Then he joined the dogs as they ran across the sand toward the surf. Shortly thereafter, they had enough wood for a fire and a nice assortment of things for making Christmas decorations.

"I think the girls will be happy with what we've collected, and I'm getting hungry," said Jason. "Let's go eat," he added as he turned the wagon toward the clearing. When they arrived, the ladies were setting the food out on the table, preparing for a picnic lunch. Jason and Barney started a fire to roast the oysters, while the girls waited to mix their berries with the shells and other beach things.

"We have a wagon full of materials to make decorations!" said Beth.

As they enjoyed their picnic lunch and oysters, Kristina informed everyone that the mare's name was Star, "after the twinkle in her eyes when she looks at you," Kristina told them. Everyone agreed that Star was a very fitting name for the mare. "Now we have to watch the colt and find a quality that will help us name him," Kristina said. "The colt is always full of energy, constantly romping with the dogs, and likes to be close to his mother at night." Everyone agreed, but no one came up with a name offhand.

Once they finished eating, they all headed out to gather their Christmas trees. The meadow was full of nicely shaped cedars, and a little farther away was a nice cluster of pine trees. "All in all, I think we need at least six Christmas trees," said Barney. "We need them for our homes, as well as the station, the church, and the schoolhouse," so they spent the rest of the afternoon picking out the best tree for each location. Then they loaded the trees on the wagon with the decorating materials and headed back home to Northard Woods.

"Keeper Daniels and the station's carpenter have volunteered to build stands for the trees and fasten them securely to the bottoms," said Jason.

"Well, then, we should take all the trees to the boathouse," answered Barney.

"And we'll take all the decorating materials to the schoolhouse, where there's plenty of room," added Mrs. Gray. "Mrs. Bridges wants to involve the schoolkids in the decorating process."

It was a cold, crisp December morning when Edward and Kristina went to the station to see Keeper Daniels. They arrived at the boathouse just as Barney, Barnacle, and Cocoa were returning from their morning beach patrol.

Christmas was two weeks away, and the holiday feeling was in the air. The ladies of the villages were busy in their kitchens, baking cakes, pies, cookies, and many other holiday treats, and everyone was excited about the upcoming festivities.

Barnacle ran over to Kristina and nibbled her hand, looking for a treat. "I don't have anything," she told Barnacle as she stroked his head. "I'll give you some apples later, and perhaps a sugar cube," she told her horse. Then, when Cocoa came running over for her pat on the head, Kristina asked, "Okay, girl, and how are you this morning? We've come over to see if Keeper Daniels has mounted the stand on the Christmas tree. We're ready to put it up in the front room," she told the dog. "We've made lots of decorations at the schoolhouse, and we're anxious to get going, if the tree's ready."

Keeper Daniels and the station carpenter had all the trees ready. The keeper asked Edward and Kristina to drop a tree off at the schoolhouse and the church on their way home. When they reached the schoolhouse, all the children ran out to greet them, eager to help with the tree.

"I hear you may be joining our staff next term," Mrs. Bridges said to Kristina.

"Perhaps, if Daddy decides to stay here and can find work. He's retiring from the shipping company in the spring," Kristina told her.

"That would really be nice," Mrs. Bridges replied. "Two elementary teachers are up for retirement," she said, winking. "When Shanna finishes her studies, hopefully she will be joining us also!" Then Mrs. Bridges said, "Bring the tree on in, and we'll place it up on the stage, where the children can decorate it later. Speaking of the children, I could really use some help with this year's church Christmas program. A couple of our teachers are off-islanders and are leaving to be with their families for the holidays. I'm hoping that you and Shanna will consider helping me. If we do a good job, and it's a success in the church, we'll perform it again at Old Christmas," the teacher added.

"I would love to help!" Kristina exclaimed. "I'm sure Shanna will be excited, too. When I see her later today, I'll ask her about it, and I'll let you what she says before nightfall."

That evening, Kristina asked Shanna about helping Mrs. Bridges with the program, and she eagerly agreed. Then the girls contacted Mrs. Bridges, and they began to put their plans into action. First they would take the children on a picnic to get acquainted. Then they would assign speeches and start practicing for the program.

Most of the children were making progress with their speeches, except for little Caleb Midgett, who was Miles Midgett's younger brother. The little fellow was scared to death to get on the stage and say his speech. All he had to say was "Merry Christmas," but each time he tried, he froze and was unable to utter a single word.

During dinner one night, Shanna told her family about the problem little Caleb was experiencing, no matter how much they coaxed him to say his speech. "He really wants to be in the show, but he freezes each time he walks across the stage," she told them.

"Make him a sign that reads 'Merry Christmas' with cardboard, glue, and glitter," said Stan. "Then fasten it to a stick and let him hold it up as he walks across the stage."

"Stan, you're a genius!" Shanna said and gave her brother a peck on the cheek. "Most of the time you aggravate the living life out of me, but this time you really came through!"

Little Caleb's problems were solved. Shanna made the sign, and everyone agreed that Caleb would probably be the star of the show. The practices went well as the children learned their speeches, and finally the program and the Nativity scene were ready.

In the early afternoon of Christmas Eve, Mrs. Bridges met Kristina and Shanna at the church. They had a few odds and ends to complete to be ready for the program that night. Stan, Miles, and a few of the boys had installed a curtain fashioned out of bedsheets, wire, and safety pins that could be opened and closed during the performance. Mrs. Bridges, Kristina, and Shanna stuffed small bags with several pieces of hard candy, one apple, and one orange each to be given out to everyone at the end of the program. The children had drawn names for the gift exchange, and each child had a present under the tree. Everything was ready for the big night.

The villagers began to arrive for the program just around dark. Edward, Beth, and Kristina arrived in their festively decorated wagon, pulled by Barnacle sporting a Christmas wreath around his neck. All of the villagers had decorated their wagons for the holidays with colored lanterns along the sides. The menfolk stayed outside discussing the weather and going over the fine points of each wagon's decorations until they were scolded by their wives to come inside the church.

Stan and Miles operated the curtain at the direction of Mrs. Bridges, and the program began. All the children got through their speeches without much difficulty. Little Caleb stole the show when he walked up and stopped at center stage, then held his sign up high and smiled. The boys closed the curtain, and the Nativity scene began as soon as everyone got into their places. All who attended jubilantly enjoyed the Christmas program.

At the end of the program, the wrapped presents were handed out to the children, and everyone received a small bag containing the candy and fruit. Mrs. Bridges thanked folks for coming and offered a special thanks to Kristina and Shanna for their work with the children, making the program possible. She also thanked Stan and Miles for their curtain work, and then turned the conclusion over to the preacher.

The preacher reminded everyone how lucky they were to have their health and the love of their families, as well as the fellowship they shared with their friends. He asked everyone to clasp hands as they sang "Silent Night," and then he dismissed them with a Christmas prayer. When the program was over, folks hugged each other, chatted a little longer, and then went to their wagons to wrap up in blankets and sing Christmas carols all the way home.

❧34❧

THE SNOWSTORM

Christmas dawned clear and cold, and the island children were already up, seeing what Santa had brought them. After they opened their own presents, they would visit each others' homes to see what their friends got for Christmas. There were many homemade toys, such as small wooden wagons and boats, as well as baby buggies and other mail-order toys from Sears Roebuck and Company.

After a morning of visiting and fellowship, everyone looked forward to their family Christmas dinners. Turkey, wild goose, boiled drum, ham, sweet potatoes, pone bread, and all types of baked desserts would be enjoyed by every household. The head of the home would ask the Christmas blessing to thank God for the love of family and friends, for the blessings of the past year, and for taking care of everyone in the coming year. A final request would be to bless the hands that prepared the food for the nourishment of the physical bodies. Then everybody would say, "Amen." The younger folks would be wringing their hands and twisting with anticipation of the upcoming feed, thinking that the blessing would never end. If there was anyone who was alone for any reason, the islanders would provide a way for them to join in the fellowship of celebrating Christmas.

Barnacle, Cocoa, and Barney were relaxing at the boathouse after their big Christmas dinner, and Keeper Daniels joined them. The keeper noticed clouds racing across the sky at a very high altitude on such a clear day. "I think we're in for a spell of bad weather," he told Barney. "Notice how Barnacle is very fidgety and nervous today? He's prancing around in an excited manner and can't seem to get settled in any one place. Perhaps we should check the long-range weather reports on the wireless," so they went to the station where their fears were confirmed. There was a winter storm brewing with a cold air mass racing down from the Canadian Maritimes, and a mass of Gulf moisture coming up the coast from the south. The center of the low was forming near South Carolina, headed up the Eastern Seaboard.

All stations were placed on a winter storm alert. "We have to warn the villagers," said Keeper Daniels. Then he instructed the wireless operator to send the information on up the line, and soon the word was out. Everyone began to gather extra wood and prepare their dwellings for the upcoming winter storm. As the low-pressure area came up the coast, the warm, moist air mass collided with the frigid air from the north, creating a massive snowstorm.

As the snowstorm approached the island, a high-pressure area drifted across the Virginia capes and stalled, blocking the low from proceeding northward. It snowed Saturday night and all day on Sunday, and some of the drifts were waist-high. The wind blew thirty knots from the northwest, then shifted to the northeast and blew just as hard. The temperature then dropped and the sound froze solid as far as the eye could see; it stayed frozen for days. Finally, the high-pressure area began to weaken and drift to the northeast, out to sea, followed by the low. As the bad weather cleared, everyone hurried outside to evaluate the situation.

Blizzards were rare on the island, and folks were not equipped for such harsh winter weather conditions. They struggled to dig paths and to care for their animals. Their wagons were of no use in so much deep snow, and the boats could not transport supplies, so everything basically came to a standstill. Keeper Daniels sent word around for the menfolk to meet at the station. Plans had to be made to clear the snow between people's homes and establish a line of communication with the families that lived outside the villages.

All the menfolk who could get to the station met with Keeper Daniels and the crew. Norman Scarborough told the keeper that he had seen an old sleigh in a barn at Aaron Hooper's house. "Then we'll need to figure out a way to get to Clarks as soon as possible to determine if the sleigh is usable," announced the keeper.

"How in the world are we going to get to Clarks in this deep snow?" asked several of the men.

Keeper Daniels replied, "I believe Barnacle will be able to get us there. He's much larger and stronger than the Banker ponies we have." Then he told Jason, "Either you or Barney can ride him there, since he trusts both of you."

"Okay, I'll go to the corral and make ready," answered Jason as he headed out the door. However, he returned quickly to inform the keeper that Barnacle was nowhere to be found.

"Now, where did he go?" sighed the keeper. "Just when we need him, he takes off somewhere."

"Listen," said Barney. "I hear a dog barking over on the beach." Then they saw a large sleigh headed their way.

"Would you look at that!" said Keeper Daniels. Sitting in the sleigh were Cocoa and Aaron Hooper, as Barnacle pulled them toward the corral. "How did you know to bring that sleigh?" the keeper hollered.

"I didn't," answered Aaron. "That fool horse and dog showed up on my front porch and wouldn't leave until I followed them. The horse went straight to my barn, and I thought he wanted some grain or hay. But when I opened the door, he went straight to this old sleigh. Then I hitched him up to the harness, but before I could bridle him, he took off! I had to run and jump into the sleigh and grab the pooch by her scruff. Barnacle headed straight up the beach in the deep snow and frozen sand, and we made good time, because he never stopped until we got here."

"Well, what do you know about that!" Keeper Daniels said. "We were just looking for Barnacle to help us reach you to see about the sleigh! Here he's already cleared a path to the beach and brought you back with the sleigh. Plus he's shown us the best way to travel along the surf line, where the snow is packed hard, almost like a road. Now we can check on the isolated families that live outside the villages. I believe Old Hazel about that horse. He's incredible!"

While the grown-ups were taking care of business, the young folks were having a heyday. There were massive snowball fights, and everyone had at least one snowman, snowwoman, or some sort of snow sculpture in their yard. The snow was soft and powdery, perfect for snow cream.

Everyone loved snow cream whenever there was enough snow to make it. They would mix up their favorite recipe for homemade ice cream and place the mixing pan outside to chill. Then they would fold in the snow to a desired consistency. It was important to make sure the mixing pan was very cold to prevent ice from forming in the snow cream. The end result was always a smooth, heavenly treat.

Once the line of communication was established and everyone had been contacted about the storm, Barnacle and Cocoa went out to join in the fun. The young folks had made sleds out of anything they could find, including old boards covered with bits of sail canvas. Then they headed for the beach to slide down the hills. Barnacle, Cocoa, and Tar romped and played in the deep snowdrifts while Stan, Shanna, Kristina, and friends had a day full of fun. Back to the station, they started a massive snowball fight that eventually included some grown-ups.

According to the villagers, snowstorms like this one only occurred along the coast about every ten years, when conditions were just right. The snow made things tough on folks for a couple of days, but it also brought a lot of fun. People helped one another however they could. Then the weather cleared, and out popped the sun. Soon only small patches of snow were left on the dunes, in spots that were shaded from the direct sunlight, and then the rain came and washed the snow away.

The weather remained mild but cold until the end of December. The villagers celebrated the New Year by shooting their shotguns on New Year's Eve at the stroke of midnight. The next day, they ate black-eyed peas and hot cheese biscuits in order to start the year off right. According to the villagers and local tradition, if you ate black-eyed peas on New Year's Day, you would have good luck in the coming year!

Of course, there were always New Year resolutions to be made, like promises to wives by their husbands to give up bad habits, such as drinking. Normally the promises only lasted until the next reason to celebrate. A few resolutions were made with good intentions, and some people benefitted from their life-changing experiences. However, most resolutions would last for just a few days and life would continue on without much change.

The first week of January was slipping by, and soon it would be Old Christmas. There were many activities planned, and everybody hoped the weather would be mild so that they could keep on celebrating. The kids would be repeating the same Christmas program that they had performed at church on Christmas Eve, with the same Nativity scene and the same speeches, right down to little Caleb Midgett and his Christmas greeting sign.

On the day before Old Christmas Eve, the largest domestic bull would be loaded down with hard candy and fruit. Then the bull would begin his journey throughout the northern villages to visit every child's house and pass out the bounty. People would always join in the journey, and soon there would be a large crowd of folks walking along, singing Christmas carols, and enjoying fellowship with friends and neighbors.

As was the custom, the Old Christmas celebration started at noon, on Old Christmas Eve, with outside activities for everyone. The men enjoyed the oyster shoot, which was handled just like a turkey shoot, except the prizes were bushels of oysters. Hot dogs and hamburgers were served for lunch, and the outside activities continued until dark. The children's Christmas program was enjoyed by all, and at the very end Santa came into the room with gifts, stirring up more Christmas cheer than the stewed chicken and pie-bread dinner they would soon eat.

After dinner, the traditional oyster roast would begin, where many New Year resolutions would be broken by the consumption of Old Christmas cheer. Most of the women with small children would head home around midnight, along with some of the old folks. After midnight the main floor would be cleared of tables and chairs, and a local band would make ready for the dance that would finish up the celebration. The young folks would dance into the wee hours of the morning. Every once in a while, a disagreement would bring a lot of pushing and shoving, and sometimes a punch would find its mark, but usually the bystanders quickly broke up these scuffles. Then folks would shake hands and keep dancing.

Most all of the Old Christmas celebrations would end on a positive note, although the rumors the next day would have as many as a dozen people with broken bones and major injuries. The after-the-fact news of the scuffles made good conversation around potbellied stoves, multiplying in size and intensity until word of a brawl was circulating around the island in the distant villages. These instances reminded everyone that a good word about anything is soon forgotten, and a bad word about anything only gets worse each time it is visited.

"Long live the celebrators of Old Christmas," the villagers said.

❧35❧

EASTER BASKETS

Just before school started, Mrs. Bridges received letters from the off-island teachers stating that they had decided to give up their teaching positions and would not be back. She immediately contacted Shanna and Kristina to see if they would be willing to fill in for the remainder of the current school year until the school board hired new teachers. Both girls agreed to accept the temporary positions and looked forward to working with the kids.

Every morning Kristina would hitch Barnacle to the wagon, once he and Cocoa returned from beach patrol, and they would head off to school after they stopped to pick up Shanna. One morning the colt was darting in and out of the bushes, nipping at Barnacle's feet as they went along. Barnacle scolded him a couple of times and then playfully nipped back at him. The colt was almost as tall as his father now.

"Look," said one of the small girls riding in the wagon with them. "He's quicker than a lightning flash! See how he nips the heels of the big horse and then gets away before he gets nipped?"

"What did you call him?" Kristina asked the little girl.

"I said that he's as quick as a lightning flash," repeated the girl with a smile.

"That's it! We will call him Flash! You just helped me name the colt," Kristina told the little girl. "He is as fast as lightning!" she proclaimed, and from that day on, Barnacle's son became known as Flash.

The long winter began to give way to spring, and the sand hills were turning green with new grass. The wildflowers in the marshes and meadows began to bloom, and the island was transforming into a warm-weather paradise. The schoolchildren were feeling the effects of the warm weather, too, and were absolutely busting at the seams to get outside. After having been cooped up during the cold winter months, they had become much harder to manage.

One Friday, Mrs. Bridges met with Kristina and Shanna after school. "Thank goodness next week is Easter," she said to them. "We have school on Monday and Tuesday, and then we're off for the rest of the week. I wanted to talk to you girls about helping me plan a picnic and Easter egg hunt for the children. The weather has warmed early this year, and from all indications it's supposed to be favorable next week for the event. Since you two have the primary classes, I thought you could plan some fun and games for them, and prepare them for the egg hunt. We'll have the hunt behind the church, since there's a very large meadow there and plenty of places to hide the eggs.".

Kristina and Shanna sent notes home with their students, asking the parents to help their children decorate six boiled eggs for Easter, and send them to the church by nine o'clock on Wednesday morning. They also helped each child weave a basket with a handle to carry their eggs once they found them. The baskets were made from large blades of grass that the students had gathered earlier that day from the cattail plants growing behind the school.

When the big day came, the children brought their lunches, eggs, and Easter baskets. While they played with Shanna and Kristina, Mrs. Bridges and some of the parents hid the eggs in clumps of grass, crooks of bushes, and other such places behind the church. The children had so much fun searching for the eggs, and when all eggs were found, the adults divided them equally among the children. Then everyone finished their picnic lunches, said their good-byes, and headed home singing "Here Comes Peter Cottontail."

Flash was always getting into trouble. He was young and full of mischief, always involved where he didn't belong. Every chance he got, he went running with the Banker ponies and would stay gone for days, which worried the life out of his mother, Star. She would spend hours looking for him in the marshes and the meadows, while Barnacle was occupied with lifesaving duties. Barnacle would often have to go find Flash and force him to return home.

On one particular moonlit night, a group of young Banker ponies were passing to the east of the corral, along the surf line. The pounding of their hooves sounded like approaching thunder. Flash was the first to awaken to the sound of the ponies, and he began to nervously pace around inside the corral. Star tried to calm him and Barnacle began to scold him, but he ran to the back of the corral, then came charging to the front as if he was going to jump over the fence. Barnacle knew his colt could not clear the top of the fence because he could barely jump it himself!

Flash pulled up short on his first attempt, but tried again. This time, his rear hooves scraped the top rail, sending him sprawling to the ground outside the corral. True to his name, Flash was up in a flash, and then he took off to find the ponies. Barnacle had to go to the rear of the corral, to get up enough speed to jump the fence. He headed to the surf line, but when he got there, the young ponies were almost out of sight to the north. Barnacle followed for a short distance, then returned to the corral with Star, and they settled down for the night.

Flash liked running with a younger group of wild Banker ponies. He liked to explore the northern portion of the island, where there was plenty of fresh water and good grazing, without any dominant stallions or fussy mares to keep him in line. Barnacle completely understood the sensations that Flash was feeling. He recalled his younger days of running carefree, grazing on the sweetest of grass, running all night, and sleeping all day. This was how he had met Star. Now he was trying to calm Star and convince her that Flash just needed to run, and that he would be fine.

Barney was on watch in the tower when his eye caught movement way down the beach toward the south. He picked up the long glass and focused it in the direction of the movement. Much to his surprise, the largest herd of Banker ponies he had ever seen was headed up the surf line in a northward direction. He called down to Jason and said, "Find the keeper and ask him to come up for a look!"

Barney, Jason, and Keeper Daniels took turns looking at the herd through the glass.

"I've never seen so many of those ponies on the move at the same time, all headed in the same direction. Something is definitely up," the keeper told them. "Better alert the villagers and see if we can figure this out. When that many animals are on the move, it could mean a number of things, and sometimes the reasons are not all good."

Soon the area was lined with village folks watching the ponies walk by. The horses were in a single file, bobbing their heads, in no apparent rush. They were headed up the surf line in the same direction that the young stallions and Flash had gone. This group of ponies contained old stallions, mares of all ages, and young colts, and it seemed the line of ponies would never end.

"Have you ever seen that many ponies together?" Edward asked Keeper Daniels.

"Never," was the keeper's reply.

"Where are they going?" asked Kristina.

"I don't know that either," responded the keeper. Then they heard Barnacle call from the corral.

"You should let him out or he'll jump over," Edward told Kristina.

"He won't leave Star," Kristina replied.

"He'll kick a rail out of the fence to let her out if he takes a notion," the keeper said. "Our best chance of finding out what's going on with the ponies is through Barnacle and Star. They're usually a big part of whatever is happening," so Kristina let them out of the corral. As Barnacle approached the ponies, they stopped instantly and allowed him to take the lead. With Star following closely behind, Barnacle led the herd on up the surf line.

"Did you see the Raven among those ponies?" asked Kristina.

"If he was, I never set eyes on him, which is very strange," said Keeper Daniels. "The Raven is an extremely dominant male and is serious about his leadership role among the Banker ponies. Barnacle is the only stallion that has ever backed him down. Now the herd accepts Barnacle as their leader whenever he is with them, and even the Raven follows him without question. The fact that the Raven is not with them could have something to do with why such a massive herd is on the move. They must be headed up near the New Inlet Meadows. It's the only place with enough grazing and fresh water to support that many horses."

Edward replied, "I think we should go and see exactly what they're up to."

"The weather conditions are favorable for the next couple of days, but at this particular time I can't spare any men for the trip," said the keeper. "With the warm weather coming on, we have a ton of maintenance work to do around the station."

Edward responded, "Both Kristina and Shanna have a couple of days off, and I believe Stan is home for Easter. Perhaps a camping trip is in order. I think I'll go to Cedar Hammock and see if Hazel wants to come along."

When Edward discussed the camping trip with the Grays, Stan and Shanna got excited about sleeping under the stars for a couple of nights. Edward and Kristina left for Cedar Hammock the very next morning in a sixteen-foot sprit sailor that Edward had purchased. Hazel spotted them on their shoreward tack about mid-morning and greeted them at the landing behind her house. "What brings you folks down here this time of day?" she asked. When Edward and Kristina told her about the herd of horses, she said, "This movement of Banker ponies took place yesterday?"

"Yes," Edward told her.

"Come to think of it, some of my stock was acting kind of funny all afternoon," Hazel said. "That young mare I just purchased from Aaron Hooper kicked the top rail off the corral and ran off yesterday, and I haven't seen her since. I had to hurry to fix the rail or the rest of my stock would have gotten loose, too." Then she said, "You are staying for dinner, I hope," as she took salt mullet from a stone crock. "I'll soak this fish and fry it up with some stewed potatoes. After we eat we'll plan our trip to see what's up with those ponies. We'll need to think about our every move, as well as the food and gear we will need to take to complete our quest," she added.

"One of us will have to bring the girls back on Sunday, before dark. They have school on Monday," Edward told Hazel, "but Stan is off all next week, so the rest of us can stay up in the meadows with him."

"I'll pack my big tent. It will sleep all of us," Hazel replied.

Then Edward told Kristina that they needed to head home. "It gets cold early in the evening this time of year," he said. "After all, it's only April."

"I'll walk down to the landing and see you off," said Hazel.

The wind was kicking up from the southwest as Edward and Kristina pushed off. They waved to Hazel as she hollered, "I'll see you bright and early tomorrow morning. Make sure you are up and ready to go!"

"We'll be ready and raring to go alright!" answered Kristina as she and her father pulled away.

Edward made a small tack to the south to get offshore, and then he turned the skiff northward. They had a fair wind all the way home and made good time getting back to Northard Woods. On their way home from the landing, they met up with Stan and Shanna, who were excited about the camping trip. They asked about Hazel.

"She's coming with us," Kristina told them.

"Good," said Shanna. "I love to hear her stories around a fire at night, about how life used to be 'way back when.'"

"We all need to get a good night's rest. We have a very big day tomorrow," said Edward.

❖36❖

BULL SHARKS

Before light the next morning, Hazel pushed her skiff off the beach behind her cottage and moved out to deep water with the shove stick. The evening before, after Kristina and Edward left for Northard Woods, she had contacted Norman Scarborough and asked him to care for her stock until she returned. She had packed her skiff with large pieces of canvas for a tent, dry goods, canned food, fishing gear, and her double-barrel shotgun with an ample supply of shells. She raised the sail and took off in the southwest wind toward Northard Woods, feeling prepared for whatever they might come across in the New Inlet area.

At the station, Barney helped Edward, Kristina, Stan, and Shanna put their gear in the wagon, then he took them to the landing. He helped them load their gear in their skiff, and just before Edward pushed off, Barney handed him a pump-action shotgun and a couple of boxes of shells. "Keeper Daniels told me to give this to you," he said, "just in case you need it."

Edward, Stan, and the girls met up with Hazel on the outer edge of the reef and struck sail for a conference. After deciding that Kristina and Shanna would ride with Hazel, while Stan remained with Edward, they raised sail again and moved briskly along in the early-morning twilight. Kristina and Shanna talked for a little while but soon settled beneath the canvas on blankets and were lulled fast to sleep by the sound of the rippling water. Both skiffs tacked offshore in order to get around the shallow water near North Hammock Bay.

A few days before the mass movement of the Banker ponies, the Raven had gathered a few of the younger stallions and led them north to check out the spring grazing grounds of New Inlet Bay. When they passed the corral at Chicamacomico, Flash had joined them, followed by Barnacle and Star soon after. When they reached the meadows, they saw the small island full of rich saltwater grass in the middle of the inlet. A couple of the younger stallions started to plunge into the water to head for the grass, but the Raven forced them to remain on shore.

The Raven knew he would need a large supply of fresh water in order to support the sizable herd of Bankers headed to the area. When he found the right spot he settled his small group for the night. Suddenly, in the middle of the night, he was awakened by a panic-filled scream for help. One of the young stallions had ventured out toward the island and was in belly-deep water screaming at the top of his lungs. The Raven rushed to his aid and found the water around him red with blood.

As soon as the Raven entered the water, he felt extreme pain in his legs and hips. The water was churning and thrashing with small bull sharks, and they were taking softball-sized chunks from him with repeated bites. All the commotion woke the sleeping horses, and many of them started toward the water, but they stopped short when the Raven scolded them. Unsure of what to do next, they watched the Raven pull the smaller stallion up onto the newly discovered island and collapse onto the sand.

Both horses had suffered attacks from several sharks. They were too weak to stand, and they were losing a lot of blood. In order to control some of the bleeding, the Raven rolled over to coat his wounds with sand. Then he kicked sand over the smaller stallion to reduce his blood loss as well. He tried to calm the younger horse and prevent him from thrashing around. The less they moved, the less they would bleed. As they remained there, helpless, the blood from their wounds trickled back into the inlet, exciting the waiting sharks.

It was nearly dawn when Hazel spotted the white sands of New Inlet Bay and motioned to Edward to strike sail. They brought the boats alongside each other and decided to paddle in the rest of the way. The tide was going out, and as they slid along at a good clip, Kristina and Shanna could hear Stan hollering at them to wake up. As they came out from under the canvas, still wrapped in blankets, he yelled, "We can see the inlet, and we'll be there soon!"

"Boy, it's chilly this morning," Shanna said.

"When do we eat breakfast?" asked Stan.

"As soon as we get ashore," Edward replied. "You kids go gather some wood and build a fire while Hazel and I set up the big tent."

After the skiffs were beached and the anchors were set, Stan, Kristina, and Shanna hurried off to find wood for the fire. They ran up the crest of the bank, and on the other side of the dune, the meadows were full of Banker ponies, as far as they could see. Shanna ran quickly to tell Edward and Hazel about the ponies, while Stan and Kristina continued toward them.

As they neared the ponies, Stan noticed the commotion at the water's edge. Then they saw Barnacle running up and down the beach, kicking constantly in the shallow water. He tried several times to enter the inlet but retreated each time to the shallows of the bank. On one of his attempts he kicked a four-foot bull shark up onto the sand. The shark jumped and squirmed its way back until the water was deep enough to escape into the channel.

"Look!" said Stan. "Do you see Barnacle's hooves? They're bloody!"

"My golly," Kristina replied. "Why in the world do you think Barnacle is messing with those sharks like that?"

"I see why," Stan responded as he pointed ahead. "Look out on that little island, in the center of the inlet." Then Kristina saw the two horses lying close to the water's edge.

"Those horses have been bitten and are bleeding badly. That's the Raven," she told Stan. Then she gasped in horror. "And that's Flash, lying there beside him!" she exclaimed. Barnacle was jumping at the water's edge with Star nervously pacing the shore behind him.

Kristina told Stan to make sure Barnacle stayed out of the water while she ran for help. She was completely out of breath when she reached her father, Hazel, and Shanna. "Slow down," Edward said, "so that we can understand you. Breathe slowly and tell us exactly what you saw." As soon as Kristina explained the situation to them, they all took off running to go help Stan with the horses.

When they reached the shore side, Hazel told Kristina to stay with Barnacle and keep him out of the water. "He's not badly injured," she said. "I'll unload my skiff and come straight back here to pick you up. Then we'll cross the channel and see to the Raven and Flash. Once we determine the extent of their injuries, we'll try our best to treat them."

"In the meantime, the kids and I will begin to set up camp and build a fire," said Edward.

As Hazel was returning to the inlet, Kristina was trying her best to calm Barnacle and Star, but as she approached the shore, Barnacle tried to get inside her skiff. Knocking Hazel's things around, he almost flipped the boat. "No, Barnacle! You'll sink the skiff!" said Kristina. It was all she and Hazel could do to keep him from trying to board the small sailboat.

"I'll have to go get Shanna to stay with Barnacle so that we can cross the channel," Kristina told Hazel. Then she ran over the dune and quickly returned with Shanna, but when Kristina and Hazel boarded the skiff, Barnacle followed them into the water. Hazel used an oar to protect him from an approaching bull shark.

"We'll have to change our plan," Hazel told the girls. "Kristina, you stay here with Barnacle or else he'll keep trying to follow us over. Shanna can come with me to treat Flash and the Raven."

Shanna and Hazel pushed off while Kristina stayed with Barnacle and Star. In a very short time, they pulled the skiff up on the sand of the small island, as the bull sharks busily circled around in the channel. Shanna and Hazel set the anchor and ran over to the injured horses. Both animals were very weak from blood loss. "At least they've coated their wounds with sand to slow the bleeding," Hazel told Shanna. At first glance, it appeared that most of their injuries were on their legs and hips. "I don't believe any organs are damaged, but they have lost a lot of blood. We'll have to clean their wounds, then salve and wrap them."

One by one, they cleaned the horses' wounds, put salve on them, and wrapped them with bandages. "Both animals are too weak to stand," Hazel said, "and we need to get some water into them. Go to the skiff and get a bottle of water, the funnel, and the long rubber tube, and bring them back for me," Hazel told Shanna. When she had done as Hazel requested, Hazel said, "Now straddle Flash's neck and hold him as still as possible."

Hazel gently placed the tube in Flash's mouth and pushed it to the back of his throat. Then she put the funnel in the opposite end of the tube and poured water in it for Flash to swallow. They repeated this process with the Raven to rehydrate him also. Then Hazel headed back across the inlet to discuss the situation with Kristina and Edward, while Shanna remained with Flash and the Raven on the small island.

Hazel told Kristina and Edward how she and Shanna had rehydrated the horses. "Now we have to get some food in them, even though they are both too weak to chew," she told them. "We'll have to cook broth and continue feeding them through the tube, to strengthen them until they can graze again. As soon as they can stand steady enough, we'll build a raft and bring them back over here. The sharks will leave as soon as the fresh blood stops leaking into the water. Then their frenzy will be over," she told them.

Later, when Hazel got to the camp, Stan and Edward already had a fire going and were cooking a broth of saltwater grass and ground grain, with a little molasses for taste. Then Hazel returned to the island and fed the horses with Shanna's help. That evening, they set up a small tent and spent the night next to the Raven and Flash. Across the inlet, Kristina had set up next to Barnacle and Star to keep them from trying to get to Flash, although the sharks had already disappeared.

Early the next morning, Edward and Stan began to collect wood to build a raft, and they got lucky when they also found two empty pork barrels to use for floats. They built the raft near the water's edge and lashed the barrels to the sides. Then Hazel towed it to the small island and tied it off. Flash was holding his head up and showing signs of wanting to stand. Assisted by his motivation, Shanna and Hazel were able to get Flash onto the raft, and Barnacle pulled him back across the inlet. As soon as Flash got off the raft, he slumped down in the sand, where his mother licked his face and his father lifted his mane. Together, Barnacle and Star were soon able to get Flash over to the soft grass of the meadow, where he could eat some fresh grass shoots, drink fresh water, and lie down. Then they settled down near him, and they rested.

Kristina and Edward hurried off to help the others get the Raven onto the raft, and Stan used a second horse to help pull them back over. Kristina rode on the raft with the Raven to keep him calm. He was bleeding more severely again, from moving around, and two sharks were circulating the raft. It would be all they could do to take care of the Raven. He was still very weak and would have to be fed with the funnel and tube for quite a while. At best, they were all together and could take turns caring for the injured horses.

"I'll remain with the horses for a few more days," Hazel said. "I know you girls have to get back to school, and Stan has to report for duty on Monday. Y'all can leave tomorrow, and hopefully Edward will come back to get me in about a week. Also, if you'll please make sure to see Norman Scarborough and let him know to watch after my place for another week, I'd sure appreciate it."

At first Kristina protested. She did not want to leave Hazel by herself, but she had to leave, and she wanted Barnacle and Star to come with her.

"You know they won't leave Flash," Hazel said.

"How long will it take before he can travel?" asked Kristina.

"Both Flash and the Raven should be able to stand and graze in about a week," Hazel answered. "That's when I plan to leave them—in a week, when your dad comes. They'll be fine in the safety of the herd until they decide to travel at summer's end."

"No way," said Kristina. "My three will return to their wild ways by then!"

"Remember what I taught you," Hazel reminded her.

❦37❦

The Long Recovery

The next morning dawned a crisp April Sunday, hazy and cold. Edward, Stan, Kristina, and Shanna boarded the sprit sailing skiff, waved good-bye to Hazel, and pushed off. Standing out on a long point of marsh, Barnacle watched from the edge of the water and Kristina stared back until they sailed out of each other's sight. Then Barnacle returned to Star and Flash.

"Don't worry," Hazel assured Barnacle. "You'll see them soon, when Flash is fit for traveling."

Edward struck sail and paddled into the creek at Northard Woods Landing by lunchtime. The foursome parted ways, breaking the silence only to bid each other good-bye, and returned to their cottages. At home, Beth had made a hot lunch and was full of questions. She wanted to know all about the camping trip, and if they had figured out why such a large herd of horses had traveled north. When Kristina said she did not feel well and asked to be excused, her father told her to go and get some rest, and that he would tell Beth all about their adventure. As they settled by the potbellied stove, Edward gave his wife a detailed account of what had happened at New Inlet. Then Beth went to Kristina and said, "You don't have anything to worry about. Barnacle loves you very much. He will return to you."

"He has a lot more to think about now," Kristina told her mother. "As long as Flash is injured, Barnacle and Star will not leave him. Also, Barnacle knows that the Raven is not in any shape to lead the herd right now, so he feels those responsibilities, too. If he spends the summer with the Bankers, who knows if he will ever be satisfied to return here? Summer is the only time I have to spend with him, so if Barnacle stays up there, I'll just have to go spend the summer with the herd."

"Up there? With a bunch of wild horses? This is certainly something we will have to discuss with your father," Beth replied.

"Daddy will not only let me go, he'll go with me," Kristina said with a smile.

"Oh, I don't know so much about that," her mother retorted. "Your father received a telegram from the shipping company while y'all were gone. They want him to return to Baltimore to discuss what they consider to be a very good offer for him. He's reading the telegram now, so we should soon know what it's all about."

Hazel fed Flash and the Raven for the next three days. Flash was now able to stand, move around, and go on very short runs. His wounds were healing nicely, but the Raven's progress was considerably slower than Flash's. The herd was restless. They had eaten most of the new grass in the upper meadows, so Barnacle took part of the herd to the middle meadows, which had ample grass and water. Hazel and three mares remained with the Raven until he could stand and hobble along slowly with the other horses.

When Hazel was satisfied that the Raven could get up and down without help, and that all his injuries had scabbed over, she packed her gear and headed south, stopping in Northward Woods long enough to inform everyone that the Banker ponies were up and moving on their own. Many of the village folks had questions about the movement of the ponies, but Hazel explained that she was in a hurry to return to her home and her animals, and didn't want to take advantage of her good friend Norman any longer.

Edward had received word from his shipping company in Baltimore about a possible job as wreck commissioner, to be stationed on the Outer Banks of North Carolina. His company would be handling the salvage of all shipwrecks in the area on a contractual basis. He would have to travel to Baltimore to be officially set up in this new position, but he wouldn't have to ship out anymore.

The job would involve some travel, but nothing like before. The meeting to discuss the position was scheduled for the beginning of summer, so the family made plans to go to Baltimore as soon as Kristina finished the school year.

Kristina was concerned about Barnacle, his family, and the Banker ponies. "They'll be here when you get back," her father told her, but she protested, lamenting that she hadn't seen them or had any contact with them since their camping trip during Easter vacation. It was almost June, and no one had seen hide nor hair of Barnacle or any of the Banker ponies. "They're enjoying their summer grazing grounds," Edward assured her. "They'll come back near the middle of summer, just as you're returning home."

"But I need to see them before we leave," Kristina said.

"That may be impossible, but let's do this," her father said. "Since Mrs. Bridges and the school board have offered you and Shanna full-time positions next year, let's ask Shanna to come to Baltimore with us. Then the two of you can go shopping in the city for the upcoming school year."

"That's a very good idea," agreed Beth. "Let's go see Shanna now," she told her daughter, and the two of them headed to the Grays' house.

Barnacle was looking after the Banker herd, trying to keep up with Flash and Star, and helping the Raven whenever possible. As soon as the Raven was able to resume his responsibilities as leader of the herd, Barnacle would return home with his family. One afternoon as they were grazing near the sound side, Barnacle noticed a sailing vessel heading for shore. He thought, at first, that it might be Hazel returning to check on them, but he soon realized that the vessel was much larger than Hazel's skiff.

The tide was still ebbing, and the vessel had dropped anchor short of the mouth of the inlet. Then several small boats had been loaded into the water. This activity alarmed Barnacle, so he circled the herd and started leading them southward. The Raven was almost healed and was able to trot at a slow pace, so Barnacle moved the herd as fast as the Raven could go. They didn't stop until they were several miles from the inlet, with ample cover for them to hide.

Once the herd was safe, Barnacle selected several of the younger stallions, including Flash, to accompany him back to the inlet to investigate the approaching boats. Flash felt very good that he had been chosen for this mission, not knowing that he was asked to come so that Barnacle could keep a close and watchful eye on him. They arrived at the inlet just after dark, and Barnacle quickly realized exactly what was going on. In short order the men were unloading supplies and had begun to construct a temporary corral and catch pens.

Barnacle knew he would have to move the horses far away—to a place where no one would expect them to be. Slowly the scout horses crept back to the herd and began their journey south, under the cover of darkness, as fast as the Raven could travel. The next day, Barnacle settled them down behind some heavy brush just on the outskirts of Northard Woods. While the horses rested, Barnacle pondered a safe place where they could spend the summer undetected and safe from poachers. Then, all of a sudden, the answer came to him. Clarks Island would be a perfect place! Far enough from the sound side, it had ample water and grass, and plenty of cover. They could stay out of sight in the daytime and feed at night. Barnacle knew that, if they were careful, they could enjoy the summer there and not be bothered. He needed to get the herd down the island, just south of Clarks, without leaving signs of their trail.

Barnacle was in luck. On the very next day the wind shifted from the northeast and blew nearly gale force, causing the sound water to be very shallow in the Clarks area. That night, Barnacle moved the entire herd along the sound side, from Northard Woods to Clarks, not even a hundred yards from shore. The sound was almost dry and the sand was packed, making for easy travel. Since Clarks Island was about two miles out in the sound, the only important challenge they faced was getting across Clarks Channel, which had a few muddy spots near the center.

Very carefully, Barnacle made sure all the ponies got across the channel. Most waded through water deep enough to cover their necks, while some of the smaller ponies had to swim a short distance. Soon they were all safely concealed on the marshy banks of Clarks Island. With fresh water in three large ponds and four meadows for grazing, Barnacle hoped the herd could remain on the island until the Raven was completely healed and the poachers were no longer a threat. When the wind fell off, the sound water would return to its normal levels and cover all evidence of their trip to Clarks Island. Barnacle would allow small groups of ponies to cross over to the beach hills at night, but insisted that they return before daylight to keep their location secret and secluded.

Kristina was excited about taking Shanna shopping in Baltimore, but after the newness of the idea wore off, she started aggravating her father about visiting the horses one last time before they left. At last, he gave in, and they both agreed that they should invite Hazel to come along. On trading day, they went to Clarks and waited for Hazel to come to Mr. Midgett's store to trade for supplies. Then Kristina asked her to go with them to New Inlet on one last camping trip to spend time with the ponies before she had to return to Baltimore.

As Hazel, Kristina, and Edward were leaving to sail up to New Inlet, Cocoa would not be denied. She ran right through the screen door, and every time Kristina tried to catch her to take her home, she ran off a short distance—just enough to keep out of reach.

"Leave her alone." Edward said. "It's okay if she wants to come. She's been stuck at home by herself for a while now, and it'll do her good." When he said, "Come on, girl, get in the skiff," Cocoa crawled along the dock on her belly, uncertain about getting within Kristina's reach.

"Alright, you can come," Kristina told her dog. Then, with one big leap, Cocoa jumped aboard and took her normal place on the bow cap at the front of the boat. They met Hazel just outside the reef and turned both boats north. With a fair southwest wind behind them, it didn't take long to sail the ten miles up to New Inlet. Upon arrival, they found a large vessel anchored near the entrance to the inlet with several men standing on the deck.

Edward sailed to the vessel's side and yelled to the men, who said they were from the army. They had heard of the many Banker ponies roaming the islands and had come to catch them for government use as army mounts and to pull wagons. The horses would be trained at the nearest base, and then transported to Norfolk, Virginia, and other army installations along the East Coast.

"Oh, Lord!" said Hazel. "First they wanted them for farm animals, and now they want them for government use."

"Have you seen any ponies around?" Edward asked the men.

"We've seen plenty of signs of them, but no animals," answered the men.

"Barnacle has moved them to safety," Kristina whispered to Hazel.

"We need to check and be sure," Hazel replied.

❧38❧

Missing Ponies

When they had finished their conversation with the men on the deck of the boat, Hazel and Edward decided to tie their skiffs together. Edward would paddle them south along the shoreline while Hazel and Kristina followed the land trail on foot. Cocoa jumped out of the skiff as soon as he could and disappeared into the brush. Shortly they heard her barking off in the distance. "I think your dog has picked up the scent of the horses and is already on their tails," Hazel said. "We must hurry before the government scouts catch up with us."

As they reached a small clearing, two men came out of the bush on horseback. They identified themselves and stated their business. Then one of them said, "Is that your dog, barking up ahead?"

"Yes," Kristina replied. "She came here with us. She loves to run ahead and check things out along the way."

"It seems she's looking for the herd of horses that made all these tracks," the man replied. "She's acting funny, though. She's at the end of this trail where the horses entered the water, just staring offshore, barking as if she sees something. But there's nothing out there," he insisted. Before he and his buddy turned to ride away, the man told Hazel and Kristina to keep straight along the path, which would take them to the shore side. "You're dog is just around the next bend," he said.

Hazel and Kristina continued around the bend and soon joined Cocoa at the end of the marsh. She was pawing the sand and barking when they approached her. "This is where the herd entered the water," Hazel said. "Now to find where they came back to shore so that we can follow their trail."

After a few minutes, Edward arrived with the skiffs, and they all sailed a little farther down the shore to make camp for the night. Later, as they were sitting around the fire, they discussed their plans to locate the herd of Bankers.

"I believe they traveled down the sound side when the wind blew hard from the east," Hazel told them.

"But how far did they travel is the next question," Edward answered.

"We'll just have to continue along until we find their trail again," added Kristina.

"That could take a very long time," Edward said. "I think we should go back to Northard Woods tomorrow and get some help tracking them."

"I'll go in the morning," Hazel said. "You and Kristina can continue south. Cocoa will follow you on the shore and alert you if she finds any sign of the ponies. I'll organize a search from Northard Woods to Clarks, and if we haven't found the horses by then, we'll regroup and plan what to do next," she declared. The next morning, Hazel was gone by first light. Then Edward paddled while Kristina and Cocoa walked along the shore, trying to find the place where the horses had come out of the water.

Barnacle and the ponies were very comfortable on Clarks Island. The Raven had healed and was nearly ready to resume his duties as lead stallion. After a while, Flash and some of the other younger stallions grew tired of the same old surroundings every day. They longed for a change of scenery and the pursuit of new adventures. Barnacle could see this restlessness growing in their eyes, and knew that he would soon have to come up with a plan to ease their anxiety.

That night, just after dark, Barnacle woke Flash and a couple other young stallions and led them across Clarks Channel, up the south dyke. Very careful not to leave any tracks, they walked in the center of the creek, all the way to the beach road. Soon they would come to a freshwater pond where travelers watered their mounts. There would be plenty of tracks to mix with their own and conceal their movement all the way to the beach.

Once they reached the beach, there were a myriad of tracks leading off in many directions. Here, the young stallions could run up and down the surf in the cover of darkness to their hearts' content, then return to the safety of Clarks Island in the early mornings, along the same path. Barnacle practiced with the horses for several nights, and when he was convinced they were sufficiently careful, he allowed them to come and go on their own.

On one of their trips to the beach, when Flash and three of the younger stallions had not returned by daylight, Barnacle knew he had to go look for them. The Raven had recovered from all injuries and had resumed his duties as leader of the herd. When Star put up a fuss and wanted to come with him to find Flash, Barnacle knew she would slow his search; he needed to travel fast and stay near cover, especially during the daylight hours. However, Barnacle also knew that if he didn't bring Star along, she'd sneak out and follow him anyway, so he decided to wait until dark and they would all go look for Flash and his friends.

Barnacle and Star carefully worked their way toward the beach after dark. In the moonlight, it was easy for Barnacle to find the ponies' tracks. They had run along the surf for about three miles. Then their tracks went into the water. He stopped and listened for them but could only hear the sound of the surf, so he and Star continued down the beach. They searched all night but could not pick up Flash's trail, and as daylight drew close, they returned to cover. Barnacle was puzzled and bewildered. He knew he'd have to extend his search into the daylight hours in order to find his son and the other stallions.

Two days earlier Flash had led his friends to the beach, along the path his father had showed them several times. They were very careful to use the creek to hide their tracks until they reached the pond, where all the horse tracks ran together. At the beach, the young stallions took off to the south, and romped and played in the surf for hours. On their way back to the trail, they decided to take a swim and cool off, so all three trotted into the water and swam over to the sandbar. The young stallions followed Flash as they walked down the edge of the bar and jumped back into the slough to swim to shore.

As soon as Flash entered the deep water, he knew he had made a mistake and tried to warn his friends, but it was too late. He had led them into a rip current. All four of them were swiftly carried about two hundred yards offshore. All they could do was swim and try to keep their heads above water. Before long, their leg muscles began to burn with exhaustion, but they kept kicking, trying to find the bottom. They were in deep water, well over their heads, and were being swept seaward.

The Gull Shoal Station crew was on their way up the beach for a day of friendly competition to practice the overturned lifeboat drill with the Chicamacomico crew. Keeper Edward O. Hooper spotted the ponies through his glass as they were swimming offshore. "That's odd," he told his crew. "You hardly ever see Banker ponies swimming that far offshore. I believe they are caught in a rip current in that outlet and are in trouble. They look like young ponies, swimming against the current instead of side to it, and if we don't help them, they'll surely drown." Then the order was given. "Stop the wagon and launch the boat! This'll be good practice for us," said Keeper Hooper.

Soon the surfboat reached the ponies, which were too weak to resist or help the men. The crew lashed the ponies to the surfboat, with two on each side, and started rowing back to shore, parallel to the rip. When they got to shore, the ponies were unable to stand, so the crew used the wagon horses to pull the ponies, one by one, up onto the beach. Completely exhausted, the ponies remained there for about half an hour. "We can't leave them like this," said Keeper Hooper. "We must get them on their feet." Then, as one man pulled on the head of each horse, another man pushed from behind. Finally, after quite some difficulty, all four ponies were standing.

The young stallions vomited seawater and tried to collapse back onto the sand. "Don't let them go down," warned Keeper Hooper. "We must walk them as much as possible. There's no telling how much seawater they have in their bellies. Put the ropes on them, and we'll take them on up to Chicamacomico and put them in the corral. Keeper Daniels can contact that old woman from Cedar Hammock. She'll know exactly how to fix horses with their bellies full of saltwater."

The Gull Station crew proceeded up the beach, stopping each time one of the ponies got sick. When they reached the beach across from the Chicamacomico Station, Keeper Hooper first led the extremely weak ponies to the corral. Then he found Keeper Daniels and gave him the account of what had occurred.

"I know one of those young stallions," said Keeper Daniels. "His name is Flash. He's the offspring of Barnacle, the large chestnut stallion found in the wreckage of the *Sylvia*. His mother is a local mare the kids have named Star. We've not seen Flash or any of the ponies he runs with since a bull shark incident at New Inlet, when he was severely bitten and almost died. His owner—or might I say, 'the girl who looks after him'—had to take a trip to Baltimore with her parents a few weeks ago. Her name is Kristina, and she's a local schoolteacher. Her father was just appointed as wreck commissioner for this area and had to go to Washington to get official. Kristina and her father looked for days before they left but couldn't find any sign of the horses. The girl was fit to be tied and refused to leave until Old Hazel from Cedar Hammock promised to keep looking for the ponies until she found them and protect them until Kristina returned from Baltimore."

"Then you must contact this Hazel at once," said Keeper Hooper.

Keeper Daniels sent for Barney and Jason. He told Barney to go find Hazel, quickly, and he told Jason to stay with the ponies. "Try to get them to drink some fresh water, and whatever you do," he told Jason, "don't let them lay down. Keep them on their feet," Keeper Daniels insisted. Then he said, "We have a full day of drilling ahead of us, and both crews can use the practice, especially on the overturned lifeboat drill."

Jason labored with the ponies, trying his best to get some fresh water into their systems. He knew he should only give them small portions of fresh water at a time, even though they tried to gulp large amounts. Their bellies were on fire from all the saltwater they had swallowed, but if the ponies drank too much water, they would try to lie down. Jason knew he'd never be able to get them back on their feet by himself, so he walked them around the corral, allowing them small sips only.

Barney found Hazel at Cedar Hammock Marsh and asked her what she was up to. "I'm headed off to look for those horses," Hazel confessed. "It's as if they have vanished from the face of the earth! Not only did I promise Kristina I'd find them but also that I'd have Barnacle, Star, and Flash waiting for her when she came home, and she'll be back by the end of the week."

"Then, boy, do I have news for you! Flash and three other stallions are at the station with Jason!" Barney exclaimed. "They've just been rescued by the Gull Shoal crew, who found them, almost drowned, about three hundred yards out in the ocean. According to Keeper Hooper, the ponies had been swept through an outlet between two sandbars by a strong rip current. Their bellies are full of salt water. They've been down a few times, and we really need your help."

"Praise the Lord!" was Hazel's response. "All we have to do is to walk them for a couple days and give them fresh water until the salt is purged from their bodies. Then we'll start them on small portions of food, so they regain their strength." After she grabbed a few of her things, she and Barney headed their mounts northward to the Chicamacomico Station corral.

❧39❧

GOVERNMENT TAKEOVER

Barney and Hazel moved their mounts to a gallop as they approached the village of Clarks. They waved to the Gull Shoal Station crew as they returned to their station after a day of drilling with the Chicamacomico crew. Neither one had noticed the two dark forms that had been following them in the fading light since they had passed the Clarks Island entrance. Barnacle had recognized Hazel from a distance, while he and Star were out looking for Flash, and had followed them closely, moving silently behind a line of brush along the sound.

Barnacle knew, from the many times Hazel had come to his aid, that if Flash and his friends were in trouble, she would be ready to help in any way she could. He moved Star along at a good pace in order to keep up with Barney and Hazel, but was very careful to stay hidden by the bushes. As they neared the Chicamacomico Station, Barnacle and Star could not believe their eyes. There, in the light of a lantern, stood Flash and his friends. After countless hours of searching for them, they had made their way home! When Barnacle grabbed Star by the tail to prevent her from running to greet Flash, she made a disapproving moan to her mate, but held fast in the shadows.

Jason met Hazel and Barney at the corral and was so glad they had arrived to help with the horses. He had been giving the ponies small sips of fresh water, trying to keep them on their feet. Just as soon as Hazel took one look at their swollen bellies, she said, "We have to get a solution of oil and water in them to induce vomiting or bowel movements and to purge them of the salt water," she said. Then, suddenly, she asked, "Did y'all just hear something in the shadows a minute ago, like a horse whinny?"

Before Jason or Barney could respond, Star appeared from the shadows. Barnacle was trying to hold her back by grasping her tail in his teeth, but he realized there was no use, so he let her go and she went scampering to the fence with Barnacle close behind.

"Well, would you look at that!" said Hazel as she opened the gate and let them in. "I've been looking for all of you, for days, fearing the worst, and you were fine all along! I knew you two were following us here," she told the horses, "hiding your movements all the way. You're just a bunch of sneaks!" Barney and Jason laughed in amazement as Star gently nuzzled Flash.

"Alright, boys, let's get started with the treatment. We have a long night ahead of us," said Barney.

On the night before departing from Elizabeth City for Southard Woods, Kristina could barely sleep. She woke her parents and Shanna very early the next morning, and they all went to breakfast, long before the cook arrived. She and Shanna were anxious to get back to the island and chatted about what they would do first when they got home.

"You girls need to stop talking and eat your breakfast so that we can get down to the dock," Edward told them.

"Yes," Beth added. "I'm sure our luggage has been loaded on the boat by now."

After breakfast they boarded the *Coastal Rambler* and were greeted by Captain Mansfield. "I'll bet you folks are anxious to get back to the banks," the captain told them. "I've heard that some big changes are about to happen down there."

"What type of changes?" asked Edward.

"I guess the federal government is going to be annexing large tracts of property and penning up all the livestock, including the wild Banker ponies," replied Captain Mansfield.

"Can they do that, Daddy?" asked Kristina.

"Honey, the federal government can do what it chooses to do. We'll have to wait until we get there for more information about what's going on," Edward told his daughter. Then Kristina's thoughts drifted to Barnacle and his carefree hours of running the marshes and surf line.

The *Coastal Rambler* made sail and headed down the river into the sound and was soon gliding southward. It wasn't long before the vessel turned into the wind and struck sail, just behind the reef off Northard Woods, and dropped anchor. Upon arrival, the *Sea Mullet* made fast to her side to ferry passengers and supplies to the landing.

As they entered the harbor, Hazel was waiting for them on the dock and spoke before anyone. "Edward, the keeper is waiting for you!" she said. "He needs you to accompany him to an important meeting—something about a government takeover of private lands," she told him.

"Captain Mansfield was mentioning something about that after we boarded the *Sea Mullet*," replied Edward.

"I have a wagon here, and I'll help your family get home," Hazel responded. "Keeper Daniels is waiting for you at the end of the dock."

Edward climbed into the wagon with Keeper Daniels. "What's all the talk about government takeover?" he asked him. Then, on the way back to the station, Keeper Daniels told Edward everything he knew to tell him.

"The federal government is considering a takeover of all beach property to make this a protected area: a 'national park,' I think they're calling it. They want to protect it for future generations of visitors to enjoy. The downside is that the local folks have to pen up all their livestock, the Banker ponies can no longer roam free on the island, and the island folks have to accept whatever payment the government offers for their property. They're taking total control of most of the property outside the villages. The meeting to explain it all is scheduled at three o'clock this afternoon at the schoolhouse in Clarks. We have about an hour to get there," the keeper told Edward. "I thought you should be present, since any decision made about the beaches will have a direct effect on you as the new shipwreck commissioner. I suspect there will be a full house. This thing has caused quite a stir around here since y'all have been out of town."

Hazel helped Beth, Kristina, and Shanna load the wagon with their luggage and the treasures they had purchased in the city. "We got you two new bonnets and a Sunday dress, along with some new work clothes," Kristina told Hazel. Then she asked, "Have you seen Barnacle or any member of his family?"

"I was wondering how long it would take you to get around to that," answered Hazel. "They're all fine and are waiting for you at the station corral. However, I've not seen hide nor hair of the Banker herd. It's as if they've disappeared from the face of the earth!" replied Hazel.

"I'll bet Barnacle can lead us to them," Kristina said.

"Yes, he probably can, but will he? There's a trust between horses and people, like you have with Barnacle, but there's also a trust among horses that only horses can understand, especially if they think danger is involved," added Hazel.

"I'll take Barnacle for a run, once we've unpacked all of our gear," said Kristina.

"I'll accompany you, and we should take your brown dog with us," Hazel said.

After they finished unpacking, Hazel, Kristina, and Shanna headed off to retrieve the horses, with Cocoa in the lead, barking the whole way. When they reached the station corral, Barnacle, Star, Flash, and Flash's three stallion friends were behind the boathouse.

"We should be very careful when we take them out the gate and back to your cottage," Hazel said to Kristina. "Barnacle and Star will follow you quietly, but Flash and those other three are feeling much better since recovering from their near-drowning experience, and if given any quarter, they might bolt and be gone!"

As they were speaking, Barney walked out of the stable. "Well, hello! What are you ladies up to?" he asked. When Hazel informed Barney that they had come to retrieve the horses, he said, "Take the station wagon and tie the young ponies to the back of it, until they are safely inside your corral. Otherwise they're liable to take off. I'll come along with you and return the wagon to the station," and soon all six horses were safely in the corral at Kristina's cottage. They decided they would wait a few days to continue their search for the Banker ponies.

Keeper Daniels and Edward arrived at the schoolhouse in Clarks and were greeted outside by Keeper Edward Hooper from the Gull Shoal Station. "We've saved seats for you two," he said. "Keeper Scarborough from Little Kinnakeet Station is watching over them until we get inside. The meeting's just about to start, and the building's packed!"

The villagers had turned out in force to attend this meeting in order to become informed about the government's plans for their property. The agenda was explained in detail to the folks at the gathering. Simply put, the federal government would take control of all beach property as well as all property between the villages. Their boundaries would exclude existing homes and businesses. Sizeable lots would be established for each dwelling, and anybody with properties impinging on government-controlled areas would be offered a fair-market price for their land. If the landowners refused to sell, the government would establish ownership by annexing the property and enlisting their authority through eminent domain laws.

The village people listened as they were told they would still have complete access to the government property and be able to continue with their livelihoods and enjoy the recreational benefits, but they would no longer control the land. All government property would become open to anybody wanting to visit the island. There would be a list of rules and regulations for the maintenance and care of said lands, which would bring on many changes for the people and animals of Hatteras and Ocracoke Islands.

Future meetings would be held farther down the island to spread the word about the federal government's plan to establish a national park in the area. The rules and regulations would be posted in each of the post offices for all to read, and the government survey crews would be arriving in the near future. They would be offering employment to anyone interested in working for them.

As the men gathered outside at the end of the meeting, Keeper Daniels said, "It looks like we'll be faced with many changes in our daily lives here shortly."

"We all have a lot to ponder," Edward added as they boarded the wagon and headed for Northard Woods.

When Keeper Daniels dropped Edward off at the cottage, Beth and Hazel were waiting for his return. "Tell us about the meeting! What happened? What do you know about all these rumors we've been hearing?" they asked anxiously.

"They're not rumors. We're going to be faced with many new rules and regulations concerning the open lands of the island," Edward said.

"How about the Banker ponies? Will they still be allowed to roam with the freedom they have always enjoyed?" Beth asked him.

"I don't think so," Edward responded. "They'll be regulated by a list of rules, which will be hung in the post office in a few days. We'll all be held accountable and expected to follow these new guidelines."

"I've heard enough. I'll see you folks later. I'm headed for Cedar Hammock," Hazel said, and out the door she went.

"Where is Kristina?" asked Edward.

"Where do you think she is?" responded Beth.

"Hmm . . . out in the stable with the horses, hey?" was his response. "I guess I had better get this over with."

"I'm glad you're the one telling her about this meeting instead of me," Beth said as Edward walked out the door and headed for the corral. When he opened the stable door, Kristina was giving Flash a belly rub.

"Oh, Daddy, please tell me it's not true about the ponies losing their freedom!"

"I wish I could, sweetheart," was her father's response.

❦40❦

Rules and Regulations

It was very hot, but a light southwest breeze was gently blowing through the window as Kristina woke up to the late July morning. She jumped out of bed and joined her parents at the breakfast table. Their conversation was totally consumed with the new regulations and how they would affect the future of the island people.

Kristina was concerned about the lifestyle of the wild ponies who had roamed free for hundreds of years. The first ponies had been shipwrecked here. They had adapted to the harshness of freezing winters and incredibly hot summers to make this area their home. Kristina thought it would be a crime against nature if they lost their freedom and had to be penned up.

"I guess we'll have to examine the regulations when they get posted and wait to see how they affect the quality of life and livestock in the area," Edward told them.

"Well, if the ponies lose their freedom here, I'll figure out some way to help them relocate to a place where they can be free," Kristina added.

"That's exactly what I am afraid of," her father replied, "some harebrained scheme of yours to buck the federal government in the interest of those Banker ponies. Remember, I do work for the government now, or did you forget that?"

"No, Daddy, I didn't forget, and I promise I won't cause problems for you.

I plan to visit Hazel as soon as we know more about these rules, and then we'll figure out how to help the Bankers," Kristina said.

There was standing room only inside the post office on the day the postmaster stapled the government regulations to the wall. Edward and Kristina waited until the crowd thinned before entering the post office to read the ten articles for themselves. According to the document, folks would still be able to use the beaches in the same manner as they had in the past. The government was promising to come forth with a plan, with limited rules and regulations, which would protect and preserve the beaches for everyone's enjoyment, without affecting free and open access in any way.

Two of the articles caused considerable concern among the island folk. One of them explained how much money, per acre, the landowners would receive for the large parcels of land outside the villages, which ran from surf to sound. This article prompted the village folks to elect a spokesman to deal with the government officials. They were being offered much less money for their property than some of them had paid! Other landowners had inherited their holdings, which had been part of their families and passed down for generations. They did not want to sell at any price.

The second article addressed the handling of livestock on open lands. In the past, all the animals had enjoyed roaming and grazing to their heart's content, anywhere they chose to do so. This new regulation would require everyone to pen their stock during certain times of the year, and to brand or mark them in an identifying manner. There would be times when the horses could use the grazing meadows on the open lands, but they would have to be accompanied by their owners or an agent representing the owner. Their days of running carefree in the surf line were coming to an end.

"That's just not fair," Kristina told her father. "The animals are going to lose their freedom, and there's nothing we can do to prevent it." As they left the post office and headed back to the cottage, they met Hazel near the entrance to the landing road.

"Have you folks read the new regulations at the post office?" she asked them.

"Yes," they both replied.

"What did it say about the domestic stock and the Banker herd?" she asked.

"Everyone will have to pen their stock and put identifying marks on them," Edward answered. "The government will give the local folks three weeks to make these arrangements, and then they're going to round up all the remaining stock for official use," explained Edward.

"That doesn't give us much time," Hazel said.

"What are we going to do about the wild Banker ponies?" asked Kristina.

"The first thing we have to do is to look after our own stock," Hazel answered. "We need to come up with some sort of way to mark them so they can be easily identified as private stock," she added.

"The articles at the post office state that, in a couple of days, we can pick up colored tags to fasten to their ears for that very reason," Edward told them.

"What about the Banker ponies?" was Kristina's next question. "We have to help them."

"Help them? We can't even find them," Hazel said. "Even if we do find them, there's no way we can mark them all or take care of them."

"There are so many of them, and they've lived here too long to be penned up and domesticated," Edward replied.

"There must be something we can do to preserve their way of life!" Kristina pleaded.

"Perhaps there is a way," said Hazel.

The island soon became a hubbub of activity, with folks trying to conform to the new rules and regulations implemented by the government. Everyone hurried to repair their corrals, round up their stock, and begin the marking process with the ear tags. After the three-week period, any livestock not properly tagged would be claimed by the government.

After Barnacle, Star, Flash, and the three young stallions were tagged, Kristina went to Cedar Hammock to help Hazel with the marking of her stock. When the work was finished, they relaxed on Hazel's back porch, overlooking Cedar Hammock, and enjoyed a cool drink.

All of a sudden, Hazel broke out in a fit of laughter. "Whatever are you laughing about?" asked Kristina.

"I was just thinking of the fun those government men are going to have when they run up with Old Scratchum and his band of unmarked wild hogs!" answered Hazel.

"If they're not careful, they'll lose the seats of their government pants!" laughed Kristina.

"Boy, I'd give anything to see that show," added Hazel.

"So . . . any stock that's not marked belongs to the government at the end of the three-week period. Is that right?" asked Kristina.

"That's how I understand it," answered Hazel. "I've been pondering for quite a while on the fate of our local Banker herd, trying to figure a way they can remain free and not become the property of the government. Let's go in the house and fix a meal, and I'll let you in on what I've worked out."

After eating, Hazel filled Kristina in on her thoughts. She had already sent a letter to her sister, Hattie, explaining the changes taking place on the islands of Hatteras and Ocracoke. Hattie lived south—on Hog's Island, near Shackelford Banks—and on a prior visit to her house, Hazel had noticed that the wild ponies roamed free there and were actually protected by the government. Much to Kristina's delight, Hazel had already formulated a plan to move the entire herd to the protection of Shackelford Banks.

The next day, Hazel and Kristina went to Northard Woods to share Hazel's plan with Edward and Keeper Daniels. The four of them met in the tack room, and Hazel explained her thoughts to them. "We need to stay ahead of that government deadline, but first, we must find those horses!" she told them. "If we let one of the already-tagged stallions go free, he will most likely lead us to the herd, and as soon as we find them, we'll start moving them southward to safety." Hazel agreed with Keeper Daniels when he warned her that she would need several friends to help her with the move.

"I'll take my wagon down to the island's end and provide the chuck for that part of the journey," Hazel volunteered. "Hopefully we can get the Howard boys in Ocracoke to help us move the ponies across Ocracoke Island. Then my sister, Hattie, will be waiting for us on Portsmouth Island. As far as she knows, there are no government plans to take over Portsmouth Island. The horses will be safe there," said Hazel. Then she reminded the keeper, Edward, and Kristina that they only had one week left before all untagged horses would be rounded up and taken away from the island. "And don't forget about the government meeting next week in Kinnakeet," she added. "Now that we've settled on a plan of action, all we have to do is locate the ponies, work out a timeline, and locate more helpers to get this journey started," Hazel concluded.

The last week of July was upon them. Miles Midgett and Luther Hooper went on to Ocracoke to meet up with the Howard boys. Everyone else who had agreed to help was busy gathering supplies for the big move.

Hazel and Kristina chose Flash's youngest stallion friend to lead them to the Bankers. When they released him from the corral, he hung around outside the fence for a while until Edward tied Barnacle, Star, Flash, and the other two young stallions up inside the corral and put rope hobbles on their front legs to keep them from jumping the fence. Then the stallion snorted, turned south, and took off.

Hazel and Kristina were mounted and ready to follow the stallion to the ponies. At full gallop he led them straight to the trail at Clarks Island and out to Clarks Channel. They followed the pony across the channel, up onto Clarks Island, and over to a large meadow, which was full of ponies as far as the eye could see. Hazel and Kristina stayed hidden by the brush and allowed the stallion to rejoin the herd. Then they slowly retreated back to Northard Woods to share the location of the herd with their crew of friends.

Time was running out and the crew was anxious to get under way, so they left early the next morning with plans to gather the herd and drive them to the Kinnakeet meadows for the first night. Hazel and Kristina would catch up with them the next day and bring Cocoa with them to scout ahead and help manage the herd.

Edward was concerned about what might happen once the ponies reached Portsmouth Island. He knew Kristina had to take Barnacle with her to help the Raven lead the herd to safety and keep the younger stallions in check. Not sure how to approach the subject, Edward came right out and asked Kristina what she would do if Barnacle chose to stay down south with the Bankers. She told her father that she didn't know the answer to his question, and that she could not imagine life without Barnacle, Star, and Flash. When Beth shared her concern about Kristina getting back in time for the next school term, Kristina grinned and said, "Don't worry, Mom. Shanna and I will not be late for school! We're teachers now!"

❦41❧

Freedom Plan

Kristina got out of bed before daylight the next morning and went to the guest room to wake Hazel. "Get out of bed, you sleepyhead," she told her.

"It seems like I just laid down a few seconds ago," Hazel answered.

"We have a big day ahead of us," Kristina said, "and we need one of Mom's big breakfasts to get us going."

"You won't get any argument from me on that! I'm starved," Hazel replied. When they went to the kitchen, Beth had breakfast ready for them and the table was set. Edward was sitting at the table having his morning coffee, reading a telegram he had received about a wreck near Pea Island.

"You're up early this morning, Dad," Kristina said.

"I wanted to talk to you and Hazel before you left this morning," he responded. "The main thing I want to ensure is that you stop at each station along the way and check the weather conditions you're facing. Also, I want you to send word back to us and let us know how you're doing, and how your journey is progressing. In other words, stay in touch."

"We will. I promise," Kristina told her father. After they finished breakfast, they all walked out to the corral together.

"Are you going to take all the horses?" Beth asked.

"We have to, Mom. If we leave any behind, they'll follow us the first chance they get," Kristina replied.

"I guess you're right," responded Beth.

"Just be careful, and remember to keep us informed," Edward said as he let the horses out of the corral.

"I'll take care of them," Hazel promised.

"Y'all look after each other," Edward told them.

"I love you, Mom and Dad, and I'll see you near the end of August," Kristina said as she and Hazel started out. Cocoa took the lead and started barking right away. The Midgett boys joined Hazel and Kristina at Southard Woods, and the Hooper boys joined them as they entered Clarks.

"When we get to the entrance of the Clarks Island trail, we should let Barnacle go alone to get the herd and bring them out," Hazel said.

"Do you want to tell him, or do you want me to tell him?" asked Kristina.

"Oh, you don't have to worry about that," Hazel said. "Barnacle knows exactly what is going on. He'll communicate with the Raven, and I believe they'll bring the herd out together. It'll be much better to let them manage the herd than for all of us to go tromping back there. We don't want to scatter the ponies and end up having to round them up again."

As they reached the beginning of the trail to Clarks Island, Kristina released Barnacle and said, "Go get 'em, boy." Cocoa took off barking, too, but when Kristina called her, she came back to her mistress.

When Star, Flash, and the two young stallions started to follow Barnacle, one of the Hooper boys tried to stop them until Hazel told him to let them go. "It will seem more natural that way, and the less we have to do to with herding those ponies, the better. Most of them have only seen people from a distance and have never had any interaction with them," Hazel added.

As Barnacle and his companions headed down the trail, Kristina said, "We'll give them about an hour, and if they don't come out by then, we'll go in after them."

"In the meantime we can water our horses at the freshwater pond and relax ourselves," one of the Midgett boys suggested.

Before the hour was up, one of the Hooper boys pointed and said, "Lord, would you look at that!" Out of the marshy trail came the Raven, bobbing his head and sniffing the air. Behind him was the longest line of Banker ponies any of them had ever seen. It took about fifteen minutes for all of the horses to come out. Barnacle was at the very end of the string of ponies, with his family ahead of him. The Raven led the ponies straight toward the freshwater pond but wouldn't let them approach until everyone moved out of the way. Then he allowed the ponies to drink, keeping himself between the herd and the humans.

"Give them room," Hazel told the group. "I count about four hundred head. We'll let the Raven and Barnacle take the lead, and we'll ride on the left and right flanks to keep them headed south. You Midgett boys can take the east side, and you Hooper boys can take the west. Kristina and I will bring up the rear with the supply wagon."

Cocoa was whimpering and ready to go. "Stay, Cocoa," said Kristina. "You can join Barnacle after the ponies finish with their drink."

"Okay, Barnacle, head 'em south," Kristina told him. Then Barnacle joined the Raven for a few seconds, and they bobbed their heads up and down. Then, after a whinny, Barnacle took the lead. The Raven trotted around and around the herd until they slowly began to move off in a southerly direction. The Midgett boys took the east flank, and the Hooper boys took the west. Kristina let Cocoa join Barnacle at the lead, then she and Hazel followed along a few yards behind the Raven. Their long journey to Portsmouth Island had begun.

As the roundup crew approached the meadows of Little Kinnakeet, about five miles north of Little Kinnakeet Lifesaving Station, they noticed a rider approaching from the south at a full gallop. It turned out to be Norman Scarborough, who had been to Kinnakeet Village to visit his mother. He circled the herd far to the west so that he would not spook them, quickly approaching Hazel and Kristina. "They know you're coming and what you're up to!" he shouted.

"What in thunder are you yelling about?" asked Hazel.

"The government men! They're waiting for you at the entrance of Kinnakeet Village with a seizure order signed by a federal judge, empowering them to take custody of all the unmarked Banker ponies," he said.

"That's not what the rules say on the post office wall in Northard Woods,"

Kristina said indignantly. "The people of Kinnakeet should have three weeks to gather their stock after the meeting yesterday," she said.

"Yes, but they've twisted the rules of the posting because the Bankers that are with you came from Northard Woods. They know you're trying to get a big herd of untagged horses to a free-ground area, and the government wants those horses," replied Norman.

"What are we going to do now?" Kristina asked Hazel.

"We'll let the horses graze in this meadow for a couple of hours. You and I will go see Keeper Hooper at Little Kinnakeet Station to see if he can help us. Go ahead and signal Barnacle and the Raven so they can stop the herd. Also, signal our flank riders to come in so that we can let them know what's going on," said Hazel.

After the herd was settled in the meadow, Norman, Kristina, Hazel, and Cocoa headed off to consult with Keeper Hooper. As they neared the Little Kinnakeet Station, they saw Keeper Hooper in the drill field, practicing the breeched buoy drill with the surfmen. "Good," said Hazel, "the keeper's outside. Maybe we'll be able to talk to him without drawing undue attention."

Keeper Hooper listened intently as Hazel explained the scrape they were in. "It just aggravates the life out of me the way the government changes the rules to suit whatever they are trying to do," Hazel said, agitated.

"I know what you mean," said Keeper Hooper, "but when you're dealing with the government, they always have the upper hand. This seizure order sounds like an official document, especially if it's signed by a federal judge. The best thing for y'all to do is avoid contact with the officials," he said.

"How in the name of common sense are we going to sneak a herd this size past them?" asked Kristina.

"I have a couple ideas," Keeper Hooper said. "Come into the tack room for a cool drink, and I'll discuss them with you. I'm amazed that the government would implement rules that would be so aggravating to folks." Then he shouted to Surfman Number One and said, "Nelson, take over for me and keep the men drilling. I'll be back shortly," as he, Kristina, and Hazel walked toward the station.

When they got inside the tack room, Keeper Hooper began the conversation. "You could rest for a while until it gets dark. Let the government agents think you've bedded down for the night and then make a beeline for the cover of Cape Woods," he told them.

"You mean for us to run the ponies at gallop speed, during the night, to get by the agents at Kinnakeet?" asked Hazel.

"That's exactly what I mean," responded Keeper Hooper.

"I'm afraid the herd will end up scattered from never to gone," Hazel answered.

"Well, I do have another idea," Keeper Hooper said. "Do you remember Roscoe Meekins and his son, Vernon?" he asked. "They're working in the southern hammock area of Big Kinnakeet, cutting ship timbers for the Newbern Shipbuilding Company. They know the south hammock area better than anyone, and I believe they would help you slip that herd past the agents to the safety of White Oak Trail, leading down to Cape Woods," he added.

"All those ponies?" Kristina asked.

"Well, maybe not all at one time," said the keeper. "We have word of a low-pressure system coming across the sound. The wind's going to switch to the northwest, blow gale force, then end up to the northeast. This will expose the shoals on the sound side and provide a route around the village and the agents for the ponies you've already marked. Just wait for the blow, then gallop your marked ponies to the sound-side trail. When the agents see you, they'll give chase. At that point I'll have Roscoe and Vernon help you sneak the unmarked ponies through the South White Oak Pass," Keeper Hooper said.

"That just might work," added Norman. "I'm familiar with the opening through the marshes to the pass. I can help lead the ponies through the trail."

"Barnacle will have to lead the sound-side run," Hazel added. "He can take Star, Flash, and the four marked stallions with him on the westward route to the shoals. When did you say the wind shift is going to get here?"

"Tomorrow, around noon," the keeper said.

"I think Barnacle should take about half of the younger, faster unmarked stallions with him," said Norman, "at least enough to make the agents think we are making a run for it."

"How about Star?" asked Kristina. "She'll surely be caught."

"She's marked. They'll have to release her," answered Norman.

"Then it's decided," Hazel said. "We'll wait for the shift in wind. Then we'll line up on the shore side to the north of the village. We'll make sure the agents see us gathering there, and then we'll take enough of the herd through so that they think it's our primary path." Then she asked the keeper if he would contact the Meekins men and arrange passage for the slower ponies to get through the pass.

"I'll be glad to arrange that for you," he responded.

They all agreed on the plan, said their good-byes, and went back to the herd to explain the plan of attack to their friends.

"Do you think we'll have any trouble getting Barnacle to lead his group through the sound trail?" Kristina asked Hazel.

"Not if you and Cocoa go along with him," Hazel responded. "The Midgett boys can go with you. They always like a good run! I'll take the Hooper boys and Norman with me through the pass with the rest of the herd, and we'll meet you at the entrance of Cape Woods," Hazel said.

Early the next morning, they moved the entire herd just north of Kinna-keet Village and settled on the shore side to wait for the shift in wind. When two government agents approached them and said they were going to take charge of the herd, Kristina informed them that there were still a few hours left before the three-week time limit was up.

"You only have until midnight before we move in and assume control of those ponies," one of the agents said.

"Well, please let us spend what time we have left with them," responded Kristina.

"We're going to keep our eyes on you. Just relax and enjoy the day, and we will be back around midnight," the government man told them.

The wind shift came in, just as Keeper Hooper said it would. As soon as the shoals were visible, Barnacle, Kristina, Star, Cocoa, the Midgett boys, and about half of the Banker ponies bolted.

☙ 42 ☙

JOURNEY TO FREEDOM BEGINS

Sam Archer and Billy Mayes were the two young government agents assigned to keep a watchful eye on the wranglers and the herd of Banker ponies. They had seen the herd settle down on the shore side, in the cover of the scrub bushes, and the ponies appeared to be completely relaxed.

The two agents grew weary of watching the ponies, and as boredom set in, they decided to play the rock toss game to pass time. Each agent selected two rocks a piece and began to toss them at the holes they had dug, about twenty-five feet away. The toss that landed closest to the hole counted as one point, and tosses that landed in the hole counted for three points.

The agents became so intent on their competitive game that they soon forgot all about the ponies. Needless to say, the men were shocked when they saw the herd galloping to the south in a dead run, several hundred yards out on the shoals of the sound. "Boy, are we in trouble!" Sam yelled to Billy. "We need to get back and tell the chief what's happened." As the agents were running back to their temporary headquarters, they did not notice that most of the Bankers had doubled back and were headed for the entrance of White Oak Trail, led by the Raven.

Hazel, Norman, and the Hooper boys moved with caution near the end of the long line of ponies. "We need to move slowly so that we don't draw attention to ourselves," Hazel told them. As they approached the entrance to

White Oak Trail, Norman took the lead. He knew that the entrance to the trail was completely hidden by bushes. He would have to tie the bushes back with rope so that the ponies could enter the trail.

The Raven led the ponies up to the entrance of the trail and hesitated when he saw two men he did not know. Then the Raven stopped and wouldn't allow the ponies to go any farther. Hazel rode up to the front of the line to see what the holdup was, and when she saw the Meekins men, she laughed. "You don't trust them, do you, fellow?" she said to the Raven. Then Hazel patted the big horse on the head and said, "It's okay boy, lead them on in." With extreme caution, the Raven moved past the men, and the ponies followed him. Soon they were all inside the trail, hidden from outside view by the tall white oak trees.

"That beats anything I've ever seen!" Roscoe said to Hazel. "That Raven did exactly what you told him to do, like he completely understood every word you said."

"That's exactly what just happened," Hazel responded.

"Boy, that takes a load off my mind," Roscoe said.

"What do you mean by that?" Hazel asked.

"Well, I have a plan," Roscoe replied. "Up ahead a little ways, I want to lead the herd off the trail and split them up. Some of them will move along with us, and the others will scatter among the oaks. Vernon will ride the trail in your wagon, keeping me in sight. I'll ride a few yards to the left of the trail, keeping you in sight. I need you to ride a few yards to the left of me, with your eyes on that black horse and the rest of the ponies," he told Hazel.

"Hopefully, anyone who rides up will only be able to see me," Roscoe explained. "That's how Vernon and I ride when we're scouting straight timbers for keels and bow sprits for the shipyard. If anyone does happen to use the trail today, hopefully they'll think it's just another day at work for us! The trick is," he told Hazel, "if you see my signal, stop right away. It will mean that Vernon has signaled me. We'll only use signals if someone comes along. If they do, Vernon will signal me as soon as they leave." Then he asked Hazel a question. "Hazel, will the Raven stop the herd at your signal?"

"I'm sure he'll be able to do it!" Hazel said. "However, let's have Norman ride in my position, and I'll ride with the Raven to make sure," she said with a chuckle. "We could also let the Hooper Boys ride on the mid-island trail to answer questions about the herd from anyone passing that way."

"That's even better," Roscoe agreed. "Alright then, we'll exit the trail at the next clearing."

At the next clearing, Hazel peeled off to the far left, as instructed. Soon she was in position. She could see Norman but could no longer see Roscoe.

When Roscoe was able to see Norman only, he sent a test signal. After a few minutes, when the herd stopped, Roscoe felt satisfied with the arrangement and waved for them to continue onward.

Sam and Billy were out of breath when they came running up to their headquarters. "Quickly, Chief," Sam said. "The herd has taken off, out onto the shoals of the sound, galloping south at full speed!"

"Saddle up, men!" yelled the chief. "We'll take the road south and try to head them off before they reach the cover of Cape Woods." Shortly, about a dozen mounted agents headed south at a full gallop, trying to catch up to the herd. "They'll have to hug the shoreline at Opening Creek because of the deep water offshore," the chief told the men.

The ponies were just beginning to turn toward shore as they approached Opening Creek Dyke. "We have them now," the chief yelled. "Hold 'em until they come ashore, then we'll take 'em." However, instead of coming to shore, the herd turned parallel to it and continued to gallop southward.

"After them," shouted the chief. On command, the government men thundered down the top of the dyke, off the edge of the shore, and into the water. Instantly, their mounts sank up to their bellies in the soft mud, and the herd galloped past them about fifty yards offshore. Soon, they disappeared from sight behind a long point of marsh to the south. Barnacle, Kristina, and Cocoa were out front with the ponies following them, and the Midgett boys bringing up the rear.

"That yellow dog and that blonde-headed girl think they've outsmarted us," the chief told the men as they climbed back up on the shore, all wet and muddy.

"Something's just not right about this situation," he said. "Did any of you see the black stallion or the two men we saw riding with the group this morning?"

The men agreed that they had not seen the Raven or the outriders this time. Then the chief said, "They must be making their way down the road with the remaining ponies. They think they've fooled us with this small herd, hoping to draw us off their trail. We'll head back up the trail toward Kinnakeet and see if we come across them," he told his men. "Let's go!"

The government agents had not gone very far when they came up on the Hooper Boys. The chief then questioned them, saying, "I know you were with the herd of Bankers this morning, and I also know about the smaller bunch that went around us to the west, out in the sound. Now I want to know where the rest of the horses are."

"They're making their way down the island toward Cape Woods," was the reply. "We're scouting ahead, looking for fresh water and ample grazing for them," the Hooper boys told the men.

Then the chief shouted, "Onward, men! We're still between them and Cape Woods."

As the agents galloped on, one of the Hooper boys said, "Well, at least we didn't lie to them! We *are* scouting for water, and the ponies *are* headed for Cape Woods. Up ahead, there's a small path that will take us to White Oak Trail, and when we get to it, I think we should let the others know what's going on," the Hooper boy said.

The government agents rode all the way back to Kinnakeet Village, to the beginning of the trail entrance, but they never found the ponies they were looking for. "We've been snookered!" the chief told his men. "We must head back down the trail and find those Hooper boys." Then the men turned around and headed back down the trail. Eventually the chief said, "I know we've come back far enough. It's as if the two men have disappeared." Then all of a sudden, he said, "Wait. Listen. Did you hear that?"

"Hear what?" Billy responded.

"I thought I heard a horse whinny. Stop, be really quiet, and listen," said the chief. Then everyone heard it. "It's off to the east, in that oak thicket," the chief said. Then he shouted, "Billy, go select a couple guys to find us a decent opening into that thicket so that we can scout this area thoroughly." It wasn't long before Billy found the small path, and soon all the agents were on White Oak Trail.

"Where did this trail come from?" asked the chief. "I thought all this area was a swampy oak thicket."

"It is," said William. "I've heard the local folks talk about it. They say it's full of floating marsh, easy for a man to disappear beneath. It's supposed to be mosquito-infested and has a few gators living in it."

"Gators this far north? Hogwash," said the chief.

"I'm only repeating what the locals told me," Billy responded.

"Keep your eyes peeled for any hazards, men," the chief barked. "We'll continue south on this trail and see if we come across anything suspicious." When they rounded the bend, they came upon the Hooper boys talking to Vernon. "We just saw you on the mid-island trail a few minutes ago," the chief told the Hooper boys. "Do you mind telling us what's going on, and the identity of this other man?" he asked.

Vernon spoke up. "I'm Vernon Meekins, and that's my father over yonder. We ride this trail often, marking the straightest oaks we can find for our timber business. I have to keep my father in sight because of the floating marsh bogs and gators. Every now and then, we switch. Then we come back later with a wagon to cut and load the marked trees."

"Well, that explains why you're here," the chief said to Vernon, "but what about the other two men? We just saw them on the mid-island trail."

"We thought we heard horses in the oak thicket and decided to investigate," Vernon explained.

"That sounds reasonable, because that's exactly what we did. Have any of you seen a large herd of Banker ponies in the last hour?" asked the chief.

"Not in the last hour," said the Hooper boys. "We came across them this morning, up north of Kinnakeet, and rode along with them for a ways. Then we split off to the mid-island trail, where we saw you."

"I haven't seen anyone, except for my dad over in the thicket there," said Vernon.

"Well, if you see them, please let us know. We'll head on south, to the end of this trail, then we'll start back along the surf line, just in case they decided to travel the beach," the chief announced. Suddenly, the most ungodly noise arose from deep within the oak thicket. It sounded like someone or something was about to meet its end. They heard growling, snorting, screaming, a gunshot, and then silence. "What in the world was that?" shouted the chief as he started his mount toward the noise.

"Stop! Don't go in there!" yelled Vernon, "It's not safe! My dad will be out in a couple of seconds; he'll tell us what happened."

Sure enough, in a little while, Roscoe came out dragging a seven-foot gator at the end of a rope. "Daggone thing tried to grab my mount's leg," he said.

"I'm surprised those gators are this far north," said the chief.

"This thicket is full of 'em," replied Roscoe. "Better stick to the main trail unless you know what you're doing back here," he told the men.

"You can count on that," said the chief. "Come on, men. Maybe they took the beach route."

Hazel froze as she saw Norman's signal. It meant that someone was on the main trail. Hazel immediately stopped the Raven and the herd, and they all stood motionless. Then, out of the blue, a gator slithered out of a mud hole and grabbed one of the mares by the hind leg. Hazel thought the commotion would cause them to be discovered for sure. Quickly, Norman came over and grabbed the gator by the tail and the Raven started kicking it. Then Roscoe shot the gator, pried his teeth off the mare's leg, and drug the gator away. The mare's leg was bleeding badly but was not broken.

❦43❧

ANGRY OLD BUCK

Kristina, Barnacle, Star, and the Midgett boys, along with the smaller herd, slowed their gallop to a canter as they approached the Haul Over area, just outside of Cape Woods. They climbed up onto the shore and made their way across the open ground to Jennette's Sedge, where they stopped at the first freshwater pond they saw.

After Cocoa had a drink, she ran ahead, following the scent of some small animal. When Kristina called her, she came running back. "Stay here, girl! I need you to stay at the edge of this sedge and let us know if any unfriendly government men come around," she told the dog. Then, as if Cocoa understood, she headed to the edge of the grass line at the beginning of the sedge. For a little while, the riders dismounted and relaxed around the pond.

"How far out in front of them do you think we are?" Kristina asked the Midgett boys.

"They'll be along in a while, probably about thirty minutes," came the reply.

"They number close to three hundred," the taller boy said. "They still have to make their way through that gator-infested bog on White Oak Trail. I'd say we have about an hour before they show up," he added.

Cocoa remained on guard, just as her mistress had instructed. Crouched in the cover of the brush, she kept a watchful eye on the open ground, where all the trails came to an end, right before the sedge. All of a sudden, a rabbit jumped out of the brush and headed toward the beach. Cocoa went after the rabbit and was hot on its trail when the government agents entered the open ground from White Oak Trail. The chief spotted Cocoa and told the men to follow that brown dog. "She'll lead us to the herd," he said, and as Cocoa ran after the rabbit, the chief and his men chased after Cocoa, back toward Kinnakeet.

"That's a very smart dog you have there," said one of the Midgett boys. "She warned us about the intruders, and now she's leading them away in the opposite direction!"

"Yeah, right," said Kristina, "and we'd better hope that rabbit doesn't turn around and run back this way!"

Norman Scarborough arrived at the open grounds, entered the cover of the sedge, and went to the watering hole where his mount could drink and rest a bit. When Kristina and the Midgett boys knew it was safe, they came out of the brush to meet him. "The others are at the edge of the trail," Norman told them. "They're ready to cross the open ground at my signal."

"Bring them on," Kristina replied. "The government men are halfway back to Kinnakeet, chasing Cocoa, and she's down behind a rabbit. Right now is a great time to bring them over!" she exclaimed. Then Norman gave the signal, and before long, all of the ponies were safe in the cover of the sedge. Shortly, Hazel rode up, leading a small, limping mare.

"What happened to her?" asked Kristina.

"A gator," Hazel replied. "Nothing's broken, though. She'll be okay after we rest tonight," Hazel added.

"That's something I wanted to talk to you about," said Kristina. "I think we should press on after a short rest and drink break. We still have to get through Trent Woods. Old Buck and his bulls are there, and it's rutting season," she continued. "You know how cantankerous wild cattle can get this time of year! They're just beginning to mate and will soon be moving to their fall grazing grounds in the Chicamacomico meadows, until after Old Christmas. Plus, there's no telling how long Cocoa will keep the government men away before she doubles back."

"You're absolutely right," Hazel agreed. "The trail into Cape Woods is narrow, but safe passage should be easy."

The Raven took the lead. Barnacle lagged behind the wagon, stopping to look back every now and then as if he was missing someone. "Don't worry," Kristina said. "She'll be along as soon as she finishes with that rabbit." Barnacle continued to lag behind until he caught sight of the brown dog ears flopping toward him.

Cocoa ran up to Barnacle, and they joined the ponies at the back of the herd. "Is Barnacle happy now?" Kristina asked the big horse. Then he gave a snort of approval in reply and continued along the Cape Woods Trail. Just around dusk, they came to a large clearing in the woods, suitable for a bed, with plenty of space, water, and grazing for the ponies. Hazel and Kristina set up the wagon and started fixing the evening meal. In addition to the food they brought with them, they also had fresh gator tail, sent from Roscoe by Norman, along with his wishes for a safe journey.

"How 'bout that Roscoe and this fresh gator?" said one of the Hooper boys.

"Yeah," the other boy said, "he sure saved our bacon back on White Oak Trail with his quick actions." Everyone agreed that Roscoe had been very helpful. After they finished eating, they settled in for the night.

Hazel said, "I'll take the first watch." Then Norman agreed to relieve her, and the rest of the night shifts were divided among the other outriders.

The next morning dawned hot and sticky. The group had a quick breakfast and began their trek through the Piney Ridge thicket to Piney Ridge Trail. This very dark and sinister trail would take them through Trent Woods. Overgrown with vegetation, one needed a lantern or some sort of artificial light to travel there, even in the daylight hours. The trail was full of odd noises and smells, and it always seemed like someone was watching every step you took.

The Trent folks were a clannish group of people who kept to themselves. They always looked out for their kin, but they shied away from strangers and the influence of outside folks. If they knew you, they'd come out with greetings. However, a newcomer could travel the entire Piney Ridge Trail and never see a living soul.

Many a tale had come out of Trent Woods, especially during the week of Old Hallows Eve. The tales had been handed down from generation to generation. There was the ghost story about the men who were hung from the old oak trees near the pine and cactus bog. Other stories were about people who had completely disappeared from the Piney Woods Trail, never heard from again. Each time the stories were told, they usually involved more evil, as folks added to or changed them to suit their particular occasions.

Just before the Raven led the group into Piney Ridge Trail, Hazel stopped them and told everyone that they needed to have a meeting as soon as they found a place where the ponies could relax and graze. If anyone had information about the trail, they would be asked to share it, so that the group would not be caught off guard.

Hazel began the meeting. "I think most of these stories are just folklore," she said, "just a bunch of hogwash fabricated by the folks around here to keep strangers out. The trail is overgrown with vegetation and does become very dark a short ways past the entrance. I just hope the darkness and the unusual noises do not spook the horses. In order to move ahead, we must keep the trail lit at all times," Hazel told the group, and then she told them how they should proceed.

"I think Kristina and Barnacle should take a lantern to the front of the line with the Raven. The rest of you should space yourselves apart among the herd with your lanterns, and I'll bring up the rear with my wagon and two lanterns of my own," she explained. "We must keep the horses as calm as possible, and moving steadily ahead. If we let them spook and run out of control, some of them could become lost in these woods, so let's have our minds right before we get started. We should be able to make it to open grounds by lunchtime." Then she headed for the back of the line and wished all of them good luck.

As Barnacle and the Raven neared the overgrown area, both horses hesitated. Barnacle looked at Kristina and whimpered. "Go on, boy. It's okay," she told him. Then he raised his head and continued on. The lanterns lit the way, and things were fine until a late-summer thunderstorm approached. Suddenly the wind started to blow with a high-pitched howl, causing the trees to rub together and make a loud scrunching sound. As the lightning began to flash and crack above their heads, the ponies became very uneasy, almost to the point of bolting. "Steady them!" Kristina yelled. "Talk to them. Take hold of the more nervous ones, and let them know they're alright. Work to maintain control!" Then the downpour of rain struck and doused Kristina's lantern, leaving them in darkness.

Hazel knew something was wrong when the forward motion of the herd stopped. She jumped from her wagon, ran up to Norman, and said, "Pass the word and tell everyone to hunker down and hold their ground until this thunderstorm goes by." As instructed, Norman followed Hazel's orders, and soon the outriders had gathered all of the ponies into smaller groups to maintain better control and seek shelter from the weather. Once the storm died down a little, everyone lit their lanterns again and continued on down the Piney Ridge Trail, through the Trent Woods.

When the group approached the highest hill on the trail, they saw the fast-moving water running toward them, like a small flowing creek. Eventually, the push of the water made it very difficult for the ponies to maintain their footing, so they climbed the hill. From the top of the hill, they realized that the flowing water had cut knee-deep ruts throughout the entire trail, and there was nothing they could do except keep trudging along. The overhead canopy was becoming thinner, allowing for more daylight. Finally, the trail opened up to a very large clearing. At that point, everyone gathered together to relax and dry out some.

"Oh, Lord," said Norman. "Look over there! It's Old Buck and his herd of half-crazed cattle!"

"It sure is," Hazel said. "Maybe we can sneak around to the west of them, if we're lucky," she said.

"I have a better idea," Norman said.

"What might that be?" Hazel asked him.

"I say we stay right here for a while and hope they wander off to another meadow or go back into the woods," he said.

"Suppose they don't move! What then?" asked Kristina.

Norman replied, "In that case, we'll send that barking, brown, fussy dog of yours straight for Old Buck, along with Barnacle, Flash, and a few of the younger, faster stallions, to harass the daylights out of him until he gives chase! If we can get Old Buck mad enough, maybe he'll move and take the rest of his kind with him. Doesn't that sound like it just might work?" he asked, and everyone agreed.

"Then it's all settled," Hazel said. "We'll rest for a spell, have lunch, and then we'll launch a harassment attack on Old Buck, if he's still out there when we get ready to go."

When the lunch was over, the group resumed their trek in a southward direction. Old Buck was still in the meadow, so Kristina said, "Go get him, girl." Then Cocoa took off, barking and growling.

At first the cattle did not pay any attention to Cocoa, so she ran right up to Old Buck and grabbed him by the tail. Buck spun around, flinging Cocoa to the side, and she rolled over a few times but went right back at him. Then Barnacle and the Raven came charging in, kicking and nipping at Old Buck, too. Finally, the two stallions and the dog were able to cut the mean bull out of the herd and isolate him. Then Old Buck pawed the ground and took off after them, away from the meadow. However, in an instant, he turned around, gathered his herd, and began stampeding back toward the outriders and ponies.

❦ 44 ❦

HATTIE BRINGS NEWS

The group of outriders looked up to see red-eyed Old Buck charging with fury, stampeding straight toward them, and flanked by angry cattle on all sides. "Get mounted!" yelled Hazel as she ran toward the wagon. "We've got to get these ponies moving! Head them to the beach where the sand is soft. Their legs are much longer, their hooves are much larger, and they'll fare much better in the soft sand than the cattle. I'll move the wagon and the injured mare off to cover and wait. If the cattle follow you, I'll try to slip around to the west of you guys. Let's go!" she said, as she cracked the whip above the lead horse.

Kristina, Norman, and the Hooper and Midgett boys hurried the herd to the beach. Cocoa, Barnacle, and the Raven had not given up on Buck. Cocoa was dragged along behind him, still grasping his tail with her teeth. Barnacle and the Raven were running alongside, nipping at the big bull's feet. Still, Old Buck did not change direction. He was headed straight for the wagon at full ramming speed.

The impact caved in the side of the wagon, broke the tongue, and splintered the wheel spokes. The force of the blow stunned the big bull. He stood up and walked off a few paces, then crumbled to his knees. The rest of Old Buck's herd stopped and gathered around him, unsure of what to do next.

One of the spokes from the rear wheel had hit the injured mare square between the eyes. The mare crumbled and fell, with blood flowing from her mouth and nose. Still tied to the wagon, the rope had drawn tight around her neck, and she could barely breathe. Hazel jumped to her feet and yelled, "Quick, everybody! Load the supplies on some of the stronger stallions, and I'll see to this injured one. Maybe we can get out of here before Old Buck comes to his senses."

While the supplies were being transferred, Cocoa, Barnacle, and the Raven positioned themselves between Old Buck and the outriders. Then Norman ran up to the stunned bull and tied him securely to the wrecked wagon. In the meantime, Hazel cut the rope from the mare's neck and wiped the blood from her eyes. "She's only stunned," said Hazel. "Help me get her to her feet so that we can be on our way.

"We need to move as fast as we can," Hazel continued. "Perhaps we can reach the safety of Creeds Hill Lifesaving Station before Old Buck comes around and gives chase! Y'all go on ahead, and I'll move this mare as fast as she'll go. We'll see you there!" Hazel shouted. Then the outriders and ponies took off in a flash. Hazel moved the mare along at her own pace, and Barnacle and the Raven brought up the rear, stopping to look back every so often. Cocoa was last in line, still growling and scolding the cattle.

Old Buck finally got to his feet and was infuriated to be tied to the wagon. He kept crashing into it, trying to get loose, and was finally able to free himself of his restraints. However, a small piece of wagon about the size of a shed door was still tied to the rope, and as the big bull took off after the ponies, the piece of wagon bumped along behind him. This inconvenience slowed Buck down just enough for Hazel and the injured pony to catch up with their group. The herd and the outriders had gathered near the station corral under the protection of Barnacle, the Raven, and Cocoa, who were still keeping a lookout for the charging cattle.

Keeper Austin and the crew at Creeds Hill Station came running outside when they saw the large group of ponies and heard the commotion. They waved their arms and shouted at the cattle; somehow, all together, they were able to stop the stampede. Old Buck lingered for a while, watching the animals. Then the enraged bull ran up within a few yards of them and stopped.

He pawed the ground, bellowed, snorted, shook his head from side to side, and made a few short, threatening runs at them.

When Old Buck saw his herd wandering off, losing interest in the chase, he chewed the rope in half to free himself of the wagon debris. Then he followed behind them, stopping to look back a time or two with a scolding, threatening stance. When Old Buck was no longer in sight, the outriders refilled their drinking water containers and rested. Then they moved on toward the Creeds Hill Lifesaving Station. They had promised Keeper Daniels they would stop at each station and let him know how they were doing.

Keeper Austin of Creeds Hill welcomed Hazel and the outriders. He told them that Keeper Daniels of Chicamacomico had wired ahead to all stations, asking about their well-being and their progress. Then he said he would wire Keeper Daniels back and let him know that everyone was safe at Creeds Hill. Hazel thanked him, and then she told the group that they had better be moving on toward Hatteras if they hoped to get across Slash Creek and through Sticky Bottom before nightfall.

The trail around Slash Creek took the herd out to the beach, almost to the surf line. They made this trek without too much difficulty, to the outer edge of Hatteras Village. Hazel and Kristina stopped by John Stowe's Trading Post to pick up a few needed items. Then they rejoined the herd headed for the Sticky Bottom Trail. Because this trail was very narrow, the ponies had to walk in columns of two on their way to the open beach, where they planned to stop for the night. If they varied from the trail by just a few feet, they'd become mired in the soft, sticky, bottomless pools of mud, where many animals had met their end. "We've got to keep the horses together, tight on the trail and moving," Hazel warned, "if we're to get across here all in one piece," she added.

Slowly they moved the entire herd through the Sticky Bottom Trail without incident to the lower end of Hatteras Village, and they were soon able to enter the meadows just north of Hatteras Inlet. As the outriders settled the ponies and looked for a place to bed down, Hazel approached Norman and suggested that they go scout around. First, she made the others aware of what she and Norman were fixing to do.

Hazel explained, "If we're going to cross the inlet early tomorrow morning, we've got to see if the tide is ebbing or flowing. This will determine where we enter the water, in order to make a smooth, safe crossing. We'll be back by the time you have a fire started and are settling in to cook." Then she and Norman headed to the inlet to check on the tide and find a good crossing spot. Cocoa chased after them, but Kristina called her back. Then Cocoa returned slowly with her head hung down.

"It's okay if she wants to go," said Hazel.

"Alright, then, go on," Kristina told her dog. Cocoa yipped with excitement as she joined Hazel and Norman. Then Barnacle joined them, too.

"Would you look at that!" said Kristina. A big chestnut stallion, a brown dog, Hazel, and Norman all headed off together to find the safest place to cross the inlet.

As the foursome approached the inlet, they could tell the tide was ebbing. There was a long sandbar on the ocean side that stuck almost halfway across the channel. "The tide is still running out," Norman said, "and it's almost eight o'clock. If we can get back here tomorrow morning, near nine o'clock, we can swim the ponies across at slack water before we run out of sandbar."

"That's exactly what we'll do," Hazel replied. Then they returned to the others and explained the plan for the next day. Hazel asked Kristina to go with her to help change the bandages on the injured mare's leg. After they had completed the task, Hazel asked her what she was going to do if, at the end of their journey, Barnacle decided to stay with the herd.

"Dad and I have discussed this," Kristina said, assuring Hazel that she was dreading such a situation but would deal with whatever the case may be.

Kristina and Hazel decided to walk down to the sound before returning to camp. Cocoa was walking along beside Kristina when her ears perked up, as if she heard something. "What is it, girl?" Kristina asked the dog. A low growl came from Cocoa's throat. Off to the west they could hear a steady, scraping noise, and men talking. It sounded as if someone was paddling a skiff, coming toward them. Then they saw the lantern light and three people standing in a small boat: one woman and two men.

Hazel shouted out, "Is that you, Hattie?"

The woman answered, "Sure is! That you, Hazel?" the woman asked.

"Yes, it's me," was Hazel's reply. "What in the world are you doing on this side of Hatteras Inlet?" Hazel asked her sister.

"I came up to Portsmouth and got tired of waiting there, so I decided to come to Ocracoke, where I met up with these two Howard boys. Then we came on here, looking for you. We have some disturbing news for you. The government has dispatched an entire unit of soldiers to Ocracoke to catch up to you and take charge of the ponies."

"Where are they now?" asked Hazel.

"At this point, all we know is that they landed at Roanoke Island yesterday and are taking smaller sailboats down here," said Hattie. "News of your whereabouts is all up and down these islands, ever since Creeds Hill wired your location to Chicamacomico. Therefore, I suggest no more contact that gives away your location. We anchored a sprit sailor inside the inlet and paddled to shore to find you."

"Come on with us," Hazel said. "We're headed back to camp. By now, they'll have some food ready, so we can eat, and you can meet the rest of the outriders. We have to tell them about the soldiers."

Back at camp, Hazel introduced her sister to everyone and told them about the soldiers. "At this point, all we know is that we're ahead of them. We don't know how much of a lead we have, so we need to plan our next move very carefully. We must get this herd across the inlet in the morning and move down Ocracoke rapidly to stay ahead of the soldiers," Hazel insisted. "Right now, we all need to get a good night's rest so that we'll be fresh in the morning."

Kristina had a hard time falling asleep, thinking about the excitement of the upcoming day. As she listened to Cocoa snoring away, she said, "I wish I could fall asleep as fast as you, Cocoa."

Hazel, Norman, and Hattie were up before sunrise the next morning, scouting out the inlet and the tides. Just as Hazel and Norman had anticipated, the water was ebbing at a good pace and was almost at the bottom of low tide.

"It'll be slack water soon," Hazel said to Norman. "We should get back, wake the troops, and get the ponies moving."

On their way back to camp, Hattie was the first to see the white puffs of sail on the distant horizon. "There they come," she told Norman and Hazel, and sure enough, there were about two dozen sails in the distance.

"They're coming down the back of the reef on an offshore tack," said Norman. "When they begin their inshore tack, that'll bring them up to Rollinson's Channel, where they can enter the inlet and possibly land very close to us."

"You're right," Hazel responded, "or else they may pass the channel entrance and head for Ocracoke Inlet to get ahead of us."

"In any case I think it's time we get a move on it," said Hattie as they neared the campsite. When they arrived, everyone already had most of the gear packed.

"Bring all your gear and supplies down to the johnboat," said Hattie. "The Howard boys and I have a wagon on the other side of the inlet. We'll off-load and pack it for you so that you can move on down the island with the ponies after you cross the inlet. You can hold up when you get to Blue Heron's Hammock, where there is plenty of cover to hide the ponies. These boys and I will take the sprit sailor on around and meet you there." Then they all headed down to the inlet to begin their crossing.

After the supplies were loaded on the johnboat, the outriders began to swim the first group of ponies across the channel. The tide had slacked; the crossing went fairly smooth and without incident. Then they loaded the supplies onto the wagon from the johnboat and began to move the ponies southward. Norman agreed to remain behind to scout the government vessels. He wanted to see whether they came into Hatteras Inlet or continued down the sound to Ocracoke Inlet.

Norman watched the vessels enter Rollinson's Channel and head for the shore. Then he decided to go back across the inlet for a closer look. As the boats entered Hatteras Harbor, he knew something was wrong. He counted only twelve, although he was sure Hattie had mentioned "a couple dozen sails." This meant that half of the boats must have continued on their offshore tack toward Ocracoke.

✵45✵

The Capture

Norman galloped his pony at top speed to reach the inlet before the current got too strong. He had to catch up with the herd and warn them that the government might be ahead of them. As he entered the inlet area, it was getting dark. He rode toward the same shoal they had used earlier and soon realized that it was half-covered with water. The tide was beginning to run in the inlet at a much faster pace than before.

Norman knew his horse could not make it across the channel unless he got off the horse's back. He dismounted and clung to the saddle horn by wrapping the reins around his left wrist, leaving his right hand free for paddling. Then he paddled with his free hand and kicked hard with his feet to help the pony all he could. They finally made it across the channel, although they had been swept a long ways back to the sound side of the inlet.

Norman and the pony had to walk about a mile, through soft mud, before they could climb up onto the marsh. Then he found a deep pool of water out in the muddy bottom where he washed himself and the pony. A freshwater pond provided a quick drink before they continued.

It was about midnight when Norman reached the herd at Blue Heron Hammock and woke everyone. "What's all the excitement about?" Hazel asked him.

Norman replied, "The government has sent vessels ahead of you to Ocracoke Inlet, and you have a regiment of soldiers behind you at Hatteras

Harbor. My guess is that the ones ahead of you are there to block your passage to Portsmouth Island. The ones in Hatteras will cross the inlet at the next slack water, and you'll be boxed in between two regiments of soldiers. The government is serious about stopping you and gaining control of these Banker ponies," Norman assured them.

"What do we do now?" asked Kristina.

"Group meeting," said Hazel. "Obviously, we must formulate a plan. We've got to figure a way to get around the government folks to the south of us," she told the group. Then they gathered more firewood and built up the fire, made fresh coffee, and began brainstorming on what to do next. Before they got the coffee poured, Hattie and the Howard boys came walking out of the shadows. "Why do you have such a large fire?" asked Hattie. "You can be seen for miles!"

"We're in turmoil," said Hazel. "We have a regiment of soldiers in front of us and a regiment behind us. They'll try to box us in for the next couple of days at least."

"There must be some way to outflank them and get around," said Kristina.

"With this herd?" replied Hazel. "It's much too large to make a clean getaway."

One of the Howard boys spoke up. "Perhaps we can help," he said. "Up ahead a few miles, there's another hammock, called Molasses Creek Hammock, with enough cover to hide this herd, plenty of fresh water to support it, and grass to provide grazing for quite some time. We suggest you take about a third of your ponies, make a run for the Ocracoke Inlet, and cross over, allowing the soldiers to see you as they cross the reef to enter the harbor. Maybe you can fool them into thinking you've made it to the safety of Portsmouth Island. Then take the rest of the herd to Molasses Creek and hide them until the soldiers lose interest and leave the area. We'll sail to Ocracoke Harbor right away and do some scouting for you," the Howard boys told them. "One of us will come to Molasses Creek Hammock and report on the movement of the soldiers at Ocracoke Village."

Everyone agreed with the plan, and they were eager to get started. It was decided that the Midgett boys, Kristina, Barnacle, and a few of the faster, younger stallions would hightail it for Ocracoke Inlet and cross with the slack morning tide. Then they would wait until it was light enough for the soldiers to see them landing at Ocracoke Harbor. Soon they got their group together and took off to the south end of the island, running at a full gallop.

Hazel, Norman, and the rest of the outriders moved the remainder of the herd to the safety of Molasses Creek Hammock. The Howard boys and Hattie sailed the inside route, closer to the island. They made short, shallow tacks, arriving about half an hour ahead of the larger boats, which were ferrying the soldiers.

As daylight appeared on the horizon, the vessels began landing the soldiers. Kristina, Barnacle, and the small group of ponies waited until the boats were close enough to guarantee that the soldiers would see them before coming out of the scrub bushes. They were only a few hundred yards from the water's edge, and they began to slowly walk toward the channel.

Before they could reach the water, a solid line of soldiers came running out of the brush, completely surrounding them and blocking their path to the inlet. A uniformed officer approached and said his name was Sergeant Walter Thurman. He said he was in charge of the soldiers, who had orders to take the outriders into custody and impound the herd. Instead he would take them to the Ocracoke Lifesaving Station, where they would be treated as guests for a few days. Sergeant Thurman assured them that he knew the majority of the herd was still to the east of them. He also explained that a regiment of soldiers was on its way south from Hatteras to round all the ponies up into one large herd and take them to a corral near the Ocracoke Station.

After Kristina and the Midgett boys were escorted to the station, their horses were placed in the corral. Then they were taken to the crew's quarters, where they waited to meet Sergeant Thurman and the station keeper. Just as soon everyone was gone, Barnacle jumped the fence and headed up the island at a fast gallop.

Hattie and the Howard boys had observed what was happening from a distance. They went to the station to see if they could talk to the Midgett boys and Kristina, but were told about the meeting and asked to come back later.

As they were leaving the station, it was decided that one of them would go to Molasses Creek Hammock and inform the others of these latest happenings.

Hazel knew something was wrong when she saw Barnacle approaching them alone at a full gallop. His entire body was gleaming with sweat, so much that his coat was entirely white. Barnacle ran up to Hazel, then stopped and nuzzled her hands. "What's wrong, boy?" she asked the big horse. "How'd you get separated from the others?" When Barnacle reared up on his hind legs and whimpered, Hazel thought something must be wrong. She led Barnacle to the wagon to dry him off and rub him down, and then she went to the opposite side of the hammock to talk with the Hooper boys and Norman.

"Something must have gone wrong," Hazel told them. "Barnacle has come back all alone, covered with sweat, as if he's been running for a very long time. I'd like to take Norman with me down to the village to see what's happened. If it's okay with y'all, I'd like to leave the herd in your care. There's ample grazing, water, and cover for you here, even if the weather gets bad. You'll be fine and out of sight, as long as you stay back here in the hammock."

As Hazel and Norman moved to the outer portion of the hammock, she said, "Barnacle is rested enough so that I can ride him. You can choose a mount, and we'll be on our way. I believe Barnacle will take us to where Kristina and the Midgett boys are, and we can get to the bottom of this." After they made their way out of the hammock, Barnacle turned down the island road toward the village.

"Do you have any idea where to look?" Norman asked Hazel.

"No, I don't," was her reply, "but Barnacle does, and I've asked him to lead us to Kristina."

"Will he do that?" Norman asked.

"We can count on it," was Hazel's confident answer.

As they were coming out of the cover of the hammock, they stopped short. Right in front of them were about fifty mounted soldiers headed toward the village.

"That must be the group I saw land at Hatteras last night," Norman told Hazel.

"Probably," Hazel answered. "Let's remain hidden until they move on by us."

Norman and Hazel waited until the men were out of sight before moving out into the open themselves. They followed at a safe distance behind the men so that they would not be discovered. They only traveled a short distance down the road before Barnacle turned down a narrow trail, well hidden from anyone passing by.

"Where is he taking us now?" asked Norman.

"I don't know yet, but if we're patient, we'll see," Hazel responded.

Barnacle brought them to a small clearing and stopped. There, peeking through the brush, were the Howard boys, watching the soldiers pass. "What are you guys doing here?" Hazel asked them.

Both men spun around on their heels at the same time. "Man! You gave us a start!" one of them said. "We're looking for you! How did you find us?"

"Barnacle brought us to you," Hazel said. Then she asked them about Hattie. The Howard boys told Hazel that Hattie had remained behind at the Ocracoke Lifesaving Station, along with Hazel's friends.

"Are they in trouble?" asked Hazel.

"That, we don't know," one of the Howard boys replied. "When we left to come find you, Kristina and the Midgett boys were guests at a meeting with the station keeper and a Sergeant Thurman. Hattie was hoping to see them after the meeting."

Hazel said, "Alright, let's head to the station."

Hattie arrived at the station just as the meeting was breaking up, and she asked the keeper if she could talk to the Midgett boys and Kristina. "Yes, they're in the galley," the keeper told her. "The cook is feeding them now, and the sergeant said they were free to go as soon as the lieutenant arrives from Hatteras and talks to them."

"That's great news!" Hattie said. "Which way is the galley from here?"

"Down the hall and to the left," the keeper told her. "You can follow me. I'm on my way there now."

Hattie followed the keeper into the galley, where Kristina and the Midgett boys were eating breakfast.

"Hungry?" the keeper asked her. "If so, have a seat."

"No, thanks. I'd just like to speak to those fellas for a minute," Hattie told the keeper. Then she asked them what was going on, and they filled her in on the capture. "They tell me you're free to go after you talk to some lieutenant," Hattie told them.

"That's what they told us, too," Kristina said. "The Ocracoke Station keeper wired Chicamacomico to let all the folks back home know what's happened. Keeper Daniels and my dad are on their way to try and help us get out of here," she said.

"I'll go find Hazel and let her know what's going on," Hattie replied.

"Tell her to keep the rest of the herd hidden until the sergeant lets us go. Then we can all talk," Kristina told Hattie. "As long as we have the majority of the herd hidden, we still have some bargaining power. Tell Hazel not to come here. So far, you're the only one that they know for sure is connected with us. From here on out, we'll have to meet secretly until Dad and Keeper Daniels arrive." Hattie agreed and headed back to the sprit sailboat to wait for the Howard boys.

As they approached the outskirts of the village, Hazel, Norman, and the Howard boys remained well behind the mounted soldiers until they determined where the soldiers were going. They watched as the soldiers stopped at the station and dismounted. Then a small group of them went inside. The lieutenant instructed the sergeant to take the rest of the men down to the inlet, near the channel, to set up camp and block all access to the south.

"You're free to go," the lieutenant told Kristina. "You and your friends have broken no laws. I know there are a lot more ponies and riders out there, and I want to talk to all of you and schedule a meeting with the district commander. He'll be here in a couple days, so meet with your friends and let me know something by tomorrow." Then he walked them to the front door and allowed them to leave.

❦46❦

The Blue-Eyed Lieutenant

When the Howard boys returned to the sprit sailor looking for Hattie, she told them that Kristina and the Midgett boys were being released by the soldiers that afternoon. Then she said, "Go find Hazel and tell her to meet us at James Spencer's Store so that we can decide on our next course of action. Mr. Spencer has a few tables inside his store where folks can sit and enjoy a snack, drink, or a hot cup of coffee," she told them.

Everyone arrived at Mr. Spencer's store at about the same time. When they were seated, Hazel asked Kristina to fill them in on her conversation with the lieutenant.

"Actually, he's a very nice, polite man," she told the group. "He knows there are many more ponies and riders out there and wants all of us to meet with his commander to work out a solution to this situation."

"Did you say 'very nice' in your description of the lieutenant?" Hazel asked.

"Yes," responded Kristina, "and very handsome, too."

"Oh, my," said Hazel, "the next thing you know, you'll want to give the ponies to him."

"I wouldn't go that far," answered Kristina, "but he is a very likable person."

"Well, I think we should wait until your father and Keeper Daniels arrive before we agree to any meeting with the commander," Hazel said.

"What about the ponies at Molasses Creek—and the Hooper boys?" Norman asked.

"We'll leave them there tonight. In the morning we'll go get them and bring them to the corral. Kristina can talk to her handsome lieutenant and work out a meeting schedule that includes Edward and Keeper Daniels so that we can all attend together."

"My 'handsome lieutenant'?" Kristina asked.

"Yes," said Hazel, "but don't allow your judgment to become clouded by his big blue eyes when you're making arrangements that concern all of us." Hazel laughed out loud.

"I didn't mention the color of his eyes to you! How did you know?" asked Kristina.

"Hattie noticed and told me," Hazel answered. "I figured you would be the best one of our group to deal with him," Hazel added.

"Whatever," Kristina replied. "That being the case, I have questions. Do you think it's wise to bring all the ponies into the station corral? What about losing our bargaining leverage?" she asked.

"I like our chances," Hazel replied. "They already know the size of the herd and what our intentions are. They've blocked our progress southward, but they seem ready to negotiate. If we bring the rest of the herd in, it will appear that we're being cooperative. Having you deal with the handsome lieutenant will help," she told Kristina, "and I know your dad and Keeper Daniels will have a few tricks up their sleeves."

Hazel continued, "I overheard Mr. Spencer talking to another Ocracoker about a storm making up near here. They were talking about flocks and flocks of shorebirds headed inland across the sound, which is another reason to bring all of the Bankers into the corral. At least they'll be together where we can look after them. Tomorrow's another day." Then it was decided that they would all spend the night at the Howard houses and proceed in the morning.

Edward and Keeper Daniels were aboard the *Coastal Rambler*, bound for Ocracoke. They had just finished with the transfer of supplies and passengers to a smaller vessel in Hatteras and were coming out Rollinson's Channel, bound for the Ocracoke harbor. They joined Captain Mansfield in the wheelhouse and sailed into a brisk southwest wind. "You'll be at the Ocracoke dock by first light," said the captain. Then he asked Edward if he would like to take the wheel for a while.

"Sure," Edward responded. "She's a might smaller than I am accustomed to, but she looks like she handles well."

Captain Mansfield replied, "When you switch the main jib on a downwind tack, she tends to drift and lose the wind. If you're not quick, she tends to slip backward until she catches the wind. When we reach that point offshore, at the beginning of the inshore tack, I'll show you what I mean. You'll have to hold her tight into the wind until the last second. Begin your turn when the main sail flaps, then switch the jib quickly while holding her tight to the leeside. If you do that, she'll scoot, grab the wind, and almost tack to port all by herself."

"I'll give her a try," Edward replied.

"Just hold her steady for about another hour. Then we'll begin the port tack, and you'll see what I mean," said the captain.

"Just so long as the two of you get us to Ocracoke Harbor by mid-morning," said Keeper Daniels. "That's all I'm concerned about! Until then, I'm going below to turn in for the night."

"You're in good hands," Edward told the keeper as the *Coastal Rambler* cut a smooth path through the four-foot waves of the southwester.

The outriders got up very early the next morning, and everyone except Kristina and Hattie headed off to Molasses Creek to bring in the herd. The Hooper boys met the outriders in a concealed hammock, and Hazel updated them on the plan. Very soon, the group had the herd up and moving toward a corral near the Ocracoke Station.

As soon as they arrived at the station, Kristina and Hattie went to see the young lieutenant. When they told him that their friends were bringing the rest of the herd into the corral that very morning, the lieutenant was glad that they had decided to cooperate. Then he smiled and said, "Not all of the ponies are going to be put to government use."

The lieutenant explained that the district commander would be bringing a livestock expert with him to size up the herd. "We have decided that any horse too small to make muster will not be used and will be returned to you," he said. This was good news to Kristina and Hattie because they knew most of the ponies in the herd were of the smaller, Banker type.

The lieutenant continued, "However, the Bankers will only be allowed to live freely on the uninhabited offshore islands. They will no longer be able to live freely on the occupied islands of Hatteras and Ocracoke." At that point, Hattie coughed and suggested that they go outside since the outriders would be arriving soon with the rest of the herd. As they were walking to the corral, the lieutenant told them that the commander would arrive around three o'clock that afternoon, when he wanted to meet with everyone and assess the stock.

Hazel, Norman, and the Midgett and Hooper boys were just closing the corral gate on the last of the ponies when Kristina, Hattie, and the lieutenant walked up. With the gate finally closed, Barnacle and the Raven started pacing back and forth nervously. Also, Cocoa would not stop barking or running in and out of the corral through a hole she had dug under the fence.

"Get in there and calm those animals down," Hazel told Kristina. "If you don't, Barnacle and that Raven will jump out or kick the fence down."

"Hush, Cocoa," Kristina scolded the dog.

"I'm sorry," Kristina told the lieutenant, "my dog stays with my horse and is not used to seeing him penned up." Then Kristina called to Barnacle and the Raven, and both of them came to her on command. Kristina spoke to the big horses in a soft tone, telling them everything was going to be okay. As they stopped pacing and began to show signs of settling, the rest of the herd also began to relax.

"Good," said Hazel. "Now maybe we'll be able to control them." Then Hazel chuckled and said, "So, this is your handsome lieutenant? He really does have big blue eyes, Kristina! No wonder you like him," she added.

Kristina was embarrassed and blushing from head to toe, but she did find a few words to say. "Well, I do think he's handsome and very nice," she said, loud enough for the lieutenant to hear her.

"Well, I think you're very nice also," the lieutenant replied. "Maybe when we get this settled, we can spend some time together," he told Kristina. "Perhaps," was the only answer he received, along with her smile.

The *Coastal Rambler* struck sail and glided into Silver Lake, near the mouth of Ocracoke Harbor. Soon Captain Mansfield shouted, "Anchor aweigh," and the vessel settled in the middle of the lake. After the process of off-loading passengers and supplies ended, Edward and Keeper Daniels boarded the first passenger skiff to shore. As they neared the dock, one of their friends, Harvey Spencer, yelled hello. He owned a twenty-four-foot fishing sloop and had just dropped the main mast and the jib set down, and was preparing to lash them to the deck.

"What's up?" Keeper Daniels hollered. "I guess you know we're in for a big blow," he said. "The glass is as low as I've ever seen it." Then he saw all the fishermen getting ready for the storm as they bustled about, securing their vessels, adding extra lines, and lashing everything down in the inner harbor.

When they reached the dock, Edward and Keeper Daniels hurried to the Ocracoke Station and found everyone gathered around the corral, checking out the ponies. Kristina immediately went to her father's side. "I'm so glad to see you, Daddy," she told her father. "I know you and Keeper Daniels will be able to help us reach a solution to the situation we're in."

The lieutenant came over and introduced himself. Then he said, "My commanding officer will be coming in this afternoon with a livestock evaluator to decide which horses might be useful to us. I'm not the expert, but it appears to me that most of these ponies are too small for pulling large wagons and field hardware."

Edward agreed with him. "Most of them are shipwrecked Banker ponies," he said.

The lieutenant qualified his evaluation by saying, "Even so, I've seen three that may pass muster as workhorses." Then he pointed as he spoke. "That big black stallion, the chestnut stallion next to him, and that tan-colored stallion over there. That chestnut stallion must be twenty-one hands high, and the tan stallion looks young, but very strong."

Keeper Daniels excused himself to go see the Ocracoke keeper to inquire about the approaching storm. When he returned to the group, he informed them that they had more to worry about than the fate of the ponies. "According to the last message received by the Ocracoke keeper, we're in for a gale," Keeper Daniels told them. "This storm is coming from Bermuda. The maximum winds are up to ninety miles per hour, and it's traveling west at twelve miles per hour. The storm's being blocked to the north by a high-pressure area. We'll be experiencing storm conditions by nightfall as it passes just to the south of our location on its current westward track. The ponies will have to be released so that they can seek shelter in a protected hammock. There's no protection in that open corral, and there are not enough barns around here to shelter them. We'll have to settle that situation after the storm has passed."

The lieutenant was hesitant to let the ponies go. He wanted to wait for his company commander and the livestock expert to evaluate them first. Finally, with a lot of coaxing from everyone, the lieutenant gave in and told them to release the herd. Hazel helped put his mind at ease when she told him that the ponies would not go far. "They'll huddle together in the protection of the closest hammock and be easy to round up after this storm passes."

When Edward opened the gate, the Raven and Barnacle were the first ones out, followed by Flash and the rest of the ponies. They took off to the north, headed for Molasses Creek Hammock, with Cocoa running next to Barnacle, barking nonstop.

"Come back here, Cocoa," Kristina yelled, and the dog stopped and looked back before she turned and ran off again. Then Kristina yelled a second time. "Barnacle has enough to worry about without having to look after you, so come back here right now," Kristina commanded. Then Cocoa came cowering back to Kristina and settled at her feet. At that point, Keeper Daniels and Edward said they had to go see the Ocracoke keeper.

When they arrived at the Ocracoke Station, Keeper Daniels asked the Ocracoke keeper what they could do to help prepare for the storm. The Ocracoke keeper informed them that everything had been battened down, and they were welcome to stay at the station until the storm passed.

Keeper Daniels told Edward, "We've got to talk to the young lieutenant and let him know that there's no way he can leave his men camped in tents out on that beach. They'll have to come back here. Some of them can stay in the boathouse, and some can stay in the station, but at least they'll be sheltered from the weather."

It wasn't long before Keeper Daniels and Edward found the lieutenant on his way to the tack room with his commanding officer and the livestock agent. The lieutenant made the introductions and then explained why they had released the horses. The commander was satisfied with the fact that the ponies would be easy to round up after the storm, and now he just wanted to help the lieutenant relocate the men under his charge before the storm hit.

❧47❧

THE HERD SPLITS UP

Keeper Daniels and the outriders sat on the east porch with the Ocracoke Station keeper and watched the winds grow stronger. As the clouds began to race westward the Ocracoke keeper said, "Thus it begins!"

The approaching storm was to the south of Bermuda, moving at twelve miles an hour to the west, with maximum sustained winds of ninety miles per hour. If it held true to its path, the center would pass over the north end of Portsmouth Island, and the strongest winds and storm conditions would come across Ocracoke. Even though the storm was still well out to sea, the southeast gale-force winds were beginning to push the sound water toward the mainland. By dark, the shoals were completely dry as far the eye could see, and the vessels in the harbor were resting on the ground. The sound water was completely gone.

When the herd of ponies reached the cover of Molasses Creek Hammock, they all settled in, except for Flash and a few of the younger stallions. Instead, they kept going—through the marsh, toward the shore side—until Barnacle caught up with them and made them return to the hammock. Flash remained very unsettled and kept pacing around the corral, trying to excite the younger ponies.

Flash managed to get most of the herd excited, and all of a sudden the hyped-up horses broke for the sound side. The younger ponies took off after them, and some of the older ponies joined as well. Barnacle gave chase and tried to turn the horses around, but they raced on after Flash, and this time Flash didn't stop. He continued past the marsh, out onto the shoals, and turned south, with his followers thundering behind him.

Barnacle stopped at the edge of the shore and called to the ponies, but they continued southward in an excited gallop. He headed back to the hammock alone, wondering how he would make Star understand that their only son was gone—and might not return.

Flash continued south on the offshore sandbars of Ocracoke Inlet. He felt a sense of danger he didn't completely understand, and a strong feeling that moving farther south would ensure the safety of his followers, as well as himself. Therefore, they thundered on, slowing down only once to swim across a small channel. From there, they climbed up on the shoals and galloped south, down the length of Portsmouth Island, until they reached the Turn Again Bay hammock. Then the ponies drank from several freshwater ponds and rested. Flash decided to settle there, in the cover of the hammock, where he felt sure they would be safe during the storm.

Barnacle tried to comfort Star. They both realized that they may have seen the last of Flash. Barnacle was also becoming restless himself, feeling a strong urge to take what was left of the herd and head north, away from the storm. He was torn, though, because he didn't want to leave Kristina and Cocoa. As Barnacle became increasingly unsettled, Star tried to calm him, but to no avail. Then they heard a familiar sound. Faintly from the south, they heard Cocoa barking.

As the barking grew louder, Barnacle knew that, somehow, Cocoa had gotten away from Kristina and was headed his way. When Cocoa arrived at the hammock, she did her best to get Barnacle to follow her. She barked nonstop and nipped at Barnacle's heels. Then she ran toward the sound and back again, several times. Finally, it was all Barnacle could take, and he headed off after Cocoa, with Star and the Raven and the rest of the herd behind him. The horses followed Cocoa to the sound side and out onto the shoals, and then they took to the north to escape the fury of the oncoming storm.

Barnacle, the Raven, and all the ponies made it safely to a small hammock on the northern end of Ocracoke Island, but Cocoa kept urging them on by barking constantly and acting weird. Finally, Barnacle and Star took off with Cocoa out onto the shoals, heading toward Hatteras Inlet. About half of the herd followed them, and the other half remained with the Raven on the north end of Ocracoke.

Barnacle, Star, Cocoa, and their smaller herd of Banker ponies didn't even slow down until they neared the Trent Woods. Then they moved to the east through the marsh and found shelter from the storm under the cover of the Trent Woods.

Back at the Ocracoke Station, the wind was howling from the east. Hazel and Kristina decided to go to the porch on the lee side. As they approached, Kristina noticed that the galley window was open to the outside and that Cocoa was gone. The dog had been asleep on a blanket provided by the cook just a few minutes ago when Kristina had gone to talk to her dad and Hazel in the dayroom. She ran to the window and called for Cocoa, but all she could see was blinding rain. She knew that Cocoa had gone to join Barnacle.

The storm continued throughout the night. As the center of the storm approached to the south of them and passed over Portsmouth, the wind shifted to the southwest. As expected, the sound water came rushing back in, but did not get high enough to have much effect on the station or the island. Folks were able to get out and check for storm damage by mid-morning. The sound tide was up to the top of the docks, and a few tree limbs were scattered around the village, but other than a sign or trashcan blown over, there appeared to be very little damage.

After helping the station crew clean up around the yard, the outriders and the lieutenant headed out to look for the ponies in hopes of returning them to the station. The commander and the stock expert stayed behind to divide the corral into sections so that they could easily separate the ponies into smaller groups for evaluation. Edward and Keeper Daniels helped the Ocracoke keeper monitor wireless messages about the storm's movement and intensity.

Hazel told Kristina to listen out for Cocoa. "Wherever she is, Barnacle will be close by," she said. "When we get to the hammock, you should call her a few times," Hazel added.

After about an hour of traveling on foot, they reached the hammock, and Kristina began to yell for Cocoa. All was quiet, and the marsh was full of water, all the way up to the high ground of the hammock.

"The tracks end here," said Norman. "With the marsh so full of water, there's no way to determine which way they went after they left high ground."

Kristina continued to call for Cocoa, but to no avail. "It's apparent that they've left here," said the lieutenant. "I have to return and report to the commander."

"There's no sign of the ponies," Hazel told Kristina. "We might as well go back and ask Keeper Daniels and your father to help us figure out our next move. If we can't find the ponies, our work here is finished. The effects of this storm could have scattered the animals to never and gone. It might take a very long time to find them, if we find them at all."

"Alright, let's go back with the lieutenant," Kristina agreed, "but I hate to leave here without them."

"Yes, I agree," said Hazel, "but they're not here."

The entire group began the walk back to the station, and when they arrived the commander met them outside.

"So that's why it took you so long," he said. "You're walking. I thought you would be riding the ponies so that we could evaluate them."

"They're all gone," said the lieutenant.

"What do you mean 'all gone'?" asked the commander.

"They're not where we thought they would be," Hazel chimed in.

"Well, let's scramble the men from the boathouse and go into the villages," the commander replied. "We boarded fifty military horses in private barns before the storm hit. We must get mounted now and find those horses."

Kristina and Hazel met Edward and Keeper Daniels on the east porch at the station to talk about their next step. Keeper Daniels began the conversation by asking them if they had any idea where the herd might be. Both of them had to tell him that they had no clue.

Then the keeper said, "Well, I personally think you two should gather your group and your gear and be ready to move. Edward and I are going to contact

Captain Mansfield to see if the *Coastal Rambler* is seaworthy. If so, we will inquire about his departure plans and meet you back here around dark. Hopefully, the soldiers will be back by then with information regarding the whereabouts of the ponies. If not, there's no telling where those Bankers might be. In that case, we might as well catch the *Coastal Rambler* and go back home." He and Edward turned to leave. Once they were gone, Hazel and Kristina hurried back to their friends to bring them up to speed. Later on, they all met back at the station, just as the soldiers were coming in from their day of searching for ponies.

The lieutenant reported to the group, "We covered the island all the way up to the Ocracoke inlet, and there's no sign of a single pony anywhere," he confessed. With that news, Keeper Daniels and Edward decided that they would sail north the very next morning, aboard the *Coastal Rambler*. The livestock expert stated that he would also be heading out at the same time. The commander announced that he would stay and wrap things up, but insisted that the lieutenant return to the mainland along with the others. Then Keeper Daniels suggested that the outriders join them as well, and at first light on the next day, they all arrived at the dock, ready to go. Upon noticing that Hazel didn't have her gear with her, Kristina said, "Where are your things, Hazel? Why haven't you packed?"

"I'm not going back home just yet," Hazel told her. "I've made arrangements with Norman to watch my stock for a few days once he gets home. I'm going to hang here for a little longer and then go home with my sister, Hattie, for a while."

"What are you up to?" Kristina asked Hazel.

"Oh, nothing," was Hazel's response.

Kristina replied, "You are up to something, and you're not telling me. Let's walk to the end of the dock where we can have a private talk."

"I do know a couple of things," Hazel began, "and so do you, if you have allowed yourself to ponder them. I know that Flash is a lot like Barnacle and wants to lead a herd of his own. I think he took most of the younger ponies with him and headed south, away from the storm and away from the influence of Barnacle and the Raven." She paused, then continued.

"Let's see. What else do I know? I know that Barnacle, Star, and Cocoa are with a bunch of ponies, probably headed north, because they know that sooner or later you will return to Northard Woods. The Raven has the remainder of the ponies somewhere, maybe even close by. You and I both know that the herd was getting way too large and difficult to manage, and the lead animals know it, too. They will all fare much better in smaller groups.

"Hattie and I are going to hang around here until we know the ponies are safe, and we will be keeping an eye on the government men until they leave. You must go back to your life in Northard Woods. You're a schoolteacher now, and the children need you. I'm sure that Barnacle, Star, and Cocoa will return there soon. I don't know how long it will take, but keep your eye out for them. After the soldiers leave, Hattie and I are going to sail her skiff southward along Portsmouth Island and down to her home at Hog Island. I have a sneaky feeling that before we get to her cottage, we'll come upon Flash and his new herd of ponies. If so, I'll send word to you." Then she said, "The blue-eyed lieutenant will be on board with you," and they both smiled.

❦48❧

The Scattering of the Ponies on the Islands

Hazel, Hattie, and the Howard boys remained on Ocracoke and said their good-byes. Then Keeper Daniels, Edward, Kristina, and the lieutenant boarded the *Coastal Rambler* and soon departed from Ocracoke Harbor, headed for the northern Outer Banks. They had a fair wind to the north as the storm crossed the sound and went inland.

The first stop was Hatteras Village. Captain Mansfield turned the *Coastal Rambler* into the wind, ordered the sails secure, and dropped anchor. When the transfer of passengers, mail, and supplies was completed, the *Coastal Rambler* continued north. Keeper Daniels joined Edward on deck, and they chatted as they sailed up the sound.

The keeper commented that the lieutenant and Kristina had been spending a lot of time together, locked in conversation, and Edward agreed. "There might be something brewing," he told Keeper Daniels. "I'll mention it to her at dinner tonight, since I am especially interested in where all this conversation is leading," he said.

That night Edward asked his daughter about the new relationship. "We're just friends, enjoying each other's company on this trip back home," she told him. "He's from Boston, and he's on his way back home. His grandfather is ill, and he has a few days to visit his family before rejoining his company of soldiers. We've exchanged addresses and will write each other, but that's all," she explained.

"I was just wondering what to tell your mother about this," her father kidded.

"You don't have to worry about that either," Kristina told her father. "I tell Mom everything. She and I have a lot to talk about when we get together."

"That's what I am concerned about," he began, but Kristina cut him off.

"Dad, it's all good!" she said. "You have nothing to worry about! I'm going back home to start the school term, and the lieutenant is on his way north, for Pete's sake."

"I'm not worried about the short term. It's just that you've developed a certain twinkle in your eye and a giggle in your voice since you two met," her father replied.

Kristina smiled and batted her big green eyes at her father. "Oh, Daddy, you know you are still the main man in my life."

Hazel and Hattie stayed on the dock until the *Coastal Rambler* was almost out of sight, gliding steadily along on the wind, headed northward. "They'll be off Northard Woods by first light tomorrow, even with the stops and connections," said Hazel. Then she announced her idea. "Let's go talk to the men at Ocracoke Station and see if we can ride along with them to search for the ponies."

"I have a better idea," Hattie told her sister. "Let's take my boat, sail up the island, and do our own search. We'll have a much better chance of getting close to the ponies if we sail quietly along than we will if we ride with a mounted group, making a bunch of noise." Hazel agreed, and they headed for Hattie's sprit sailor.

The wind was still blowing a stiff breeze from the southwest, so Hattie and Hazel glided along the shore at a nice pace. As they hugged the shoreline Hazel sat up in the bow with a long glass, scanning the marsh for any sign of ponies. She saw the mounted soldiers to the far right of Tar Yard Creek Hammock. They were circling in and out of the hammock in a search pattern, looking for the ponies. Suddenly a speck of black glistened in the sun and caught Hazel's eye.

Far away, out on the beach hills, Hazel saw the Raven leading a group of ponies around the mounted searchers, headed in the opposite direction. She felt satisfied when she saw them quickly pick up speed and disappear in an oak thicket, a good ways south. "There goes the Raven and his group," she told Hattie, "and I really don't think those soldiers have any chance of finding them. That Raven's been leading them on a merry chase!" Hazel chuckled. Then Hattie tried to have a look at the ponies, but they were all gone.

"Are you sure you saw them?" Hattie asked Hazel.

"Keep watch on the far side of that oak thicket, just before those beach hills, and you'll see them emerge in that hollow yonder," Hazel replied.

"Ah, yes, I see them now. The searchers are way north of them," Hattie said. "They'll never find them at this rate."

"That's what I'm talking about," replied Hazel. "Let's go back to the village and talk to them when they return from their pony hunt."

"Okay, let's get moving," replied Hattie. "We'll get back long before the soldiers do and have plenty of time to eat before we meet them at the station." Then she turned the skiff toward the south and began an offshore tack.

The two sisters arrived at Ocracoke Village in the early afternoon. Then they docked the sprit sailor and headed over to see the Ocracoke Station keeper. As soon as they met up with him, the sisters inquired about the search party looking for the ponies. The keeper told them that the soldiers would be arriving just ahead of dark. Then he said, "The section commander and sergeant will be having dinner with me tonight in the officers' galley. You two are more than welcome to attend, if you wish." Hazel and Hattie politely accepted the invitation, knowing that it would be the ideal place to gather information concerning the whereabouts of the ponies.

The dinner conversation that evening revolved entirely around the missing ponies. The commander informed the dinner guests that his department had more important things to deal with than chasing ponies they couldn't find. He announced that most of his men would be traveling to the north end of the island and leaving soon. Four troopers would stay behind along with the sergeant—long enough to return the mounts to the villagers. Then they would catch the next freight-boat passage to Elizabeth City, and from there, they would all head north where they were needed. This was just the news that Hazel and Hattie wanted to hear. As soon as they could, they would ask the

Ocracoke keeper to wire this information to the Chicamacomico Station and share the good news with the folks up there.

Finally the government ended its search, as well as its desire to acquire Banker ponies. The stock expert had reported to Washington that the Banker ponies were not of hearty breeding. He reported that they were too small, as a rule, and would not make satisfactory mounts for the military. According to the government, if the ponies did return, they would have to be penned up on the inhabited islands. However, they would be allowed to run free on the islands unoccupied by people.

Hazel and Hattie stayed on Ocracoke until the sergeant and the four troopers were completely out of the picture. Then they began their journey south in Hattie's small sailboat to her cottage on Hog Island. After they crossed Ocracoke Inlet, they hugged the shoreline along the sound side. The storm had crossed the sound and turned northward, providing a light northwest wind and allowing them to sail twenty miles easily on the first day. By dusk, the sisters found a small protected bay and stopped for the night. As they walked up onto the small sand beach, Hattie noticed tracks and called for her sister. "It appears that about fifty ponies have crossed this sand beach since the last high tide," she said.

"These could be some of the ponies we're looking for," Hazel told Hattie. "I have a feeling that Flash is the lead stallion of this bunch. He's always been free to roam, and he's been itching to lead his own group of ponies to new adventures."

The sisters built a cook fire, ate a meal, and settled down for the night. Then, sometime after midnight, Hazel was jarred awake by the pounding of hooves. She couldn't see the ponies passing by, but Hazel knew there were many. It took about five minutes for the sound to fade toward the south.

"That was a huge bunch," Hattie said, as she rubbed her eyes in a half-asleep stupor.

"They're headed south," Hazel replied. "Perhaps we'll come across them tomorrow." Then she rolled over and went back to sleep.

The next morning, the sisters continued their journey south, sailing very close to the shore, keeping a watchful eye for any sign of the ponies. They had sailed about ten to twelve miles and could see the mouth of Drum Inlet when Hazel told Hattie to hold off a bit. Then, as she stood on the bow-cap of the sailboat, straining to see through a long glass, she pointed and said, "See that point of marsh over there? After we get around it, the beach is flat and free of vegetation, and you'll be able to see all the way to Drum Inlet," Hazel said.

Just as they cleared the point, Hazel caught a glimpse of a chestnut-colored stallion and became almost speechless. At first she thought it was Barnacle. Standing in the meadow was a full-grown stallion watching over a herd of about 250 ponies as they grazed.

"He looks so much like his father," Hazel said, knowing instantly that the horse was Flash. Hazel admired how intent he was on keeping his group together. When a few of the younger ponies began to move forward, Flash quickly corrected them and forced them back to the herd. However, when Hazel called out to Flash, he stopped and turned to face the boat. Then he came down to the edge of the shoreline and allowed the ponies to follow him.

Before long, all of the ponies were lined up on the shore, staring at Hazel and Hattie. When Hazel got out of the boat and walked over to Flash, the big stallion bent his head down so that she could pet him. Then Hazel said, "Well, fellow, you finally have what you want now. Lead your herd wisely, and have many prosperous and wonderful adventures." Then she got back in the boat, and Hattie pushed off shore, headed for Drum Inlet.

Hog Island was just on the other side of Drum Inlet, sheltered somewhat from the ocean by the barrier islands to its east. Hazel and Hattie sailed smoothly across the inlet, entering the sheltered sound where they struck and secured the sails. They used a push pole to move the boat the last hundred yards to the dock connected to Hattie's cottage. After they secured and off-loaded the boat, Hazel asked Hattie if they could sail down to Cape Lookout Station the very next day. She wanted to send word north as quickly as possible and update the outriders on the locations of Flash, the Raven, and their herds.

The journey north on the *Coastal Rambler* seemed to fly by for Kristina. She had exchanged addresses with the young lieutenant, and they had agreed to write to each other. As she was on her way to shore onboard a smaller passenger boat, her mind wandered back to the lieutenant until she was jarred to reality by her father's voice warning her to sit down. He cautioned her that the small boat was about to make its last tack and enter the harbor near Northard Woods. As she sat, her thoughts shifted to Barnacle, Star, and Cocoa. "I wonder where my horses and dog are right now," she said aloud.

"Hopefully making their way back home," her father replied.

"You don't have much to worry about with that lot looking out for them," said Keeper Daniels. "They'll be along, and it won't surprise me if they return in a few days," he added.

"I hope you're right," Kristina answered.

Everyone was glad to be back at Northard Woods. The Chicamacomico Station crew met them at the dock and gave them rides back to the village. When Edward and his daughter reached their cottage, Kristina ran to greet her mother. "Oh, Mom," she said," I have so much to tell you!"

"Don't forget about the handsome young lieutenant," her father kidded her.

"What's that?" said Beth.

"I'll tell you all about it, Mom," Kristina replied.

"Well, come on in. I have the evening meal all ready, and you two can tell me all about it after we eat," she said.

After dinner they settled on the back porch to enjoy the splendors of the evening. Edward started the conversation by reminding Kristina that the summer was almost over and a new school term would be starting very soon. She responded by telling her father that she and Shanna would be meeting with Miss Bridges the next day. Then Kristina brought her mother up to speed about her southern adventure, including the lieutenant and the scattering of the ponies. Then they heard a soft whinny coming from the corral.

"Are there any horses in the corral?" asked Edward.

"Not to my knowledge," Beth replied.

❧49❧

Two Big Cats

Early the next morning, there was a rapping at the front door of the cottage. Edward answered it, and there stood Keeper Daniels with a message for Kristina. "I came over as soon as I received it," the keeper told Edward.

"Well, come on in and have some coffee," said Edward. "I'll wake Kristina. She has things to do today and needs to get moving anyway."

Kristina read the wire. "Hazel has seen the Raven!" she exclaimed. "He's safe, with a sizable herd on Ocracoke. She has also spotted Flash. He's on the south end of Portsmouth Island with a large herd of his own. Both herds seem to be fine for now, leading carefree lives, and roaming the beaches to their hearts' content."

"That's great," Edward said. "At least you know where Flash is, but I don't think he'll be back. It was clear to see that he was hankering for a command of his own. At this point, it would be very hard for Flash to be number two in command, which is exactly where he'll be if he comes back here, next to his father."

"I just wonder where Barnacle, Star, and Cocoa are—and how they're faring," said Kristina. "We heard some noise near the corral last night, and when we got out there, we found tracks, but no ponies," she told the keeper.

Keeper Daniels replied, "All you can do is keep fresh water in the trough and some food in the bins. Check 'em each morning and see if anything disappears." Then, as the keeper turned to leave, he thanked Edward for the coffee and wished them good luck in finding their animal friends.

Kristina and Shanna went to see Mrs. Bridges, and the three of them discussed the upcoming school year. The weather turned in early September, beginning with three northeast storms, one right behind the other. The temperature dropped off in a hurry, and the first month of school was wet and blustery.

Edward had several wrecks to reconcile, and due to the weather he was gone for long periods of time. Kristina and Beth spent a lot of time indoors, but Kristina checked the water trough and food bins daily. For a while, all the water and food remained undisturbed. Then one morning, some of it was gone and there were small hoof tracks all around. Kristina knew the tracts did not belong to her horses.

Eventually the wind moderated and shifted light to the southwest, warming up enough for Beth and Kristina to sit on the porch with light jackets. They were enjoying such an evening as Edward returned from work. He was carrying a large jar of molasses that he had retrieved from one of the wrecked vessels.

"I'll put this molasses out in the barn entrance to keep it cool," said Edward. "Then you can get it in the morning and pour it into smaller containers," he told Beth.

"We're so glad to see you," Beth replied. "Come on in and eat, and tell us all the details about your latest jobs. We always enjoy the stories you bring home from your adventures as shipwreck commissioner."

"Well, first of all, I stopped by the post office on my way home," said Edward. "Kristina has two letters. One is from Hazel, and the other is from you-know-who!"

"Daddy, will you stop teasing and give them to me, please?" Kristina asked her father. When he handed them over, she immediately went inside to read them.

The news from Hazel was all good. She indicated that she had enjoyed the time she was able to spend with her sister, Hattie. She had taken the supply boat from Cape Lookout to Ocracoke and was waiting for the *Coastal Rambler* and Captain Mansfield to bring her home, and she was hoping to be back to Northard Woods by the end of the week.

The letter from the lieutenant made Kristina's heart skip a beat. He was scheduled to be in Elizabeth City for two weeks around Thanksgiving, and he wanted Kristina to meet him there for the holiday. She knew she couldn't be away from her family and friends during Thanksgiving. Instead, she would have to figure out a way to get the lieutenant to spend the holiday with her on the island. Edward and Beth both agreed that he would be welcome to spend Thanksgiving in Chicamacomico. "Tell him that there's going to be a big covered-dish feed at the schoolhouse on Thanksgiving Day," said Beth.

Kristina promptly returned the lieutenant's letter and invited him to spend the holiday with her family and all of their friends. In her correspondence to the lieutenant, she mentioned the big Thanksgiving feast at the schoolhouse, where the village folks would gather and give thanks, share their food, socialize, and catch up on all the latest gossip. Kristina suggested that he bring news about the latest inventions and changes taking place around the world that were going to have profound effects on people's lifestyles. She told him that she was already looking forward to seeing him again, and then her mind shifted to Hazel. Kristina couldn't wait for Hazel to return either, and she knew Hazel would help her find her animals.

Cocoa was very uneasy. As soon as the rain stopped, she was ready to leave the cover of Trent Woods and continue up the beach. However, Barnacle and some of the ponies were not in such a big hurry. They were very tired and needed to graze and find water in order to gain adequate strength to continue the journey. Two of the mares were ready to give birth, and Barnacle knew they had to stop and rest. He kept the ponies in the meadows for a while and allowed them to graze, and then he moved them to the Cape Woods area.

Cocoa ran out of patience. She left her friends and headed north. When she stopped at the Big Kinnakeet Lifesaving Station for water, the cook recognized her. "Doesn't that brown Lab right there belong to the girl from Chicamacomico?" he asked one of the crewmen.

"I think you're right," replied the crewman.

Then the cook said, "Take her these scraps and see if she's hungry."

When the crewman called for Cocoa, she lowered her head and crawled forward to the tin of food. She ate every bite while the crewman and cook removed the sand spurs, thorns, and burs from her coat. They washed her down with fresh water and brushed her with a currycomb to clean her coat. Then Cocoa jumped up, licked their hands, and took off. When she got a few yards away, she looked back and barked her thanks, then headed on her way up the beach. Finally she could see the lights of Northard Woods in the fading light.

When Cocoa reached the Grays' cottage, she barked a couple of times and Tar came out to meet her. Then the two dogs took off, past the station, and straight to Kristina's cottage.

Kristina heard the dogs barking as they neared the station. "That's Cocoa," she shouted as she ran past her parents and out the front door to the porch. Cocoa jumped from the ground and landed right on Kristina's chest, knocking her to the floor. "Let me up, Cocoa, so I can look at you!" she said, laughing as Cocoa licked her face.

"Look, Mom and Dad! It's Cocoa!" Kristina said, beaming with happiness. "She's home now, and Barnacle and Star will be here soon. I just know it," she told them.

"She looks great," said Beth. "Someone has even brushed her coat! Look how shiny and clean she is!" Beth exclaimed.

"She does look clean and well fed," Edward commented. Then he said, "Tar's here for a visit. Maybe you should give them a treat. I'll bet they would love some of your biscuits and leftover gravy, heated up," he suggested politely.

"Come on in, guys," Kristina told the dogs, and both of them followed her into the kitchen, wagging their tails. "You two eat up and rest well tonight. We're going to find Barnacle, Star, and the ponies tomorrow morning," she told the dogs as she stroked their heads.

Hazel arrived on the *Coastal Rambler*, on the back of the reef, west of Clarks Village. Then she boarded Aaron Hooper's smaller vessel, along with everybody and everything headed for shore. After being gone for such a long time, she was ready to get back to her cottage and check on her things.

Norman was waiting for her at the dock with a wagon. She had a few extra parcels that Hattie had given her to bring home. Their conversation on their way to Hazel's house was all about her trip down the sound to Hattie's house, as well as her accounts of seeing The Raven, Flash, and all the ponies. They both agreed that the Bankers would be much safer in smaller herds, scattered among the islands.

When Hazel asked Norman about the well-being of her animals and the condition of her yard and cottage, he assured her that everything was fine. When she asked about Cocoa and Barnacle, Norman said, "I got wind that the brown dog returned home a few days ago, but I haven't heard or seen anything regarding the ponies." When they reached the watering hole abreast Clarks Island, Norman stopped long enough for the two ponies pulling the wagon to take a drink.

Hazel had an uneasy feeling. It was bothering her so much that she finally mentioned it to Norman. "I feel as if someone or something is watching us right this very minute. I feel a presence and a sense of danger right here, right now."

"Ah, it's just your imagination," Norman responded as he examined the tracks in the sand around the edge of the watering hole. He saw deer tracks, bird tracks, some wild boar tracks, and then he saw some tracks that really got his attention. They looked like the tracks of a very large cat. Then he called Hazel to come have a look.

"They're too large to be from a panther," said Hazel, "but they could be from a cougar. A few cougars crossed the sound a couple years ago and caused a ruckus around here for a while."

"If that's the case, people will have to look out for their smaller animals for a while, until someone catches them," Norman told her.

"Especially those who have had new colts this past summer," Hazel replied.

"Folks will have to be on guard for a while," Norman repeated, and they both agreed to spread the word to everyone they saw.

Hazel said, "After I check everything out at my place, I plan to go up to Northard Woods this weekend while the girls are out of school. We'll probably go searching for the missing ponies. I'll be sure to alert the folks up that way about the tracks we've seen." Soon they arrived at Hazel's cottage, and Norman helped her off-load her parcels. As he turned the wagon around and started toward the road, Norman told Hazel that he would spread the word back in Clarks for folks to be on the lookout for another cougar problem.

"That's a good start," said Hazel. Then she expressed her sincere thanks to Norman for looking after her things and told him good-bye.

Two male panthers, about two hundred pounds each, had made their way to Long Shoal by clinging to a large floating tree. They had barely escaped death from a much larger dominant male, which had chased them on the mainland to the water's edge near Gull Rock Bay. The two smaller animals had jumped into the water and floated away with the tree on a fair west wind. The larger male, satisfied that he was rid of his rivals, stopped at the edge of the marsh and scolded them as they drifted out of sight.

Once the panthers entered the open sound, where the waves were much larger, they had a hard time keeping their balance on the tree log. With no food or drinking water, they became more agitated as they floated away. Several times, they jumped into the water and tried to catch small fish, but the fish got away. Although extremely agile on the land, the panthers were very clumsy in the water. They were so thirsty that they lapped up a few mouthfuls of salt water, which instantly made them sick to their stomachs. By the time the tree grounded on Long Shoal, the panthers were snarling at each other.

Up on Long Shoal they found a few crabs in the shallow water and were able to catch a few small fish. However, when they saw their log drifting around the point, headed for deep water, both of them took off to catch it. After a very long, fast swim, the panthers pulled themselves back onto the log and resumed their questionable journey. They finally came to rest on a sand beach about a hundred yards from the watering hole, where Norman and Hazel had seen their tracks. The big cats had been startled by the approaching wagon. Now they were hiding in the bushes, remaining very still, watching.

⚶50⚶

CAPTURE OF THE CATS

Barnacle had been feeling an urge to move his group of ponies up the island, back to the Cedar Hammock meadows. Out of Cape Woods they proceeded, very cautiously toward the surf line. He kept them moving up the beach until they reached a sheltered hammock north of Little Kinnakeet Station. There he let them rest, graze, and drink from a watering hole near the cover of the scrub bushes. Barnacle felt very uneasy the entire time they rested, as if someone or something was watching them. As soon as possible he moved the ponies back to the beach, to the surf line, where they could see in all directions and know if anyone or anything was approaching them.

As the ponies rested, the two panthers watched them from the brush, keeping a special eye on the smaller colts born during the late summer. The colts weren't moving as fast as the others, and their mothers were lagging behind to help them along. Barnacle turned the lead over to one of the senior stallions and went to the end of the line to assist the mares with their colts. Still unsteady on their feet, the colts wobbled along as fast as they could as Barnacle nipped at their heels to hurry them on their way. The two big cats crept along the brush line, parallel to the herd, keeping their focus on the two small colts.

Barnacle stopped his herd as they entered the beach path to the west of Gull Shoal Station. He entered the brush long enough to check out a watering hole near the grass line, and when he felt it was safe he beckoned the ponies to come in for a drink. Then he placed himself between the brush and the two mares and their colts. After a quick rest he hurried them back to the surf line, where they continued their journey north.

Hazel was just heading out of Cedar Hammock Marsh along the sand road to Clarks when she heard high-pitched screams coming from the direction of the beach path. She crossed the road and continued out toward the beach. As soon as her wagon cleared the brush line, Hazel caught sight of a small mare, down and bleeding from several deep gashes in her back. Then Hazel saw Barnacle and another stallion between two big cats and the bleeding mare. Two colts were cowering behind Barnacle as he and the stallion fought fiercely to protect the downed mare from the wild cats. To Hazel they looked like panthers. Then she recalled the tracks she and Norman had seen at the watering hole.

Barnacle and the other stallion held fast to protect the ponies. They kicked and nipped at the panthers and finally drove them back a few feet, where they crouched in an agitated posture, still on the attack.

Hazel was in a quandary. She didn't know if she should leave for help or if she should stay and try to help drive the cats away. She slowly moved her wagon up behind Barnacle and the stallion, near the injured mare and the trembling colts. Then, with some difficulty, she loaded the colts into the wagon and wrapped them in a canvas tarp. She slipped a rope halter around the injured mare and used the wagon to pull her to her feet. The mare was still bleeding badly across her back and down her legs as Hazel urged the wagon ahead.

The ponies took the lead while Barnacle and the other stallion took the rear to keep the big cats at bay. The pace was very slow, and Hazel stopped a couple of times to check the gashes in the mare's back. She shredded an old pair of her jeans and used them to help stop the bleeding with direct pressure.

The panthers continued to follow closely, steadily snarling and growling their disapproval of having missed out on what they thought would be a certain meal. When Hazel and the horses entered the south end of Clarks Village, a few people came running, and the big cats scampered off into the brush.

The villagers took care of the injured mare and "scared-half-to-death" colts while Hazel continued to Aaron Hooper's cottage. It didn't take Aaron

Hooper long to gather up some village men to help move Barnacle and his herd to the Northard Woods meadows, just south of the village. Then Hazel headed to Edward's cottage to share the good news.

Kristina and Shanna were just getting home from a day at school and were overjoyed to see Hazel and learn that the ponies had made it back home.

"We must go down to the meadows to see the ponies!" Kristina told her father.

Edward agreed and said, "We'll take the wagon. It's getting late and will soon be dark." When Edward and Kristina arrived at the meadows, Barnacle and Star came running up to the wagon and placed their heads over the side so that Kristina and Edward could stroke them.

"I am so glad to see you!" Kristina told the horses. "I'll really miss Flash— and I know you will, too—but I'm so glad you came back here. You belong in Northard Woods," she said. Then she asked her father if they could take Barnacle and Star home.

"If we can persuade Barnacle to leave the herd," Edward answered.

"Listen!" Hazel said. "I hear dogs barking, way off in the distance."

"That's Cocoa and Tar," Kristina said.

"Well, if anything can get Barnacle to go with you, it'll be that brown dog of yours," Hazel responded. "Why don't you just ask Barnacle to turn the herd over to his senior stallion and go home with you?" she told Kristina.

Kristina wrapped her arms around Barnacle's neck and whispered in his ear. "Please come home with us, boy," she said. Then Barnacle ran over to the largest stallion, and they put their heads together for several seconds. Both of them began to whinny and prance around, and then Barnacle returned to Kristina.

"You folks go on home with Barnacle and Star," Hazel told Edward. "Aaron and I will arrange care for the rest of the herd tonight," she said.

"Thank you, Hazel," Kristina replied.

At about that time, Cocoa and Tar came running up barking and covered with mud. They ran straight to Barnacle and greeted him. Then Cocoa tried to jump up in the wagon, but Edward stopped her. "You two will have to be washed off before you can get in this wagon," he said to the dogs. As they headed toward the cottage, Cocoa and Tar ran up front, barking constantly, and checking each clump of brush they came across. Barnacle and Star followed the wagon, just a few feet behind them.

"Look how those two horses follow along without even being tied to that wagon," Aaron commented.

"They've always done that," Hazel replied. "I'm really glad those two dogs got upwind and went home with them before they caught the scent of those big cats. You talk about a mess we'd have on our hands if the dogs got tangled up with those things. Can you imagine? We'll definitely need to build small fires around the herd in order to provide the protection they'll need for the night." Then she and Aaron headed to the beach to find the wood for the fires.

Kristina and Edward put Barnacle and Star in the corral. Kristina fed them and rubbed them down, taking time to do an extra-exceptional job. Then she called for Cocoa and Tar to wash them under the hand pump before feeding them the table scraps her mother had left. Inside the barn, Kristina made herself a bed in the hay with a couple of nearby blankets.

In a short while, Beth came out to the barn with a few apples and some lumps of sugar for the horses. She hugged and stroked Barnacle's head as she gave the animals their treats. As Beth was speaking very softly to Barnacle, telling him how glad she was to see him, Star pushed her head in to get some of the loving attention. "I'm glad to see you, too, girl!" she told the mare and gave her a hug.

"Are you planning to spend the night with these horses?" Beth asked her daughter.

"Absolutely," Kristina replied. "After all, today is Friday, so I have no school tomorrow."

"Well, perhaps you might want to come to the house and read the letter that came for you today," Beth told her.

"Mother, why didn't you tell me before now?" Kristina asked.

"Because this is the first time I've seen you since this morning," Beth answered.

Kristina turned and raced for the cottage with Cocoa at her heels. She entered the porch with one large step, then went inside the cottage and hurried to the table to find the letter. "Mother?" she yelled.

"It's on the nightstand, beside your bed." Beth hollered back before her daughter could ask where the letter was located.

Kristina ripped open the envelope and read the letter. The lieutenant would be arriving at Northard Woods one week before Thanksgiving, and he would be able to stay until a few days after the holiday.

"That should give you enough time," Edward said, as he and Beth listened to their excited daughter read the letter.

"Enough time for what?" Kristina inquired.

"Time enough to work your magic on him before he goes back up north," Edward said as he winked at Beth.

"Pay no attention to your father! Just visit and enjoy yourselves," Beth told her daughter.

"But he'll be here in one week! Thanksgiving is only two weeks away!" Kristina exclaimed to her parents.

"What do you need to do before he gets here?" her father asked.

"Well, nothing, I guess," answered Kristina. "We'll be out of school for the holidays, so I guess I'm ready."

"The lieutenant can stay at the station with the crew," her father insisted. "Keeper Daniels says they have plenty of room over there."

"So I guess everything is set then," Kristina said with a smile.

"With the lieutenant, yes, but we still have to deal with this big cat problem," said Edward. "Keeper Daniels knows a fellow who has a large bear trap and says he can capture the panthers alive. After he secures them he will release them on the mainland, where they should be. Would you like to go with us in the morning when we try to catch them?" Edward asked Kristina.

"Sounds exciting," she said as she left the cottage and headed for the barn to spend the night with her animals.

The next morning, Edward found Kristina sound asleep, wrapped in a blanket with Cocoa huddled against Barnacle's back, with Star asleep in front of Barnacle. Then he woke them up. Barnacle waited until Kristina and the dog were out of the way before he stood up and nudged Star awake with his nose. Then Hazel came into the barn. "Beth said to tell you that breakfast is ready," she hollered.

After Edward and Kristina ate, they joined Keeper Daniels and several men from the village and headed off to the south meadows. They were sure the cats had watched the herd all night. Sure enough, when they reached the herd, the panthers were spotted in the distance, keeping away from the lighted areas provided by the small fires.

Harland Spruill was on the island for the Thanksgiving holiday. He was a trained trapper of large animals—usually for zoos, circuses, and carnivals— and he had two large traps that were capable of catching the panthers alive. He had made an agreement with Keeper Daniels to trap the animals and return them to the mainland, for a small fee from the villagers.

Mr. Spruill followed the villagers as they moved the herd of ponies north to the Pea Island meadows. He baited his traps with raw fish and placed them one mile apart, along the trail, to leave overnight. The very next morning, Keeper Daniels announced that if anyone wanted to see the big cats, they needed to hurry to the landing. Sure enough, when they arrived at the landing, a large wire cage was on the dock containing both snarling panthers. Harland had hired a couple of men from the village to help transport the panthers back to the mainland.

"They were both in the first trap," Harland said with a grin. "We'll see you folks in a few days. I'll have a load of framing lumber on my return trip from Buffalo City for those who've placed orders with me," said Mr. Spruill.

As the vessel sailed out of sight, Edward said, "Well, that's that."

"Yes, indeed," answered Keeper Daniels. "I think we got off fairly easy, all things considered. We didn't lose any livestock or even a pet. It could've been much worse with a couple of large predators like that around."

"I'm glad we were able to catch the panthers and return them to the mainland," Kristina said.

Hazel agreed. "They're amazing animals."

❧51❧

Thanksgiving Celebration

The day the lieutenant arrived, a blustery northeaster wind was blowing in the ten- to twenty-mile-an-hour range, with a steady rain falling. Keeper Daniels had made arrangements for the lieutenant to stay at the station. Jason would be picking him up at the dock and taking him straight to his quarters. It was the last day of school before the Thanksgiving holiday, and Kristina was in a hurry to get home to see if the lieutenant had arrived. When she entered the cottage, Beth met her at the door and said, "Leave your foul-weather gear in the foyer."

"Mom, do you know if he's arrived yet?" asked Kristina.

"Yes," was her mother's response, "about an hour ago. Keeper Daniels has invited us for dinner, so you'll get to see them tonight."

"Did you say 'them'?" Kristina asked puzzled.

"Yes. He brought two friends with him," said Beth. "One of them is the editor of a newspaper based in Boston. Keeper Daniels has asked the editor to be our guest speaker at the Thanksgiving dinner get-together," she told Kristina.

That evening, Edward, Beth, and Kristina arrived at the station at about the same time as Jason, Mrs. Gray, and Shanna. They pulled the wagons on the lee side of the large galley and entered from the side door. The young officer was very excited to see Kristina. He embraced her and kissed her on the cheek. Then Edward turned to Beth. "Not serious? Yeah, right," he said, and Beth just smiled.

Keeper Daniels introduced everyone as they stood around the table, including the guest speaker, Mr. Thurman Perkins, staff editor of the *Boston Times Dispatch*. After the keeper blessed the food, they all sat down and the conversation began. Mr. Perkins explained that his newspaper was located in the town with the busiest seaport on the East Coast. His company received state and national news as well as some news from Europe and places farther away. He told many interesting stories of new gadgets, inventions, and things that would eventually change their lifestyles. The conversation made for an interesting evening, to say the least.

When the meal was completed and the kitchen was clean, the men retired to the tack room for coffee, smokes, and conversation, while the ladies remained in the galley, around the table, for coffee, dessert, and more time to visit. Kristina, Shanna, the lieutenant, and his friends slipped off to the dayroom. Both girls had agreed that the dayroom would be an ideal place for the young folks to catch up. Through the large windows and rain, they could see the ocean waves bounding high in the air as they crashed onto the beach, driven by the stiff northeast wind. When the time for visiting ended, the young folks headed off to their respective places of rest, with promises of seeing each other the next day, weather permitting.

The next morning dawned very wet and dreary, with a fine mist in the air—lighter than rain, but heavier than fog. The wind had fallen off some, but the temperature had dropped during the night, making for a very cold, raw day. It was extremely uncomfortable to be outside for any length of time, so everyone who was able remained indoors for the entire day before the Thanksgiving celebration. Thankfully, overnight, the low pressure moved offshore, far enough that the mist stopped and the wind fell out even more.

Early the next morning, Beth woke Kristina early. It was time to go to the schoolhouse and decorate for the midday Thanksgiving feast. The younger folks would decorate the meeting place while the ladies cooked. The menfolk would gather oysters, clams, fish, and other types of seafood for everyone to share.

When Kristina and Shanna arrived at the schoolhouse, it was full of young people in the midst of decorating. The entire room was full of excitement about the feast and the guest speaker. Soon, folks from the entire Chicama-comico area began arriving at the schoolhouse, with wagonloads of food for the gathering.

As the potluck feast came together, the abundance of food was a sight to behold. Three very large tables had been set up in the dining area, offering an impressive buffet. The first table was full of turkey, goose, pheasant, duck, and chicken—dishes that were either baked, stewed, fried, grilled, steamed, or boiled. The table even included a large pot of stewed beach-birds in pie-bread. The second table was covered with a variety of pork, beef, ham, and many kinds of vegetable dishes. The third table was full of seafood, including fish, clams, oysters, and shrimp. There was clam chowder and oyster stew, as well as a large pot of turtle soup, some turtle hash, and two platters of fried turtle. A separate, smaller table was loaded with a vast array of desserts.

Before the dinner began, the schoolchildren performed a play they had been practicing about the first Thanksgiving with the Indians and the Pilgrims. The play lasted about an hour. Then the local preachers—from the Holy Roller and Methodist churches—shared in the blessing of the food and offered well-wishing prayers upon the crowd gathered. Keeper Daniels then informed the audience that a special guest speaker from Boston would be addressing them after dinner, with many stories of the changing times.

As the crowd lined up for the gathering of food on their plates, the older folks were given first place in line and at the tables. Soon the conversation began with several comments like, "Boy, I wish the plates were bigger," and "Have you ever seen such a sight?" The entire crowd feasted to their hearts' content on the homemade, island-style cooking. Many trips were made for seconds before the dessert table was attacked. Gradually, the room became filled with satisfied groans, as folks patted and rubbed their bellies. Someone said, "Man, it's good to be full!"

Then menfolk went outside so some could smoke their pipes and trade fishing and hunting exploits. The ladies cleared the tables while discussing their children, their husbands, and the many tasty dishes they had enjoyed during the feast. They even traded a few recipes as they cleaned up and set out the after-dinner coffee. The smaller children ran around outside, playing tag and other games, while the teenage boys and girls gathered to talk about boyfriends, girlfriends, and the things that were important to them. Soon, a few of the older ladies called everyone back into the building. They instructed the children to go to their parents and settle down respectfully to prepare for the after-dinner guest speaker.

Mothers became busy trying to tidy up their children by straightening their clothes, combing their hair with their fingers, and giving them spit-baths with their hankies. Some children squirmed and complained, and one boy fussed that his mother was trying to scrub the skin off his face!

After everyone was comfortably situated, Keeper Daniels rose to introduce the guest speaker. He gained the people's attention by rapping on the podium with a large, wooden spoon. Everyone quieted down as the keeper invited Mr. Thurman Perkins to the front of the room. Mr. Perkins first congratulated the folks on such a fine meal. Then he greeted everyone and told them how privileged he felt to be sharing the Thanksgiving holiday with them in such an intriguing place. He commented on the quaintness, the isolation, and the beauty of the area, and told everyone that he had news of many new and exciting things that would change their lives for the better in the very near future.

Mr. Perkins began with the steam-powered engine. "It will change the way people travel," he said. "The base fuel is wood, coal, or basically any type of solid material that will burn," he explained. This burning provides the heat required to create water pressure in a vessel and generate steam, which then powers the engines. "In my opinion," he added, "these engines could be used in all types of travel, from ships to wagons. They might even replace horses someday," he added.

Mr. Perkins also talked about a new idea of lighting homes at night that could eventually replace oil lamps. He finished up his address to the group by informing them that they were entering a new era in which new discoveries were being made that would help everyone and make life much easier, "even for people like you, in such a remote location." Then Mr. Perkins suggested that they separate into smaller groups of men, women, teens, and children, and he would answer any questions they had. Accordingly, the men asked questions about the possible changes. The women asked all sorts of questions about various things, from the latest fashion to fishing. The teens were interested in the fads and gadgets, and of course the children wanted to know about new toys and games.

Mr. Perkins shared any information he could think of about life in Boston and around the world. There were many questions still unanswered, but because of the very late hour, Keeper Daniels proposed that they bring the session to a close. He stated that, if it was agreeable with Mr. Perkins, anyone who wanted to continue the discussions was welcome to drop by the station. "Mr. Perkins and his friends will be our guests for at least three more days," said Keeper Daniels.

As it turned out, the next three days of November were gorgeous, and Mr. Perkins received many visitors with all sorts of questions. Thanksgiving vacation was over, and it was time for the lieutenant and his friends to return to Boston. Kristina and many of the villagers went to the Northard Woods harbor to see the men off. Everyone wished them well as they began their journey to the back of the reef to meet the larger schooner.

Kristina was silent and reserved on the wagon ride back to the cottage, so Edward decided not to question her until they got back home. His daughter and the young lieutenant had spent a lot of time together during his short visit, and Edward was very much interested in their future plans. Shortly after they arrived at their cottage, Edward found out what he feared the most. Kristina affirmed to her father that the lieutenant was planning to ask for her hand in marriage when he returned to the island for Christmas. He wanted her to move to the Boston area, where he was currently stationed, to be with him forever.

When Edward asked Kristina what she thought about it, she was very slow to answer. All she could say was that she had mixed emotions about the situation, which was the same thing she had told the young officer. Kristina told her father that she needed more time to think before she could give a firm answer, and Edward told her he would support her decision, whatever it turned out to be. All he wanted was for her to be happy. He suggested that she spend time with her mother and seek her advice, and also to spend time with her closest friends to give them an opportunity to offer their guidance. He encouraged her to take long rides near the surf line with Barnacle and Cocoa, and visit some of her favorite places to help her make up her mind. She still had about three weeks before the young officer returned.

Kristina walked slowly out the door to the corral and called for Barnacle. He came out of the stall and trotted over to her. Then he bent his large head down and nuzzled her hands. She knew Barnacle would never fit into the Boston lifestyle, and she wondered if she ever could. Suddenly Cocoa ran from underneath the back porch and started barking. Kristina opened the gate and jumped on Barnacle's back, and they took off toward the beach as Cocoa nipped at Barnacle's heels.

Edward turned to Beth. "See what we've created," he said. "And now she'll probably go off to live in Boston."

"I don't know so much about that," Beth replied, as her blonde-haired daughter faded from sight with her chestnut horse and brown dog.

❦52❧

THE BIG DECISION

The very next morning was a clear, crisp Sunday, with a light northeast wind and a slight chill. It was Kristina's last day before she returned to school following the Thanksgiving vacation. She definitely had to visit Hazel at Cedar Hammock Marsh to seek her advice about the future.

As Kristina and Barnacle left the yard, Cocoa came out from under the porch and joined them. As they passed the Grays' cottage, Tar joined them also. Just as they were approaching the freshwater pond near Clarks Village, a rabbit bolted from the tall grass, and Tar took off in a flash with Cocoa at his heels. They chased the rabbit down the path, and soon Cocoa's barking faded. *Silly dogs*, Kristina thought to herself as Barnacle stopped at the edge of the pond for a drink.

When Barnacle finished drinking, Kristina urged him forward with her left knee, and they headed on down the road. She had never used a bridle or bit on him. In fact, Barnacle had only been tied up a few times. When Kristina wanted to go she simply talked to him and applied light pressure with her knees.

Soon they were entering the path to Cedar Hammock. The path wound past the matted floating marsh and along the long pond toward Hazel's shack. Kristina wanted to surprise Hazel, so she and Barnacle entered her yard from the partially hidden back side. Hazel was relaxing on the back porch on the lee side of the cottage.

"What're you doing?" Kristina asked Hazel.

"Just listening," Hazel responded.

"Listening to what?" Kristina asked.

"Just to life in general," Hazel replied. "For instance, I knew you were coming thirty minutes before you arrived by those yapping mutts that always accompany you." Kristina and Hazel could hear the dogs in a distant cove, coming down the shore side. "They'll be here in a few minutes," Hazel told her. "They're on the shore side of the north dyke and will be covered with mud when they get here. Keep them off the porch and out of the house when they arrive," she told Kristina. Very soon, the dogs came bounding out of the brush, covered with mud from head to paw.

Kristina yelled loudly. "Tar, Cocoa, stop!" she commanded, and the dogs froze in their tracks.

"Now get that bucket and wash them off," said Hazel. Right away, Kristina got the bucket and washed the mud off the dogs. She also made them stay on the lee side of the cottage to dry off in the sun. Barnacle wandered off to the side to munch on some marsh-grass roots.

"Now, to what do I owe the pleasure of this visit from you all so early on a Sunday morning?" asked Hazel.

"I came here seeking your advice concerning my future plans," Kristina said.

"Are you serious?" Hazel asked her.

"Very serious," responded Kristina.

"You might've come to the wrong person for counsel on matters concerning the heart," Hazel told Kristina. "Now, if it has to do with livestock, nature, or the weather, I do have experience in those areas. Let's just relax and listen to what the sounds of the marsh have to offer. I will share what knowledge I have acquired about such matters with you." Then Hazel said, "Tell me what you hear."

"Right now, at this very moment?" asked Kristina.

"Yes," Hazel replied.

"Not much of anything," admitted Kristina.

"Listen very closely," Hazel said. "Do you hear the faint cooing of a distant loon—and his mate answering him from even farther away? Listen to the sounds your two dogs are making as they roll in the salt grass, drying their coats. Do you hear their satisfied groans as they scratch their backs among the grass roots? Listen to your stallion as he crunches and grazes on the tender shoots of the salt grass. Listen to the light winds as they rustle and move the grasses around, creating peace and harmony that soothes the entire marsh.

"This marsh is the very reason I live here, in Cedar Hammock, along with my animals," Hazel continued. "It is where I've found the answers to my most difficult questions. This marsh has always taken care of me and provided for all my needs. I feel much more comfortable living out here than among the folks in the villages. You, on the other hand, must search your inner self and find your own answers," she told Kristina.

"We must each seek our own balance, keeping happiness in mind. We need to remember that it's not the gale, but the set of the sail that helps mold our decisions for our future," Hazel explained. "Relax here with me for the rest of the morning. You can help me boil the wax off that large pile of bayberries I picked yesterday to mold into candles. As the kettle boils, you can hang out on the porch in the sun and listen to the marsh to see if it has any answers for you."

Later, as they filled the large kettle with bayberry branches to be boiled, Kristina's mind drifted back to the many happy hours she had spent in this marsh. She recalled the first time she had seen the large black kettle, on her very first trip to meet Old Hazel. Kristina had seen the kettle from the bushes, sitting over a roaring fire in Hazel's yard. She was sure she had seen a child's hand sticking out of the pot, and she was convinced that the old lady must be cooking children for dinner. Needless to say, she never left her father's side until she discovered that Hazel was only boiling bayberries in the kettle.

That was a long time ago, and life was so simple then, Kristina thought to herself. She had been a very carefree child, without many pressures or major life choices facing her. No matter which path she chose, Kristina knew that the results would have a large impact on her life and the lives of those she loved so much. She was jolted back to reality by Hazel's voice.

"Come here, Kristina. Help me skim the wax off the surface of this water so that we can make ready the candle molds." Together they took the large

cast-iron ladle and began to skim off the melted wax. Then they poured it
into the candle molds, tied to three long wooden racks. When their task was
complete, Hazel placed her hands on her hips. "There are now three racks of
bayberry candles to trade at the store," she said with a satisfied sigh. "Come
along now. It's time to warm up some leftovers and put a lunch together."

After they had eaten, Kristina called for Barnacle and said good-bye to
Hazel. When Kristina mounted the large stallion and called the dogs, Hazel
waved and said, "Don't worry, girl. Things have a way of working out." Kristina
waved back and took off for the path leading out of the marsh. Hazel knew
Kristina was facing some difficult decisions, to be so young.

Kristina, Barnacle, and the dogs made their way across the marsh, past the
grassy meadows, and finally out to the beach. Slowly, they began to make their
way up the surf line. It was a fairly mild day for November. The sun was warm,
and the wind was light from the southeast. Far out over the ocean, Kristina
could see the rain clouds approaching. *The wind's probably going to shift from
the north and cause the temperatures to drop by tomorrow*, she thought to herself
as she rode along in a dreamlike state.

Cocoa and Tar were chasing the shorebirds up and down the surf line,
barking steadily as they ran along. Every now and then they would stop and
sniff the openings of sand fiddler holes, and if they caught a scent, they would
begin to dig aggressively. If they dug up a fiddler crab, it would go into an
attack mode by raising its pincers. Most of the time, the dogs just circled the
crab until it scampered into another hole.

When Kristina came to herself, Barnacle had already turned off the beach
path and was moving past the boathouse, headed for the cottage. Her father
met her at the corral gate and inquired about her visit with Hazel. She told him
they had a nice visit, but that she was still in a quandary and had no idea what
she was going to do.

"Your mother and I will discuss it with you after the evening meal tonight,"
he told her as they fed the dogs and bedded the horses down for the night.

After dinner, Kristina and her parents had a lengthy discussion. All three
of them decided that Kristina should ask for a few days off from her teaching

duties in order to visit Boston and the young lieutenant. Edward and Beth were sure that Kristina could stay with their friends who lived in the city, close to where the lieutenant was assigned.

The next morning, Kristina went to see Mrs. Bridges to ask for some time off. After listening to Kristina's reason, Mrs. Bridges made arrangements for her to take two weeks off in addition to her standard Christmas vacation. Kristina agreed that this would give her enough time to see what life would be like in Boston with the young lieutenant. As soon as she returned home, Kristina asked her father to help her make arrangements for the trip.

The day soon arrived for Kristina to leave the island. As she and her parents turned onto the landing road, they saw the very large crowd of folks gathered on the dock and along both sides of the creek.

"Are all those people here to see me off?" she asked her parents, in a surprised tone.

"Not exactly," answered her father. "They're here to see the vessel that has replaced the *Coastal Rambler*. Look south! You can see it now." Far out on the horizon, Kristina could see a huge plume of black smoke rising from the water.

"What is that?" asked Kristina.

"That's your ride," Edward answered.

"It looks like it's on fire," Kristina responded.

"In a way, it is," said Edward. "The new vessel will travel from Ocracoke to Elizabeth City, just like the *Coastal Rambler* did, to transport cargo and passengers. Most of the folks are gathered down here to see this vessel for the very first time."

Kristina kept her eyes on the approaching vessel, which was slowly materializing from the billow of smoke. Soon she could make out the lines of a very large boat.

Most of Kristina's friends were at the landing to see her off. They hugged her and wished her luck. Kristina thanked Hazel for watching over their animal friends until she returned. Then Hazel reminded her to take a few minutes and explain her departure to Barnacle.

Barnacle stood motionless as Kristina approached him. He was hitched to the wagon, but as usual, there was no bit in his mouth or bridle over his head. "You're such a smart, handsome boy," Kristina told him as he lowered his big head to her face. "You've always been a true friend to me. I've only had to ask you to take us wherever we've wanted to go, whether it was in the wagon or on your back. I'll be gone for a short while, but I'll return very soon, and it's very important that you understand this." Barnacle whimpered and bobbed his large head up and down.

Hazel was waiting for Kristina at the end of the dock. "Listen to your heart, girl, and search your inner self. Remember, only you can decide what's best for you."

As Kristina gave Hazel a big hug, she noticed that Barnacle had moved the wagon up to the edge of the creek and had his eyes fixed on her. "I hope he understands," Kristina told Hazel.

"I believe he does," Hazel responded. "He's much more relaxed compared to the last time you left. It's good that you talked to him, instead of trying to trick him again.

"What are you going to tell this one?" Hazel asked Kristina. Cocoa's big brown eyes told them that she thought she was coming along.

"No, girl. You can't come along this time," Kristina said. Then Cocoa began to whine as Kristina climbed into the small boat. The dog jumped into the boat immediately behind her and nuzzled Kristina's hand with her cold, wet nose. Hazel came over and helped lift the dog out of the boat. As the *Sea Mullet* was being shoved out of the creek to catch the wind, Kristina turned to wave to her parents. Edward and Beth waved back, and Barnacle bobbed his head. Hazel had a good grasp on Cocoa—by the scruff of the neck to prevent her from swimming after the boat. The dog finally gave up, sat down on the dock, and started howling.

Kristina boarded the larger vessel and stared into the churning water near the stern. This was the beginning of her journey. *Where would it end?* she wondered.

Epilogue

It was Kristina's ninetieth birthday, and her family members had come to Boston to celebrate and spend five days with her. The northeaster lasted for three out of the five days in the Boston harbor area. In the meanwhile, Kristina told stories to her family about growing up in Chicamacomico. Her storytelling had begun with her trip to Charleston, South Carolina, on the vessel *Sylvia*, where she had met Barnacle. She shared many memories from her childhood, throughout her teenage years, right up to the time she left Chicamacomico, and returned to Boston with the young lieutenant.

Due to the stormy weather, Kristina's children, grandchildren, and great-grandchildren had huddled in the great room, transfixed on the adventures of her youth. As she told them story after story, they only left her side to eat and to sleep. On the fourth day, the weather finally broke. It was still chilly outside, but the family was able to take an early-morning beach walk. However, just as soon as they returned and ate their breakfast, everyone gathered around Kristina, wanting to hear more tales.

On Sunday morning, shortly before her family had to leave to return to their homes, Kristina told one more story. Then hugs and kisses were exchanged, and everyone went outside. Kristina remained in the great room with her oldest son as the others pulled out of the long, winding driveway, honking their horns and waving.

"Well, Mom," said her son, "you had quite a visit, and I really believe everyone enjoyed your stories." Kristina didn't answer. Instead, she just sat quietly. A few tears welled up in her eyes and dropped to her lap as she waved good-bye from the window to the last car leaving her driveway. Then a big smile came across her face. Her son asked her what she was smiling about, especially since her family was leaving.

"That is a secret," Kristina answered. She knew her family would be returning for another visit on the Fourth of July. *More Chicamacomico stories*, she thought to herself. Then she locked her wheelchair into position, closed her eyes, and let her mind drift back to her Chicamacomico wedding to the young lieutenant.

About the Author

Hatteras Island has always been Elvin Hooper's home. He was born on July 9, 1949, in a twelve-bed hospital located in Buxton, North Carolina. The hospital was destroyed by a hurricane some years later. Just for the record, the location of his birth is also the site from which the very first wireless message was ever sent. It is now the home of a recreational park named the Fessenden Center, after the man who sent that message.

Elvin Hooper, Surfman #4,
Chicamacomico Life Saving Station
Breeches Buoy Re-enactment Drill.
Photo courtesy of Drew Wilson and *The Virginia Pilot.*

The Hooper ancestry has been a part of Hatteras Island for generations and can be traced back as far as anyone can remember. The Hoopers were connected with the United States Lifesaving Service, even before it became the U.S. Coast Guard.

Elvin grew up in the village of Salvo, formerly named Clarks, until the U.S. Postal Service changed the name of the village. Elvin attended Cape Hatteras School, located in Buxton. He later retired from the local county government—as a former high school teacher and building code inspector. Elvin has served as a director of the Cape Hatteras Electric Membership Cooperative for more than twenty years.

During one of his years as a high school carpentry teacher, Elvin's students constructed several rowboats, similar to those used before the days of

335

motorized vessels, to ferry passengers and supplies from the villages to the larger vessels offshore.

Elvin served fifteen years as Surfman Number Four on the Chicamacomico Lifesaving Service Re-enactment Team for the breeches buoy drill until the attacks of September 11, 2001, prohibited the firing of the black powder cannon—also known as a Lyle gun—used to transport the shot line to a vessel in distress.

Some of Elvin's hobbies include fishing, hunting, music, and storytelling. He still works part time as a carpentry teacher at the high school in Buxton. Elvin also works full-time for the Hatteras Inlet Ferry operation. If he's not working, you might find him singing and playing his guitar with the Chicamacomico Band, or writing his second novel, *Gull Island*.

Elvin is married with one daughter, named Kristina. He and his wife, Debra, have been married for forty years. Their family home is located in Buxton, North Carolina, in what was once known as the Cape Woods. Kristina is the name of the main character in this book, and the book is dedicated to her.